The Best Test Preparation for the

CBEST

California Basic Educational Skills Test

Written by California Educators and CBEST Experts...to prepare you to do your best on the CBEST.

 Research & Education Association

The Best Test Preparation for the

CBEST

California Basic Educational Skills Test

Written by California Educators and CBEST Experts:

Mary F. Andis, Ed.D.
Assistant Professor of Education
California State University
San Bernardino, CA

Adria Klein, Ph.D.
Professor of Education and Department Chair
California State University
San Bernardino, CA

Linda Bannister, Ph.D.
Director of University Writing Programs and
Associate Professor of English
Loyola Marymount University, Los Angeles, CA

Kathryn F. Porter, Ph.D.
Associate Professor of Mathematics
St. Mary's College of California
Moraga, CA

Charles Funkhouser, Ph.D.
Assistant Professor of Education
California State University
San Bernardino, CA

Archibald Sia, Ph.D
Associate Professor of Elementary Education
California State University, Northridge
Northridge, CA

Marie Ice, Ph.D.
Associate Professor of Reading/Language Arts
California State University, Bakersfield
Bakersfield, CA

Mary J. Skillings, Ph.D
Assistant Professor of Education
California State University
San Bernardino, CA

Aida Joshi, Ph.D
Associate Professor of Education
University of San Francisco
San Francisco, CA

Hugo Sun, Ph.D.
Professor of Mathematics
California State University, Fresno
Fresno, CA

Stanley Swartz, Ph.D
Professor of Education and Department Chair
California State University, San Bernardino
San Bernardino, CA

 Research & Education Association

The Best Test Preparation for the
CBEST – California Basic Educational Skills Test

Printed in the United States of America

Library of Congress Catalog Card Number 92-68570

International Standard Book Number 0-87891-894-9

Research & Education Association
61 Ethel Road West
Piscataway, New Jersey 08854

*REA supports the effort to conserve and protect
environmental resources by printing on
recycled papers.*

ACKNOWLEDGMENTS

Special recognition is extended to the following persons:

Carl Fuchs, Production Director, for his overall guidance which has brought this publication to completion.

Rochelle L. Stern, Managing Editor, for coordinating the editorial staff throughout each phase of the project.

Judy Walters, Senior Editor, for her editorial contributions and compilation of critical material.

Bruce Hanson, Graphic Design Manager, for his cover design and final efforts in preparing the book for press.

Contents

CBEST STUDY SCHEDULE viii

INTRODUCTION xi
  About Research and Education Association xiii
  How to Prepare and Do Your Best on the CBEST xiii
  About the Test Experts...xiv
  About the CBEST xiv
  About the Diagnostic Test xvi
  About the Review Sections xvii
  Scoring the Exam xviii
  CBEST Test Taking Strategies xix

TEST 1 1
  The Diagnostic Test

  Reading Comprehension 3
    Answer Key 22
    Scoring the Reading Comprehension Section 23
    Detailed Explanations of Answers 24

  Mathematics 29
    Answer Key 44
    Scoring the Mathematics Section 45
    Detailed Explanations of Answers 46

  Essay Writing 53
    Scoring the Essay Writing Section 54
    Detailed Explanations of Answers................................55

CBEST SUBJECT REVIEWS
  READING COMPREHENSION REVIEW 63
    Overview 65
    Key Strategies for Answering the Reading
    Comprehension Questions 66
    Sample Passages 67

MATHEMATICS REVIEW 73

    Overview 75

    Arithmetic Review 77

    Algebra Review 88

    Measurement and Geometry 94

    Key Strategies for Answering the Mathematics Questions 101

    Arithmetic Practice Problems...............................102

    Answers 104

    Algebra Practice Problems 104

    Answers 106

    Measurement and Geometry Practice Problems 106

    Answers 108

ESSAY WRITING REVIEW 109

    Overview 110

    Key Strategies for Answering the Essay Questions...............112

    Essay Scoring...115

TEST 2 121

    Reading Comprehension..122

    Mathematics 140

    Essay Writing 155

    Answer Key...156

    Detailed Explanations of Answers, Test 2 157

TEST 3 179

    Reading Comprehension..180

    Mathematics 197

    Essay Writing 209

    Answer Key...210

    Detailed Explanations of Answers, Test 3 211

Answer Sheets for TESTS 1, 2, and 3 233

STUDY SCHEDULE

It is important for you to discover the time and place for studying that works best for you. Some students may set aside a certain number of hours every morning to study, while others may choose to study at night before going to sleep. Other students may study during the day, while waiting in a line, or they may find another unusual time to do their studying. Only you will be able to know when and where your studying is most effective. Keep in mind that the most important factor is consistency. Use your time wisely. Work out a study routine and stick to it!

You may want to follow a schedule similar to the one below. The following schedule consists of an eight-week program. If you need to condense your study time, you can combine two weeks into one, thereby creating a four-week schedule.

Week	Activity
1	Use the diagnostic test by taking each section separately, and then analyzing your answers and scores for each individual section. Make sure to time yourself! Finally, determine your weaknesses and plan on focusing upon the weakest areas first, so that you feel more prepared later.
2	Study your weakest area this week. For example, if you had the most trouble on the measurement and geometry questions in the math section, you would study the geometry in the math review. After reviewing this section completely, retake only this subject from the diagnostic test (in the above case, it would be the mathematics section) to see how your score has improved.
3	Study your next to lowest scoring area this week. For example, if your essay writing skills were somewhat weak, go to the scoring explanations to determine why a certain essay received a certain score. Retake that section from the diagnostic test and note any improvement.
4	Study your strongest area this week. If you are already pleased with your score, you need not repeat this section of the diagnostic test. If you hope to raise your score even further, retake this section of the diagnostic test.

Week	Activity
5	Take Practice Test 2. This is not a diagnostic test, so you should try to simulate the testing conditions as much as possible, especially regarding time. Making sure you take the test under time restrictions will allow you to focus more strongly on both your strengths and your weaknesses. Make sure that you take this test straight through in one sitting, as a "dry run." See if your scores have improved since you last took the test.
6	Restudy any area in which you still feel weak.
7	Take Practice Test 3 under the same simulated conditions in which you took the last practice test. Notice any improvement in the amount of time you needed to complete a section. If you can keep up a good pace, you have a better chance of completing all the items on the day of the test.
8	Continue to review all unclear items. If you are unsure about what grade your essay would receive, seek the advice of a counselor or teacher at school. If you are satisfied with your scores and the time it takes you to complete the sections, you have completed your studying and are ready to take the CBEST with confidence.

CBEST

California Basic Educational Skills Test

INTRODUCTION

ABOUT RESEARCH AND EDUCATION ASSOCIATION

REA is an organization of educators, scientists, and engineers specializing in various academic fields. REA was founded in 1959 for the purpose of disseminating the most recently developed scientific information to groups in industry, government, universities, and high schools. Since then, REA has become a successful and highly respected publisher of study aids, test preps, handbooks, and reference works.

REA's Test Preparation series extensively prepares students and professionals for the Medical College Admission Test (MCAT), Graduate Record Examinations (GRE), Graduate Management Admission Test (GMAT), Scholastic Achievement Test (SAT), Advanced Placement Exams, and College Board Achievement Tests. Whereas most test preparation books present a limited amount of practice exams and bear little resemblance to the actual exams, REA's series accurately depict the actual exams in both degree of difficulty and types of questions. REA's exams are always based on the most recently administered tests and include every type of question that can be expected on the actual tests.

REA's publications and educational materials are highly regarded for their significant contributions to the quest for excellence that characterizes today's educational goals. We continually receive an unprecedented amount of praise from professionals, instructors, librarians, parents, and students for our published books. Our authors are as diverse as the subjects and fields represented in the books we publish. They are well-known in their respective fields and serve on the faculties of prestigious universities and high schools throughout the United States.

HOW TO PREPARE AND DO YOUR BEST ON THE CBEST

By reviewing and studying this book, you can achieve a top score on the CBEST. The CBEST assesses knowledge which you have gained throughout your academic career. Most of the knowledge tested by the CBEST is covered in your college or university teacher preparation programs or through other classes. While the test does not ascertain aspects of teaching such as dedication, rapport with students, and motivation, the test does assess basic skills relevant to the teaching profession.

The purpose of our book is to properly prepare you for the CBEST by providing three full-length exams which accurately reflect the CBEST in both type of question and degree of difficulty. The provided exams, based on the most recently administered CBESTs, include every type of question that can be expected on the CBEST. Following each exam is an answer key complete with detailed explanations and solutions. Designed specifically to clarify the material to the student, the explanations not only provide the correct answers, but also explain to the student why the answer to a particular question is more acceptable than any other answer choice. By completing all three exams and studying the explanations which follow, your strengths and weaknesses can be discovered. This knowledge will allow you to concentrate on the sections of the exam you find to be most difficult.

ABOUT THE TEST EXPERTS

To aid us in meeting our objectives for providing exams which accurately reflect the CBEST, test experts in the relevant subject fields carefully prepared each and every exam section. Our authors, all Californians who have distinct knowledge of the CBEST, have spent quality time examining and researching the mechanics of the actual CBEST to see what types of practice questions accurately depict the exam and challenge the student. Our experts are highly regarded in the educational community, having studied at the doctoral level and taught in their respective fields at competitive universities and colleges throughout California. They have an in-depth knowledge of the subjects presented in the book, and provide accurate questions which appeal to the student's interest. Each question is clearly explained in order to help the student achieve a top score on the CBEST.

ABOUT THE CBEST
(California Basic Educational Skills Test)

The CBEST (California Basic Educational Skills Test) is required by the states of California and Oregon for applicants requiring a first teaching or service credential. In California, unless an applicant already holds a California teaching credential, this test must be taken to obtain an issuance or renewal of an Emergency Credential. This rule does not apply in Oregon.

There are two other cases when the CBEST might be required. It may be required for those people who have not taught for 39 months or more and are re-entering the teaching profession, and for diagnostic purposes for students entering teacher education programs throughout their state. To determine if you should take the CBEST, contact:

California Commission on Teacher Credentialing
P.O. Box 944270
Sacramento, CA 94244-2700
(916) 445-7254
(in California)

or

Oregon Teacher Standards and Practices Commission
630 Center, N.E. Suite 200
Salem, OR 97310-0320
(503) 378-3586
(in Oregon)

The CBEST is given six times a year: in October, December, February, April, June, and August. The test is administered by the Educational Testing Service (ETS) under the direction of the CBEST Program. Questions regarding the CBEST can be referred to:

CBEST Program
P.O. Box 23260
Oakland, CA 94623-2326
(415) 596-5950

You may also contact your school's education department for information on applying to take the test.

The exam tests reading skills (literal, critical, and inferential comprehension), mathematics skills (arithmetic, algebra, and measurement and geometry), and writing skills (insight into a subject, writing for a specific audience, clarity, consistency of point of view, cohesiveness, strength and logic of supporting information, and overall mechanics, spelling, and usage). The CBEST consists entirely of multiple-choice questions, except for the two essays you must write. Each multiple-choice question presents five choices (A through E). The time requirement of the exam is 3 hours and 15 minutes.

The test contains three distinct sections broken down into the following areas:

1. Reading Section: There is one 65-minute reading section which contains 50 questions based on original passages of between 100 and 200 words. In a few cases, these passages simply could be short statements of not more than one or two sentences.

2. Mathematics Section: There is one 70-minute mathematics section which contains 50 questions. These questions come from three broad categories: arithmetic, algebra, and measurement and geometry. Within these categories, the following types of problems will be tested:

- Processes Used in Problem Solving–For example, identifying an operation needed to solve a problem or changing a verbal problem into one using math symbols.

- Solution of Applied Problems–For example, answering word problems including arithmetic, percent, ratio and proportion, algebra, elementary geometry, and elementary statistics.

- Mathematical Concepts and Relationships–For example, recognizing the definitions of certain terms (such as percent), and relationships shown by graphs.

All of these categories require the knowledge of arithmetic, algebra, and measurement and geometry.

3. Essay Writing Section: There is one 60 minute essay section which contains two essay topics. You must write on both topics. One topic requires you to analyze a given situation, the other asks you to write on a personal experience.

Following this preface are test strategies, examples, and suggested study techniques which will help you to properly prepare for the CBEST.

ABOUT THE DIAGNOSTIC TEST

Our diagnostic test is a full-length test designed to help you determine your strengths and weaknesses on the CBEST. For maximum benefit, simulate actual testing conditions by timing yourself and taking the test where you will not be interrupted.

Take each section separately. After each section, score yourself and review the detailed explanations of answers to determine your strengths and weaknesses. Each section offers a discussion of scoring so that you may understand what grade you must receive to pass the exam.

After you complete each section of the diagnostic test, study the reviews in Reading Comprehension, Mathematics, and Essay Writing. By reading our Study Schedule, you will be able to conform your own studying plan to your studying schedule.

ABOUT THE REVIEW SECTIONS

Our CBEST Test Preparation book offers three reviews which correspond to the subject areas you will find on the exam. These include Reading Comprehension, Mathematics, and Essay Writing. Supplementing your studies with our review will provide focus and structure and will allow you to choose a particular subject or subtopic to study. The reviews consist of the following:

Reading Comprehension Review

In this review you will be taught to recognize literal, inferential, and critical comprehension questions. You are given general strategies for answering reading comprehension questions and then you will practice these strategies on sample questions.

Mathematics Review

The Mathematics Review offers three mini-reviews on the following topics:

Arithmetic, including integers, prime and composite numbers, odd and even numbers, place value, powers and roots of whole numbers, addition, subtraction, multiplication, and division of integers, common fractions, decimal fractions, percents, and elementary statistics.

Algebra, including algebraic expressions, simplifying algebraic expressions, factoring, solving linear equations, solving inequalities, evaluating formulas, elementary probability, and algebra word problems.

Geometry and Measurement, including perimeter and area of rectangles, squares and triangles, circumference and area of circles, volume of cubes and rectangular solids, angle measure, properties of triangles, the Pythagorean Theorem, properties of parallel and perpendicular lines, coordinate geometry, graphs, and the metric system.

You will read a full review on each topic and then will be able to practice your skills in a short exercise at the end of this review.

Essay Writing Review

The Essay Writing Review focuses specifically on essay writing for the CBEST. You will learn about the types of topics you can expect to see on the

CBEST, and sample topics will be given. In addition, you will learn how the essay grade is determined so that you will be able to sharpen your writing ability to achieve a high grade.

PARTICIPATE IN STUDY GROUPS

As a final word on how to study for this exam, you may want to study with others. This will allow you to share knowledge and obtain feedback from other members of your study group. Study groups may make preparing for the exam more enjoyable.

SCORING THE EXAM

The Reading and Mathematics sections in the CBEST are scored the same way: raw scores are determined by adding together all the correct answers without deducting points for incorrect answers.

The Writing section is scored a different way. Each of your essays will be scored by two readers. The criteria by which the readers must grade are determined before the reading process begins, and the readers are thoroughly trained to grade using these criteria only. The readers are college professors from public and private colleges and universities in California and Oregon, as well as elementary and secondary school English teachers from these two states.

Two readers will read each of your essays independently. Each will assign a score from 1 to 4, with 4 being the highest:

> 4 = Pass
> 3 = Marginal Pass
> 2 = Marginal Fail
> 1 = Fail

The two scores for each essay will then be averaged to one score. Each of those averages are then combined to determine the final score, which ranges on a scale from a high of 16 to a low of four.

The basic rule when determining a passing score on the CBEST is that if you answer at least 70% of the items on each section of the test correctly, you will receive a passing grade on the entire exam. This means you must answer 35 items correctly on both the Reading Comprehension and Mathematics sections to qualify for a passing score, as well as write a passing essay based on the criterion above. Keep this in mind as you score yourself on our tests.

CBEST TEST TAKING STRATEGIES

How to Beat the Clock

Every second counts and you will want to use the available test time for each section in the most efficient manner. Here's how:

1. Memorize the test directions for each section of the test. You do not want to waste valuable time reading directions on the day of the exam. Your time should be spent on answering the questions.

2. Bring a watch to the exam and pace yourself. Work steadily and quickly. Do not get stuck or spend too much time on any one question. If, after a few minutes, you cannot answer a particular question, make a note of it and continue. You can go back to it after you have completed easier questions first.

3. As you work on the test, be sure that your answers correspond with the proper numbers and letters on the answer sheet.

Guessing Strategy

1. If you are uncertain about a question, guess at the answer rather than not answer the question at all. You will not be penalized for answering incorrectly, since wrong answers are not counted toward your final score. This means that you should never leave a blank space on your answer sheet. Even if you do not have time to narrow down the choices, be sure to fill in every space on the answer sheet. You will not be assessed a penalty for a wrong answer, but you will receive credit for any questions answered correctly by luck.

2. You can improve on your guessing strategy by eliminating any choices recognized as incorrect. As you eliminate incorrect choices, cross them out. Remember that writing in test booklets is allowed and that by crossing out incorrect choices, you will be better able to focus on the remaining choices.

TEST 1
DIAGNOSTIC TEST

Diagnostic Test

CBEST Test 1

Section I: Reading Comprehension
(Answer sheets appear in the back of this book.)

TIME: 65 Minutes
50 Questions

DIRECTIONS: A number of questions follow each of the passages in the reading section. Answer the questions by choosing the best answer from the five choices given.

Questions 1, 2, 3, 4, and 5 refer to the following passage:

Spa water quality is maintained through a filter to ensure cleanliness and clarity. Wastes such as perspiration, hairspray, and lotions which cannot be removed by the spa filter can be controlled by shock treatment or super chlorination every other week. Although the filter traps most of the solid material to control bacteria and algae and to oxidize any organic material, the addition of disinfectants such as bromine or chlorine is necessary.

As all water solutions have a pH which controls corrosion, proper pH balance is also necessary. A pH measurement determines if the water is acid or alkaline. Based on a 14-point scale, a pH reading of 7.0 is considered neutral while a lower reading is considered acidic, and a higher reading indicates alkalinity or basic. High pH (above 7.6) reduces sanitizer efficiency, clouds water, promotes scale formation on surfaces and equipment, and interferes with filter operation. When pH is high, add a pH decrease such as Sodium Bisulphate (e.g., Spa Down). Because the spa water is hot, scale is deposited more rapidly. A weekly dose of a stain and scale fighter also will help to control this problem. Low pH (below 7.2) is equally damaging, causing equipment corrosion, water which is irritating, and rapid sanitizer dissipation. To increase pH add Sodium Bicarbonate (e.g., Spa Up).

The recommended operating temperature of a spa (98° - 104°) is a fertile environment for the growth of bacteria and virus. This growth is prevented when appropriate sanitizer levels are continuously monitored. Bacteria can also be controlled by maintaining a proper bromine level of 3.0 to 5.0 parts per million (ppm) or a chlorine level of 1.0 - 2.0 ppm. As bromine tablets should not be added directly to the water, a bromine floater will properly dispense the tablets. Should chlorine be the chosen sanitizer, a granular form is recommended, as liquid chlorine or tablets are too harsh for the spa.

1.   Although proper chemical and temperature maintenance of spa water is neces-
      sary, the most important condition to monitor is

      (A)   preventing growth of bacteria and virus.

      (B)   preventing equipment corrosion.

      (C)   preventing soap build up.

      (D)   preventing scale formation.

      (E)   preventing cloudy water.

2.   Of the chemical and temperature conditions in a spa, the condition most
      dangerous to one's health is

      (A)   spa water temperature above 104°.

      (B)   bromine level between 3.0 and 5.0.

      (C)   pH level below 7.2.

      (D)   spa water temperature between 90° and 104°.

      (E)   cloudy and dirty water.

3.   The primary purpose of the passage is to

      (A)   relate that maintenance of a spa can negate the full enjoyment of the
             spa experience.

      (B)   provide evidence that spas are not a viable alternative to swimming
             pools.

      (C)   convey that the maintenance of a spa is expensive and time consuming.

      (D)   explain the importance of proper spa maintenance.

      (E)   detail proper spa maintenance.

4.   The spa filter can be relied upon to

      (A)   control algae and bacteria.

      (B)   trap most solid material.

      (C)   oxidize organic material.

      (D)   assure an adequate level of sanitation.

      (E)   maintain clear spa water.

5.   Which chemical should one avoid when maintaining a spa?

       (A)   Liquid chlorine   (B)   Bromine

       (C)   Sodium bisulfate   (D)   Baking soda

       (E)   All forms of chlorine

Questions 6, 7, 8, 9, and 10 refer to the following passage:

The relationship of story elements found in children's generated stories to reading achievement was analyzed. Correlations ranged from .61101 (p=.64) at the beginning of first grade to .83546 (p=.24) at the end of first grade, to .85126 (p=.21) at the end of second grade, and to .82588 (p=.26) for fifth/sixth grades. Overall, the correlation of the story elements to reading achievement appeared to indicate a high positive correlation trend even though it was not statistically significant.

Multiple regression equation analyses dealt with the relative contribution of the story elements to reading achievement. The contribution of certain story elements was substantial. At the beginning of first grade, story conventions added 40 percent to the total variance while the other increments were not significant. At the end of first grade, story plot contributed 44 percent to the total variance, story conventions contributed 20 percent, and story sources contributed 17 percent. At the end of second grade, the story elements contributed more equal percentages to the total partial correlation of .8513. Although none of the percentages were substantial, story plot (.2200), clausal connectors (.1858), and T-units (.1590), contributed the most to the total partial correlation. By the fifth and sixth grades three other story elements—T-units (.2241), story characters (.3214), and clausal connectors (.1212)—contributed most to the total partial correlation. None of these percentages were substantial.

6.   Which of the following is the most complete and accurate definition of the term **statistically significant** as used in the passage?

       (A)   Consists of important numerical data

       (B)   Is educationally significant

       (C)   Departs greatly from chance expectations

       (D)   Permits prediction of reading achievement by knowing the story elements

       (E)   Indicates two measures (reading achievement and story elements) give the same information

7.   The passage suggests which of the following conclusions about the correlation of story elements to reading achievement?

       (A)   That there are other more important story elements that should also be included in the analyses

(B)   That children's inclusion of story elements in their stories causes them to achieve higher levels in reading

(C)   That these story elements are important variables to consider in reading achievement

(D)   That correlations of more than 1.0 are needed for this study to be statistically significant

(E)   That this correlation was not statistically significant because there was little variance between story elements and reading achievemen.

8. The relative contribution of story conventions and story plot in first grade suggests that

(A)   children may have spontaneously picked up these story elements as a result of their exposure to stories.

(B)   children have been explicitly taught these story elements.

(C)   these story elements were not important because in fifth/sixth grades other story elements contributed more to the total partial correlation.

(D)   other story elements were more substantial.

(E)   children's use of story conventions and plots were not taken from story models.

9. The content of the passage suggests that the passage would most likely appear in which of the following?

(A)   *Psychology Today*

(B)   *The Creative Writer*

(C)   *Educational Leadership*

(D)   *Language Arts*

(E)   *Reading Research Quarterly*

10. "None of these percentages were substantial" is the last statement in the passage. It refers to

(A)   the story elements for fifth/sixth grades.

(B)   the story elements for second grade.

(C)   the story elements at the end of first grade.

(D)   the story elements at the beginning of first grade.

(E)   the story elements for all of the grades, i.e., first grade, second grade, and fifth/sixth grade.

Questions 11, 12, and 13 refer to the following passage:

There is an importance of learning communication and meaning in language. Yet the use of notions such as communication and meaning as the basic criteria for instruction, experiences, and materials in classrooms may misguide a child in several respects. Communication in the classroom is vital. The teacher should use communication to help students develop the capacity to make their private responses become public responses. Otherwise, one's use of language would be in danger of being what the younger generation refers to as mere words, mere thoughts, and mere feelings.

Learning theorists emphasize specific components of learning: behaviorists stress behavior in learning; humanists stress the affective in learning; and cognitivists stress cognition in learning. All three of these components occur simultaneously and cannot be separated from each other in the learning process. In 1957, Festinger referred to dissonance as the lack of harmony between what one does (behavior) and what one believes (attitude). Attempts to separate the components of learning either knowingly or unknowingly create dissonances wherein language, thought, feeling, and behavior become diminished of authenticity. As a result, ideas and concepts lose their content and vitality, and the manipulation and politics of communication assume prominence.

11.   Which of the following best describes the author's attitude toward the subject discussed?

(A)   A flippant disregard   (D)   A passive resignation

(B)   A mild frustration   (E)   An informed concern

(C)   A moral indignation

12.   The primary purpose of the passage is to

(A)   explain the criteria for providing authentic communication in classroom learning.

(B)   discuss the relationships between learning and communication.

(C)   assure teachers that communication and meaning are the basic criteria for learning in classrooms.

(D)   stress the importance of providing authentic communication in classroom learning.

(E)   address the role of communication and meaning in classrooms.

13.   Which of the following is the most complete and accurate definition of the term **mere** as used in the passage?

(A)   Small   (B)   Minor   (C)   Little

(D)   Poor   (E)   Insignificant

Questions 14, 15, and 16 refer to the following passage:

In 1975, Sinclair observed that it had often been supposed that the main factor in learning to talk is being able to imitate. Schlesinger (1975) noted that at certain stages of learning to speak, a child tends to imitate everything an adult says to him or her, and it therefore seems reasonable to accord to such imitation an important role in the acquisition of language.

Moreover, various investigators have attempted to explain the role of imitation in language. In his discussion of the development of imitation and cognition of adult speech sounds, Nakazema (1975) stated that although the parent's talking stimulates and accelerates the infant's articulatory activity, the parent's phoneme system does not influence the child's articulatory mechanisms. Slobin and Welsh (1973) suggested that imitation is the reconstruction of the adult's utterance and that the child does so by employing the grammatical rules that he has developed at a specific time. Schlesinger proposed that by imitating the adult the child practices new grammatical constructions. Brown and Bellugi (1964) noted that a child's imitations resemble spontaneous speech in that they drop inflections, most function words, and some-times other words. However, the word order of imitated sentences usually was preserved. Brown and Bellugi assumed that imitation is a function of what the child attended to or remembered. Shipley et al. (1969) suggested that repeating an adult's utterance assists the child's comprehension. Ervin (1964) and Braine (1971) found that a child's imitations do not contain more advanced structures than his or her spontaneous utterances; thus, imitation can no longer be regarded as the simple behavioristic act that earlier scholars assumed it to be.

14. The author of the passage would tend to agree with which of the following statements?

    (A) Apparently, children are physiologically unable to imitate a parent's phoneme system.

    (B) Apparently, children require practice with more advanced structures before they are able to imitate.

    (C) Apparently, children only imitate what they already do, using whatever is in their repertoire.

    (D) Apparently, the main factor in learning to talk remains being able to imitate.

    (E) Apparently, children cannot respond meaningfully to a speech situation until they have reached a stage where they can make symbol-orientation responses.

15. The primary purpose of the passage is to

    (A) explain language acquisition.

    (B) explain the role of imitation in language acquisition.

    (C) assure parents of their role in assisting imitation in language acquisition.

    (D) relate the history of imitation in language acquisition.

    (E) discuss relationships between psychological and physiological processes in language acquisition.

16. An inference that parents may make from the passage is that they should

    (A) be concerned when a child imitates their language.

    (B) focus on developing imitation in their child's language.

    (C) realize that their child's imitations may reflect several aspects of language acquisition.

    (D) realize that their talking may over-stimulate their child's articulatory activity.

    (E) not be concerned as imitation is too complex for anyone to understand.

Questions 17 and 18 refer to the following passage:

   A major problem with reading/language arts instruction is that practice assignments from workbooks often provide short, segmented activities that do not really resemble the true act of reading. Perhaps more than any computer application, word processing is capable of addressing these issues.

17. The author would tend to agree that a major benefit of computers in reading/language arts instruction is

    (A) that the reading act may be more closely resembled.

    (B) that short segmented assignments will be eliminated.

    (C) that the issues in reading/language arts instruction will be addressed.

    (D) that computer application will be limited to word processing.

    (E) that reading practice will be eliminated.

18. The appropriate use of a word processor to assist in making practice resemble a reading act is

    (A) detailed.   (B) desirable.

    (C) unstated.   (D) alluded.

(E)   costly.

Questions 19, 20, and 21 refer to the following passage:

In view of the current emphasis on literature-based reading instruction, a greater understanding by teachers of variance in cultural, language, and story components should assist in narrowing the gap between reader and text and improve reading comprehension. Classroom teachers should begin with students' meaning and intentions about stories before moving students to the commonalities of story meaning based on common background and culture. With teacher guidance students should develop a fuller understanding of how complex narratives are when they are generating stories as well as when they are reading stories.

19.   Which of the following is the intended audience for the passage?

   (A)   Students in a reading class

   (B)   Teachers using literature-based curriculum

   (C)   Professors teaching a literature course

   (D)   Parents concerned about their child's comprehension of books

   (E)   Teacher educators teaching reading methods courses

20.   Which of the following is the most complete and accurate definition of the term **variance** as used in the passage?

   (A)   Change   (D)   Deviation

   (B)   Fluctuations   (E)   Incongruity

   (C)   Diversity

21.   The passage supports a concept of meaning primarily residing in

   (A)   culture, language, and story components.

   (B)   comprehension.

   (C)   student's stories only.

   (D)   students only.

   (E)   students and narratives.

Questions 22, 23, 24, and 25 refer to the following passage:

As noted by Favat in 1977, the study of children's stories has been an ongoing concern of linguists, anthropologists, and psychologists. The past decade has witnessed a surge of interest in children's stories from researchers in these and other disciplines. The use of narratives for reading and reading instruction has been commonly accepted by the educational community. The notion that narrative is highly structured and that children's sense of narrative structure is more highly developed than expository structure has been proposed by some researchers.

Early studies of children's stories followed two approaches for story analysis: the analysis of story content or the analysis of story structure. Story content analysis has centered primarily on examining motivational and psychodynamic aspects of story characters as noted in the works of Erikson and Pitcher and Prelinger in 1963 and Ames in 1966. These studies have noted that themes or topics predominate and that themes change with age.

Early research on story structure focused on formal models of structure such as story grammar and story schemata. These models specified basic story elements and formed sets of rules similar to sentence grammar for ordering the elements.

The importance or centrality of narrative in a child's development of communicative ability has been proposed by Halliday (1976) and Hymes (1975). Thus, the importance of narrative for language communicative ability and for reading and reading instruction has been well documented. However, the question still remains about how these literacy abilities interact and lead to conventional reading.

22.   This passage is most probably directed at which of the following audience?

   (A)   Reading educators   (D)   Reading researchers

   (B)   Linguists   (E)   Anthropologists

   (C)   Psychologists

23.   According to the passage, future research should address

   (A)   how story structure and story schema interact with comprehension.

   (B)   how children's use and understanding of narrative interacts and leads to conventional reading.

   (C)   how basal texts and literature texts differ from children's story structure.

   (D)   how story content interacts with story comprehension.

   (E)   how narrative text structure differs from expository text structure.

24.   The major distinction between story content and story structure is that

   (A)   story content focuses on motivational aspects whereas story structure focuses on rules similar to sentence grammar.

   (B)   story content focuses on psychodynamic aspects whereas story structure focuses on formal structural models.

   (C)   story content and story structure essentially refer to the same concepts.

(D)   story content focuses on themes and topic whereas story structure focuses on specific basic story elements.

(E)   story content focuses primarily on characters whereas story structure focuses on story grammar and schemata.

25.   Which of the following is the most complete and accurate definition of the term **surge** as used in the following sentence? The past decade has witnessed a **surge** of interest in children's stories from researchers in these and other disciplines.

(A)   A heavy swell   (D)   A sudden increase

(B)   A slight flood   (E)   A sudden rush

(C)   A sudden rise

Questions 26, 27, 28, and 29 refer to the following passage:

Seldom has the American school system not been the target of demands for change to meet the social priorities of the times. This theme has been traced through the following significant occurrences in education: Benjamin Franklin's advocacy in 1749 for a more useful type of education; Horace Mann's zealous proposals in the 1830s espousing the tax-supported public school; John Dewey's early twentieth century attack on traditional schools for not developing the child effectively for his or her role in society; the post-Sputnik pressure for academic rigor; the prolific criticism and accountability pressures of the 1970s, and the ensuing disillusionment and continued criticism of schools until this last decade of the twentieth century. Indeed, the waves of criticism about American education have reflected currents of social dissatisfaction for any given period of this country's history.

As dynamics for change in the social order result in demands for change in the American educational system, so in turn insistence has developed for revision of teacher education (witness the more recent Holmes report (1986). Historically, the education of American teachers has reflected evolving attitudes about public education. With slight modifications, the teacher education pattern established following the demise of the normal school during the early 1900s has persisted in most teacher preparation programs. The pattern has been one requiring certain academic and professional (educational) courses often resulting in teachers prone to teach as they had been taught.

26.   The author of this passage would probably agree with which of the following statements?

(A)   Teacher education courses tend to be of no value.

(B)   Social dissatisfaction should drive change in the American school systems.

(C) Teacher education programs have changed greatly since normal schools were eliminated.

(D) Critics of American education reflect vested interests.

(E) Teachers teaching methods tend to reflect what they have learned in their academic and professional courses.

27. The evolving attitudes about public education are

(A) stated.   (D) unchanged.

(B) unstated.   (E) unwarranted.

(C) alluded.

28. One possible sequence of significant occurrences in education noted in the passage is

(A) Mann's tax-supported public schools, post-Sputnik pressures for academic rigor, and the Holmes' report.

(B) Franklin's more useful type of education, Dewey's educating children for their role in society, and Mann's tax-supported public schools.

(C) Mann's tax-supported public schools, the Holmes' report, and post-Sputnik pressures for academic rigor.

(D) Franklin's more useful type of education, the Holmes' report, and accountability pressures of the 1970s.

(E) Mann's tax-supported public schools, accountability pressures of the 1970s, and the post-Sputnik pressures for academic rigor.

29. Which of the following statements most obviously implies dissatisfaction with preparation of teachers in the United States?

(A) Demands for change in the American education system lead to insistence for revision of teacher education programs.

(B) The pattern of teacher education requires certain academic and professional education courses.

(C) The education of U.S. teachers has reflected evolving attitudes about public education.

(D) Teachers tend to teach as they were taught.

(E) Teacher education has changed very little since the decline of the normal school.

Questions 30, 31, 32, and 33 refer to the following passage:

HAWK ON A FRESHLY PLOWED FIELD

My Lord of the Field, proudly perched on the sod,

You eye with disdain

And mutter with wings

As steadily each furrow I tractor-plod.

"Intruder!" you glare, firmly standing your ground,

Proclaim this fief yours

By Nature so willed—

Yet bound to the air on my very next round.

You hover and soar, skimming close by the earth,

Distract me from work

To brood there with you

Of changes that Man wrought your land—for his worth.

In medieval days, lords were god over all:

Their word was the law.

Yet here is this hawk

A ruler displaced—Man and Season forestall.

My Lord of the Field, from sight you have flown

For purpose untold,

When brave, you return

And perch once again, still liege-lord—but Alone.

Jacqueline K. Hultquist (1952)

30. Which of the following is the most complete and accurate definition of the term **liege-lord** as used in the passage?

    (A) Monarch   (D) Sovereign

    (B) King   (E) Master

    (C) Owner

31. Which of the following best describes the author's attitude toward the hawk?

    (A) Whimsical   (D) Intimidating

    (B) Romantic   (E) Fearful

    (C) Pensive

32. Which of the following groups of words about the hawk carry human qualities?

    (A) mutter, brood, and ruler   (B) brave, disdain, and perch

    (C) mutter, disdain, and perch   (D) brave, brood, and distract

    (E) mutter, disdain, and skimming

33. Which of the following is the most complete and accurate definition of the term **medieval** as used in the passage?

    (A) Antiquated   (D) Antebellum

    (B) Feudal   (E) Antediluvian

    (C) Old

Questions 34, 35, 36, and 37 refer to the following passage:

Reduced to its simplest form, a political system is really no more than a device enabling groups of people to live together in a more or less orderly society. As they have developed, political systems generally have fallen into the broad categories of those which do not offer direct subject participation in the decision-making process, and those which allow citizen participation—in form, if not in actual effectiveness.

Let us consider, however, the type of political system that is classified as the modern democracy in a complex society. Such a democracy is defined by Lipset (1963) as "a political system which supplies regular constitutional opportunities for changing the governing officials, and a social mechanism which permits the largest possible part of the population to influence major decisions by choosing among alternative contenders for political office."

Proceeding from another concept (that of Easton and Dennis), a political system is one of inputs, conversion, and outputs by which the wants of a society are transformed into binding decisions. Easton and Dennis (1967) observed: "To sustain a conversion process of this sort, a society must provide a relatively stable context for political interaction, as set of general rules for participating in all parts of the political process." As a rule, this interaction evolves around the settling of differences (satisfying wants or demands) involving the elements of a "political regime," which consists of minimal general goal constraints, norms governing behavior, and structures of authority for the input-output function.

In order to persist, a political system would seem to need a minimal support for the political regime. To insure the maintenance of such a support is the function of political socialization, a process varying according to political systems but toward the end of indoctrinating the members to the respective political system. "To the extent that the maturing members absorb and become attached to the overarching goals of the system and its basic norms and come to approve its structure of authority as legitimate, we can say that they are learning to contribute support to the regime." The desired political norm (an expectation about the way people will behave) is that referred to as political efficacy—a feeling that one's action can have an impact on government.

Adapted from Easton, B. and J. Dennis, "The Child's Acquisition of Regime Norms: Political Efficacy" *American Political Science Review*, March 1967.

34. Political efficacy according to the passage is

    (A)   most likely to be found where citizen participation is encouraged.

    (B)   most likely to be found where little direct citizen participation is offered.

    (C)   in an expanding concept of political efficiency.

    (D)   in a diminishing concept of political efficiency.

    (E)   in a figurehead political system.

35. Political socialization is a process which

    (A)   occurs only in democracies.

    (B)   occurs only in totalitarian regimes.

    (C)   occurs in any type of political system.

    (D)   occurs less frequently in recent years.

    (E)   occurs when members reject the goals of the system.

36. As used in the passage, which of the following is the most complete and accurate definition of the term **conversion**?

    (A)   Transformation   (D)   Resolution

    (B)   Changeover   (E)   Passing

    (C)   Growth

37. The major distinction between the concepts of Easton and Dennis as opposed to the concepts of Lipset is

    (A)   that the concepts of Easton and Dennis are based on the wants of a society whereas Lipset's concepts are based on change of governing officials.

(B)   that Easton and Dennis' concepts are based on arbitrary decisions whereas Lipset's concepts are based on influencing major decisions.

(C)   that Easton and Dennis' concepts must have a set of general rules whereas Lipset's concepts provide for irregular constitutional opportunities.

(D)   that Easton and Dennis' concepts have no inputs, conversion, and outputs, whereas Lipset's concepts allow for no regular constitutional opportunities.

(E)   that Easton and Dennis' concepts evolve around the settling of differences whereas Lipset's concepts permit the largest conflict possible.

Questions 38, 39, 40, and 41 refer to the following passage:

Assignment: Research for a White Paper Proposing U.S. Foreign Policy

Imagine you are in charge (or assigned to) a foreign policy desk in the U.S. Department of State. Select one of the following regions (descriptors are merely suggestions):

Western Europe—A Changing Alliance

Eastern Europe—Out from Behind the Iron Curtain

The U.S.S.R.—Still an Enigma

The Middle East—History and Emotions

Africa—Rising Expectations in the Postwar Continent

South and Southeast Asia—Unrest in Far Away Places

The Far East—Alienation and Alliance

The Western Hemisphere—Neighbors; Pro and Con

Through research, prepare a White Paper for that area which will indicate:

1. a General Policy Statement toward the nations of that region;

2. a statement as to how World War II set the stage for that policy;

3. a summary of the major events since 1945 in that region which have affected U.S. foreign policy;

4. a list of suggested problems and/or possibilities for near-future interactions of that region and the U.S.

38.   In order to complete this assignment, research into which of the following disciplines (areas of study) would be most appropriate?

(A)   History, Economics, Political Science, and Language

(B)   History, Political Science, Education, Economics

(C)   Political Science, Economics, Geography, and Religion

(D)   Geography, Education, History, and Political Science

(E)   History, Political Science, Economics, and Culture

39.   Which of the following is the most complete and accurate definition of the term **Enigma** as used in the passage?

(A)   Problem   (D)   Secret

(B)   Riddle   (E)   Mystery

(C)   Puzzle

40.   Which of the following is the most appropriate secondary school audience for the assignment?

(A)   Students in a World Geography class

(B)   Students in a World History class

(C)   Students in a Content Area Reading class

(D)   Students in an Economics class

(E)   Students in an American Government class

41.   "White Paper" as used in the passage is best defined as

(A)   a special research-based report which analyzes, summarizes, and/or proposes U.S. Foreign Policy.

(B)   a research-based paper which dictates U.S. Foreign Policy.

(C)   a paper which white-washes previous U.S. Foreign Policy.

(D)   a quasi-official but classified government report.

(E)   a research-based paper which includes items 1, 2, 3, and 4 as specified in the passage:

Questions 42, 43, and 44 refer to the following passage:

Beginning readers, and those who are experiencing difficulty with reading, benefit from assisted reading. During assisted reading the teacher orally reads a passage with a student or students. The teacher fades in and out of the reading act. For example, the teacher lets his or her voice drop to a whisper when students are reading on their own at an acceptable rate and lets his/her voice rise to say the words clearly when the students are having difficulty.

Students who are threatened by print, read word-by-word, or rely on graphophonemic cues, will be helped by assisted reading. These students are stuck on individual language units which can be as small as a single letter or as large as phrases or sentences. As Frank Smith (1977) and other reading educators have noted, speeding up reading, not slowing it down, helps the reader make sense of a passage: This strategy allows students to concentrate on meaning as the short-term memory is not overloaded by focusing on small language units. As the name implies, assisted reading lets the reader move along without being responsible for every language unit; the pressure is taken off the student. Consequently, when the reading act is sped up, it sounds more like language, and students can begin to integrate the cueing systems of semantics and syntax along with grapho-phonemics.

42. As a strategy, assisted reading is best for

    (A) beginning readers who are relying on grapho-phonemic cues.

    (B) learning disabled readers who are experiencing neurological deficits.

    (C) beginning readers who are relying on phono-graphic cues.

    (D) remedial readers who are experiencing difficulty with silent reading.

    (E) beginning readers who are experiencing difficulty with silent reading.

43. Language units as presented in the passage refer to

    (A) individual letters, syllables, or phrases.

    (B) individual letters, syllables, or sentences.

    (C) individual letters, phrases, or paragraphs.

    (D) individual letters, phrases, or sentences.

    (E) individual letters, sentences, or paragraphs.

44. According to the passage, to make sense of a passage a reader must

    (A) focus on small language units.

    (B) overload short-term memory.

    (C) slow down when reading.

    (D) read word-by-word.

    (E) speed up the reading act.

Questions 45, 46, 47, and 48 refer to the following passage:

The information about the comparison of the technology (duplex versus one-way video and two-way audio) and the comparison of site classes versus regular classes tends to indicate that although there was not much of an apparent difference between classes and technology, student participation and student involvement were viewed as important components in any teaching/learning setting. For the future, perhaps revisiting what learning is might be helpful so that this component of distance learning can be more adequately addressed. The question remains whether or not student participation can be equated with learning. Participation per se does not demonstrate learning. A more rigorous instrument which assesses and determines learning may need to be addressed with future distance learning studies.

45. Duplex, as used in the passage, suggests which of the following when comparing distance learning technology?

(A) One-way video and two-way audio

(B) One-way video and one-way audio

(C) Two-way video and two-way audio

(D) Two-way video and one-way audio

(E) Two-way video

46. Which of the following is the most complete and accurate definition of the term **rigorous** as used in the passage?

(A) Harsh   (D) Dogmatic

(B) Austere   (E) Precise

(C) Uncompromising

47. The author of the passage would tend to agree with which of the following statements?

(A) Learning consists of more than student participation.

(B) Duplex technology is better than one-way video and two-way audio.

(C) Student participation and student involvement are not important in learning.

(D) An instrument which assesses and demonstrates learning is not currently available.

(E) A review of learning is not important as the topic has been thoroughly researched.

48. The primary purpose of the passage is to

(A) delineate the issues in distance learning.

(B) note student participation in distance learning and question this role in learning.

(C) detail the comparison of site classes versus regular classes.

    (D)   share information about duplex technology versus one-way video and two-way audio.

    (E)   request an assessment instrument which includes a learning component.

Questions 49 and 50 refer to the following passage:

Eyes are. There is no doubt about it—they are certainly in existence. Eyes have many purposes in this world. Eyes are to see with, to be seen, to be heard, and even to be felt. I suppose they could be tasted, and in some cases could be smelled. Now anything that can satisfy all five of the body's senses must have a great deal of value.

To begin with, I shall start with the thing that enables us to see the other kinds of eyes, and that is the eye—e-y-e. It is a very delicate and effeminate mechanism, as any optician or optometrist will tell you. However, if one of these is not close at hand, just consult a hygiene, psychology, or physics textbook. It (the eye) is also very intricate; the cornea, iris, retina, and crystalline lens are a few of its main members. Each is arranged very neatly in its proper place, where it helps form a part of a very necessary whole.

49.   Which of the following is the most complete and accurate definition of the term **effeminate** as used in the passage?

    (A)   Womanish   (D)   Soft, delicate

    (B)   Unmanly   (E)   Female

    (C)   Emasculate

50.   The author's attitude about the subject discussed is best described as

    (A)   Flippant disregard   (D)   Imaginative

    (B)   Moral indignation   (E)   Humorous

    (C)   Critical

CBEST TEST 1 – ANSWER KEY

Section I: Reading Comprehension

1.	(A)	14.	(C)	27.	(B)	40.	(E)
2.	(A)	15.	(B)	28.	(A)	41.	(A)
3.	(D)	16.	(C)	29.	(E)	42.	(A)
4.	(B)	17.	(A)	30.	(E)	43.	(D)
5.	(A)	18.	(C)	31.	(C)	44.	(E)
6.	(D)	19.	(B)	32.	(A)	45.	(C)
7.	(C)	20.	(C)	33.	(B)	46.	(E)
8.	(A)	21.	(E)	34.	(A)	47.	(A)
9.	(E)	22.	(D)	35.	(C)	48.	(B)
10.	(A)	23.	(B)	36.	(A)	49.	(D)
11.	(E)	24.	(B)	37.	(A)	50.	(D)
12.	(D)	25.	(D)	38.	(E)		
13.	(E)	26.	(E)	39.	(C)		

SCORING THE READING COMPREHENSION SECTION

Your score on this section is based on the total number of questions answered correctly. You will pass the Reading Comprehension if you answer at least 70% of the test items correctly. To get an idea of how you performed on this section, determine the number of questions you answered correctly out of 50. Generally, if you have answered more than 35 of the items correctly, you will be adequately prepared.

DETAILED EXPLANATIONS OF ANSWERS

Section I: Reading Comprehension

1. **(A)** Choices (B), (D), and (E) present minor problems in spa maintenance, whereas choice (C) cannot be prevented. As bacteria and virus are controlled by both temperature and chemicals, it becomes a possible source of health problems if ignored.

2. **(A)** Choices (B), (C), and (D) are correct levels or degrees. Although choice (E) is important, it is not as dangerous as choice (A) where temperatures in excess of 104° can cause dizziness, nausea, fainting, drowsiness, and reduced awareness.

3. **(D)** Choices (A), (B), and (C) represent an inference that goes beyond the scope of the passage and would indicate biases of the reader. Although the passage explains spa maintenance, choice (E), the information is not adequate to serve as a detailed guide.

4. **(B)** The other choices (A), (C), and (D) refer to chemical or temperature maintenance. Although choice (E) helps to ensure clarity, choice (B) is explicitly stated in the passage.

5. **(A)** Choices (B), (C), and (D) are appropriate chemicals. Although chlorine is an alternative to bromine, this passage indicates it should be granular as indicated in choice (A); liquid and tablet chlorines are too harsh for spas, thus all forms are not acceptable as indicated by choice (E).

6. **(D)** Choices (A) and (B) appear to be acceptable, whereas choice (E) indicates a perfect correlation. Although choice (C) is a definition of statistical significance, choice (D) is correct as the passage is about correlational statistical significance which permits prediction.

7. **(C)** Choice (A) goes beyond the information provided in the passage. Choice (B) is incorrect as correlation cannot indicate causality, and choice (E) states incorrectly there was no variance. Choice (D) is not statistically possible. The high positive correlation trend indicates that these variables are important to consider for future research, thus choice (C).

8. **(A)** Choices (B), (C), (D), and (E) represent inferences that are based on inadequate information which go beyond the scope of the passage. As these story elements are not taught explicitly in the first grade or prior to entering school, children

apparently have picked up these elements from their exposures to stories as indicated by choice (A).

9.   (E)   Although the content might be appropriate for each of the journals, choices (A), (B), (C), and (D), the style of writing suggests that it would be most appropriate for choice (C), *Reading Research Quarterly*, as this passage reports research results.

10.   (A)   The passage provides information for the grade level and mentions if it was significant or substantial. As this statement follows information provided for fifth/sixth grades, it refers to that level, thus choice (A).

11.   (E)   Choices (A), (B), (C), and (D) all connote extreme or inappropriate attitudes not expressed in the passage. The author presents an informed concern—choice (E).

12.   (D)   For the other choices (A), (B), (C), and (E) the criteria, the role, the discussion, and the assurance for communication or learning are not provided in the passage. The passage stresses the importance of authenticity in communication—choice (D).

13.   (E)   Each of the choices is a possible definition, but the passage overall suggests that communication needs to be developed so that students' responses may become more significant and authentic—choice (E).

14.   (C)   Choices (A), (B), and (E) are not supported by the passage. Choice (D) represents an incorrect conclusion. Choice (C) is supported by the various investigators, explanations.

15.   (B)   As stated explicitly in the passage, the various investigators have attempted to explain the role of imitation in language—choice (B). The other choices go beyond the scope of the passage.

16.   (C)   As the investigators studied different aspects of language while attempting to explain the role of imitation in language, choice (C) is correct. The other choices go beyond the scope of the passage.

17.   (A)   The passage explicitly states that computers are capable of addressing the issues of practice and the true act of reading, choice (A). The other choices represent inferences that are not supported by the passage.

18.   (C)   Although the reader might make inferences to select choices (A), (B), (D), and (E), ways to use a word processor to make practice resemble the true reading act are not stated in the passage, thus choice (C).

19. **(B)** Although audiences in choices (A), (C), (D), and (E) may benefit from the information provided in the passage, the passage explicitly states that a greater understanding of the information in the passage should assist teachers—choice (B).

20. **(C)** Each of the choices is a definition of variance. However, for this passage, choice (C) is the most appropriate.

21. **(E)** Although meaning is found in the components of each choice, the passage states that we should begin with students' meaning before moving to the commonalities of story meaning—choice (E).

22. **(D)** As the passage presents information by various researchers on children's stories, the passage ends with an unanswered question that still needs to be addressed by reading researchers as provided in choice (D).

23. **(B)** Although more information may be needed about story content and story structure as indicated in choices (A), (C), (D), and (E), the main question that remains to be answered is choice (B).

24. **(B)** Each choice provides partially correct information about story content and story structure; choice (B) provides the most complete response.

25. **(D)** Each choice is a possible definition. However, choice (D) is most appropriate as there was an increased interest by researchers in these and other areas even though it has been an ongoing concern of some researchers.

26. **(E)** Choices (A) and (C) are not supported by the passage. Choices (B) and (D) go beyond the passage. The last sentence states "The pattern ... results in teachers prone to teach as they had been taught"—thus choice (E).

27. **(B)** The other choices (A), (C), (D), and (E) are not supported by the passage. Although the passage mentions that teacher education has reflected evolving attitudes about education, the attitudes are not spelled out—choice (B).

28. **(A)** Only choice (A) has the correct sequence; the other sequences are incorrect.

29. **(E)** Choices (A), (B), (C), and (D) are statements about education, teacher education, and teachers. Choice (E) statement that teacher education has changed very little implies that this lack of change could be a source of dissatisfaction.

30. **(E)** Choices (A), (B), and (D) suggest rights either by heredity or supreme authority, whereas choice (C) indicates rights just by possession. The hyphenated term "liege-lord" connotes both entitled rights and power to command respect. Thus choice (E), "master" (one who assumes authority and property rights through ability and power to control) best represents the hawk.

31. **(C)** Choices (A), (D), and (E) are not supported by the passage. Choice (B) represents a possible conclusion, but choice (C) suggests real thought about the hawk.

32. **(A)** Each of the other choices contains a term which does not refer to human qualities. The other qualities may refer to the hawk, e.g., perch or to the author of the passage, e.g., disdain.

33. **(B)** Choices (D) and (E) are incorrect because of definitions. Choices (A) and (C) are possible definitions, but feudal most clearly denotes an association to the Middle Ages.

34. **(A)** The passage explicitly states that political efficacy is a feeling that one's actions can have an impact on government—choice (A). Choices (C), (D), and (E) are not supported by the passage. Choice (B) is incorrect.

35. **(C)** Choices (A), (B), (D), and (E) are not supported by the passage. The passage states "...political socialization, a process varying according to political systems but toward the end of indoctrinating the members to the respective political system"—choice (C).

36. **(A)** Although the other choices (B), (C), (D), and (E) are possible definitions, the passage explicitly states that "a political system is one of inputs, conversions, and outputs by which the wants of a society are transformed into binding decisions"—thus choice (A).

37. **(A)** Choices (B), (C), (D), and (E) contain an incorrect concept of either Easton and Dennis or Lipset. Only choice (A) has the correct concepts for both Easton and Dennis and Lipset.

38. **(E)** Choices (A), (B), (C), and (D) each contain an area which is considered a component of culture, such as religion, education, and language. Thus choice (E) is the most appropriate response.

39. **(C)** Although each definition appears appropriate, choices (B), (D), and (E) assume that a solution is known, or has been known at one time, and could be solved. Although choice (A) suggests difficulty in solving, choice (C) suggests a situation that is intricate enough to perplex the mind. Choice (C) is most appropriate for this passage as a definition of enigma is an inexplicable situation.

40. **(E)** Although choices (A), (B), (C), and (D) may touch on such a topic, the roles and functions of governmental offices and departments are generally addressed in an American Government class, thus choice (E).

41. **(A)** Choices (B), (C), and (D) are incorrect in that a White Paper does not dictate or automatically white-wash U.S. Foreign Policy, nor is it a classified report. Although choice (E) states criteria to include in a report, it may not meet the specifications of a White Paper—thus choice (A).

42. **(A)** Choices (D) and (E) are incorrect as the strategy is for oral reading, not silent reading. Choices (B) and (C) are not supported by the passage—thus choice (A).

43. **(D)** Choices (A), (B), (C), and (E) include syllable and paragraph elements which are not supported by the passage. The passage states "...individual language units which can be as small as a single letter or as large as a phrase or sentence."

44. **(E)** Choices (A), (B), (C), and (D) are not supported by the passage. The passages states "that speeding up reading, not slowing it down, helps the reader make sense of a passage."

45. **(C)** The passage compares duplex versus one-way video and two-way audio. The reader must infer that duplex indicates two-way video and two-way audio since duplex refers to two. The other choices (A), (B), (D), and (E) are incorrect.

46. **(E)** Choices (A), (B), (C), and (D) are inappropriate for defining an instrument which assesses learning and demonstrates learning.

47. **(A)** Choices (B), (C), (D), and (E) are not supported by the passage.

48. **(B)** While choices (A), (C), (D), and (E) are mentioned briefly in the passage, the passage focuses on student participation and learning.

49. **(D)** Choices (A), (B), (C) and (E) appear to be definitions of effeminate. However, for this passage choice (D) is most appropriate since it relates to the eyes.

50. **(D)** Choices (A), (B), and (C) are not supported by the passage. The passage hints at choice (E), but the passage remains primarily imaginative, thus choice (D).

CBEST Test 1

Section II: Mathematics

TIME: 65 Minutes
        50 Questions

DIRECTIONS: Each of the questions or incomplete statements below is followed by five suggested answers or completions. Select the one that is best in
each case.

1.   If 406.725 is rounded off to the nearest tenth, the number is

(A)   406.3   (D)   406.8

(B)   406.5   (E)   407.0

(C)   406.7

2.   The mean IQ score for 1,500 students is 100, with a standard deviation of 15.
     Assuming normal curve distribution, how many students have an IQ between
     85 and 115? Refer to the figure shown below.

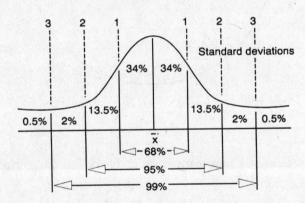

(A)   510   (D)   1,275

(B)   750   (E)   1,425

(C)   1,020

3. The sum of 12 and twice a number is 24. Find the number.

    (A) 6   (D) 11

    (B) 8   (E) 12

    (C) 10

4. Twice the sum of 10 and a number is 28. Find the number.

    (A) 4   (D) 14

    (B) 8   (E) 24

    (C) 12

5. Two college roommates spent $2,000 for their total monthly expenses. A circle graph below indicates a record of their expenses.

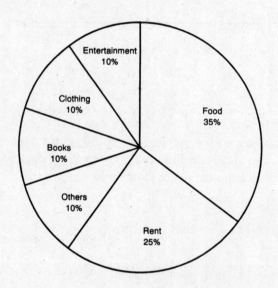

    Based on the above information, which of the following statements is accurate?

    (A)   The roommates spent $700 on food alone.

    (B)   The roommates spent $550 on rent alone.

    (C)   The roommates spent $300 on entertainment alone.

    (D)   The roommates spent $300 on clothing alone.

    (E)   The roommates spent $300 on books alone.

6. You can buy a telephone for $24. If you are charged $3 per month for renting a telephone from the telephone company, how long will it take you to recover the cost of the phone if you buy one?

    (A)   6 months   (D)   9 months

    (B)   7 months   (E)   10 months

    (C)   8 months

7. What would be the measure of the third angle in the following triangle?

    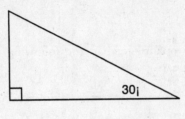

    (A)   45°   (D)   70°

    (B)   50°   (E)   240°

    (C)   60°

8. What is the perimeter of this figure?

    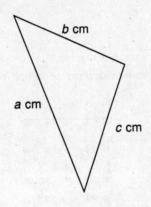

    (A)   *abc* cm   (D)   (*a* + *b* + *c*) cm²

    (B)   *abc* cm²   (E)   *abc* cm³

    (C)   (*a* + *b* + *c*) cm

9.   What is the perimeter of the given triangle?

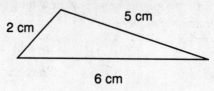

(A)   6 cm   (D)   13 cm

(B)   11 cm   (E)   15 cm

(C)   12 cm

10. Assuming that the quadrilateral in the following figure is a parallelogram, what would be its area?

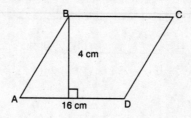

(A)   32 cm   (D)   64 cm

(B)   40 cm   (E)   64 cm²

(C)   40 cm²

11. Refer to the figure below to determine which of the following statements is correct.

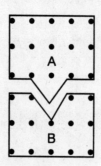

I.   Figures A and B have the same area.

II. Figures A and B have the same perimeter.

(A)   Only I   (D)   Neither I nor II

(B)   Only II   (E)   Can't be determined.

(C)   Both I and II

12. Which of the following is *not* a proper subset of {1, 2, 3, 4}?

    (A) {1, 2}   (D) {1, 3, 4}

    (B) {1, 2, 3}   (E) {1, 2, 5}

    (C) {1, 2, 4}

13. Which of the following is an example of a rational number?

    (A) $\sqrt{17}$ (D) $7 + \sqrt{9}$

    (B) $6 + 3\sqrt{7}$ (E) $2 - \sqrt{15}$

    (C) $4\sqrt{11}$

14. Which of the following statements includes a cardinal number?

    (A) There are 15 volumes in the set of periodicals.

    (B) I received my 14th volume recently.

    (C) The students meet at Room 304.

    (D) My phone number is 213-617-8442.

    (E) James lives on 3448 Lucky Avenue.

15. In a group of 30 studuents, 12 are studying mathematics, 18 are studying English, 8 are studying science, 7 are studying both mathematics and English, 6 are studying English and science, 5 are studying mathematics and science, and 4 are studying all three subjects. How many of these students are taking only English? How many of these students are not taking any of these subjects?

    (A) 9 students take only English; 6 students take neither of these subjects.

    (B) 10 students take only English; 5 students take neither of these subjects.

    (C) 11 students take only English; 5 students take neither of these subjects.

    (D) 12 students take only English; 6 students take neither of these subjects.

    (E) 13 students take only English; 4 students take neither of these subjects.

16. For the given Venn diagram find n(A ∩ B ∩ C):

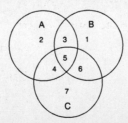

(A) 3   (D) 6

(B) 4   (E) 7

(C) 5

17. Find the next three terms in this sequence: 1, 4, 9, 16, ...

(A) 19, 24, 31   (D) 25, 36, 49

(B) 20, 25, 31   (E) 25, 34, 43

(C) 21, 28, 36

18. Assume that one pig eats 4 pounds of food each week. There are 52 weeks in a year. How much food do 10 pigs eat in a week?

(A) 40 lb.   (D) 20 lb.

(B) 520 lb.   (E) 60 lb.

(C) 208 lb.

19. Suppose that a pair of pants and a shirt cost $65 and the pants cost $25 more than the shirt. What did they each cost?

(A) The pants cost $35 and the shirt costs $30.

(B) The pants cost $40 and the shirt costs $25.

(C) The pants cost $43 and the shirt costs $22.

(D) The pants cost $45 and the shirt costs $20.

(E) The pants cost $50 and the shirt costs $15.

20. There are five members in a basketball team. Supposing each member shakes hands with every other member of the team before the game starts, how many handshakes will there be in all?

(A) 6   (D) 10

(B) 8   (E) 12

(C) 9

21. Which figure can be obtained from figure Y by translation?

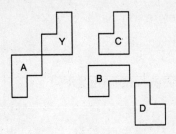

(A) a
(B) b
(C) c

(D) d
(E) None of the above

22. Which of the polygons below is a triangular pyramid?

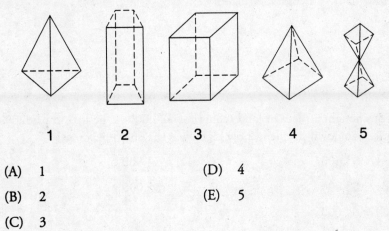

   1   2   3   4   5

(A) 1
(B) 2
(C) 3

(D) 4
(E) 5

23. The figure below represents a portion of a square pyramid viewed from above. Which of the following statements is true?

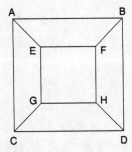

(A) Edges AE and BF intersect.

(B) Lines AE and BF intersect.

(C)   Line segment CG intersects plane DHB.

(D)   Face CGEA intersects plane DHB.

(E)   Line CG intersects line AB.

24.   Below is a rectangular pyramid ABCDE.

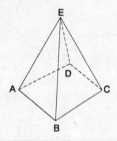

How many vertices does it have?

(A)   3   (D)   6

(B)   4   (E)   7

(C)   5

25.   Tom bought a piece of land selling for $20,000. If he had to pay 20% of the price as a down payment, how much was the down payment?

(A) $2,500   (D) $4,500

(B) $3,000   (E) $5,000

(C) $4,000

26.   A Macintosh LC computer sells for $3,200 to the general public. If you purchase one in the university, the price is reduced by 20%. What is the sale price of the computer?

(A) $640   (D) $2,560

(B) $2,000   (E) $3,180

(C) $2,410

27.   In order for Sue to receive a final grade of C, she must have an average greater than or equal to 70% but less than 80% on five tests. Suppose her grades on the first four tests were 65%, 85%, 60% and 90%. What range of grades on the fifth test would give her a C in the course?

(A)   40 up to but excluding 95   (B)   45 up to but excluding 95

(C)   47 up to but excluding 90   (D)   49 up to but excluding 98

(E)   50 up to but excluding 100

28.   A certain company produces two types of lawnmowers. Type A is self-pro-
      pelled while type B is not. The company can produce a maximum of 18
      mowers per week. It can make a profit of $15 on mower A and a profit of $20
      on mower B. The company wants to make at least 2 mowers of type A but
      not more than 5. They also plan to make at least 2 mowers of type B. Let x be
      the number of type A produced, and let y be the number of type B produced.

      From the above, which of the following is *not* one of the listed constraints?

      (A) $x \geq 2$ (D) $y < 5$

      (B) $x \leq 5$ (E) $y \geq 2$

      (C) $x + y \leq 18$

29.   Mr. Smith died and left an estate to be divided among his wife, two children,
      and a foundation of his choosing in the ratio of 8:6:6:1. How much did his
      wife receive if the estate was valued at $300,000?

      (A) $114,285.71   (D) $14,285.71

      (B) $120,421.91   (E) $125,461.71

      (C) $85,714.29

30.   There were 19 hamburgers for 9 people on a picnic. How many whole ham-
      burgers were there for each person if they were divided equally?

      (A)   1   (D)   4

      (B)   2   (E)   5

      (C)   3

31.   George has four ways to get from his house to the park. He has seven ways to
      get from the park to the school. How many ways can George get from his
      house to school by way of the park?

      (A)   4   (D)   3

      (B)   7   (E)   11

      (C)   28

32.   If it takes 1 minute per cut, how long will it take to cut a 15-foot long timber
      into 15 equal pieces?

      (A)   5   (B)   10

(C) 14 (D) 20

(E) 15

33. Ed has 6 new shirts and 4 new pairs of pants. How many combinations of new shirts and pants does he have?

(A) 10 (D) 20

(B) 14 (E) 24

(C) 18

34. The property tax rate of the town of Grandview is $32 per $1,000 of assessed value. What is the tax if the property is assessed at $50,000?

(A) $32 (D) $1,600

(B) $1,000 (E) $2,000

(C) $1,562

35. Ralph kept track of his work time in gardening. Refer to the broken-line graph below:

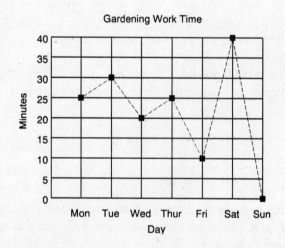

Gardening Work Time

How many minutes did he average per day?

(A) 10 min. (D) 23.05 min.

(B) 20 min. (E) 25 min.

(C) 21.43 min.

36. Mary had been selling printed shirts in her neighborhood. She made this pictograph to show how much money she made each week.

WEEKLY SALES

WEEK	
1st	$ $ $
2nd	$ $ $ $
3rd	$ $ $ $ $ $
4th	$ $ $ $ $
5th	$ $ $
6th	$ $ $ $

Each [$] stands for $12.

How many weeks were sales more than $55?

(A)   1 week

(B)   2 weeks

(C)   3 weeks

(D)   4 weeks

(E)   5 weeks

37. Find the volume of the following figure.

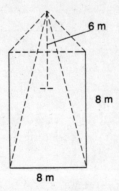

6 m

8 m

8 m

(A)   48 m²

(B)   64 m²

(C)   128 m³

(D)   192 m³

(E)   384 m³

38. The result of Mary's spring semester grades follow. Find her grade point average for the term (A = 4, B = 3, C = 2, D = 1, F = 0).

Course	Credits	Grades
Biology	5	A
English	3	C
Math	3	A
French	3	D
P.E.	2	B

(A) 3.80   (D) 2.00

(B) 3.50   (E) 1.86

(C) 2.94

39. In a biology class at International University, the grades on the final examination were as follows:

91	81	65	81
50	70	81	93
36	90	43	87
96	81	75	81

Find the mode.

(A) 36   (D) 87

(B) 70   (E) 96

(C) 81

40. One commonly used standard score is a z-score. A z-score gives the number of standard deviations by which the score differs from the mean, as shown in the following example.

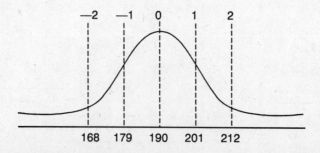

As shown on the previous page, the mean ($\bar{x}$) is 190 and the standard deviation(s) is 11. The score of 201 has a z-score of 1 and a score of 168 has a z-score of –2. Consider the mean height of a certain group of people as 190 cm with a standard deviation of 11 cm. Suppose Glenn's height has a z-score of 1.6, what is his height? (Note $z = \dfrac{x - \bar{x}}{s.d.}$)

(A)   20760 cm

(B)   190 cm

(C)   201 cm

(D)   179 cm

(E)   212 cm

41.   The cost of gas for heating a house in Riverview, Florida is $1.83 per cubic foot. What is the monthly gas bill if the customer uses 145 cubic feet?

(A) $265.35

(B) $145.00

(C) $183.00

(D) $79.23

(E) $200.00

42.   Which of the following figures below represent simple closed curves?

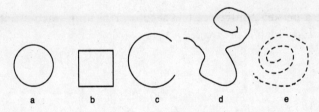

(A)   a and b

(B)   a, b, and c

(C)   c and d

(D)   d and e

(E)   c, d, and e

43.   The wear-out mileage of a certain tire is normally distributed with a mean of 30,000 miles and a standard deviation of 2,500 miles, as shown below.

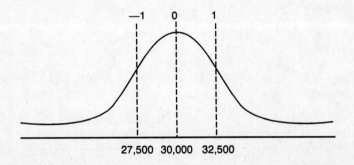

What will be the percentage of tires that will last at least 30,000 miles?

(A)   40%   (D)   55%

(B)   45%   (E)   60%

(C)   50%

44.   How many lines of symmetry, if any, does the following figure have?

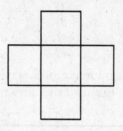

(A)   1   (D)   4

(B)   2   (E)   5

(C)   3

45.   Suppose a person 2 m tall casts a shadow 1 m long when a tree has an 8 m shadow. How high is the tree?

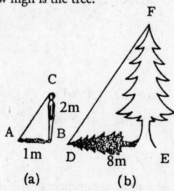

(A)   8 m   (D)   16 m

(B)   10 m   (E)   18 m

(C)   14 m

46.   How many 12 oz. cans of orange juice would it take to give 75 people an 8 oz. orange juice?

(A)   112 cans   (D)   900 cans

(B)   75 cans   (E)   50 cans

(C)   600 cans

47. A car rental agency charges $139 per week plus $0.08 per mile for an average size car. How far can you travel to the nearest mile on a maximum budget of $350?

    (A) 2,637 mi.   (D) 1,737 mi.

    (B) 2,640 mi.   (E) 4,375 mi.

    (C) 2,110 mi.

48. Suppose 4 people have to split 50 hours of overtime. Twice the number of hours must be assigned to one worker as to each of the other three. Find the number of hours of overtime that will be assigned to each worker.

    (A) 10 hrs. for the first three workers; 20 hrs. for the 4th worker.

    (B) 8 hrs. for the first three workers; 16 hrs. for the 4th worker.

    (C) 9 hrs. for the first three workers; 18 hrs. for the 4th worker.

    (D) 11 hrs. for the first three workers; 22 hrs. for the 4th worker.

    (E) 12 hrs. for the first three workers; 24 hrs. for the 4th worker.

49. Peter took a 1,500 mile trip in 5 days. Each day, he drove 30 miles more than the day before. How many miles did he cover on the first day?

    (A) 375 mi.   (D) 240 mi.

    (B) 294 mi.   (E) 250 mi.

    (C) 230 mi.

50. Mr. Reagan needs 75 m to enclose his rectangular property. If the length of the property is 5 m more than the width, what are the dimensions of his property? Note the figure below.

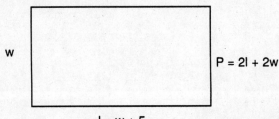

w

$P = 2l + 2w$

$l = w + 5$

    (A) w = 16.25 m; l = 21.25 m   (D) w = 17.50 m; l = 20.00 m

    (B) w = 18.25 m; l = 19.25 m   (E) w = 35.00 m; l = 40.00 m

    (C) w = 13.00 m; l = 24.50 m

CBEST TEST 1 – ANSWER KEY

Section II: Mathematics

1.	(C)	14.	(A)	27.	(E)	40.	(A)
2.	(C)	15.	(A)	28.	(D)	41.	(A)
3.	(A)	16.	(C)	29.	(A)	42.	(A)
4.	(A)	17.	(D)	30.	(B)	43.	(C)
5.	(A)	18.	(A)	31.	(C)	44.	(D)
6.	(C)	19.	(D)	32.	(C)	45.	(D)
7.	(C)	20.	(D)	33.	(E)	46.	(E)
8.	(C)	21.	(C)	34.	(D)	47.	(A)
9.	(D)	22.	(A)	35.	(C)	48.	(A)
10.	(E)	23.	(B)	36.	(B)	49.	(D)
11.	(B)	24.	(C)	37.	(C)	50.	(A)
12.	(E)	25.	(C)	38.	(C)		
13.	(D)	26.	(D)	39.	(C)		

SCORING THE MATHEMATICS SECTION

Your score on this section is based on the total number of questions answered correctly. You will pass the Mathematics if you answer at least 70% of the test items correctly. To get an idea of how you performed on the section, determine the number of questions you answered correctly out of 50. Generally, if you have answered more than 35 of the items correctly you will be adequately prepared.

DETAILED EXPLANATIONS OF ANSWERS

Section II: Mathematics

1. **(C)** 7 is in the tenth's place. Since the next digit (2) is below 5, drop this digit and retain the 7. The answer, therefore, is 406.7.

2. **(C)** The mean IQ score of 100 is given. One standard deviation above the mean is 34% of the cases, with an IQ score up to 115. One standard deviation below the mean is another 34% of the cases, with an IQ score till 85. So, a total of 68% of the students have an IQ between 85 and 115. Therefore, 1,500 x .68 = 1,020.

3. **(A)**
$$12 + 2x = 24$$
$$2x = 24 - 12$$
$$2x = 12$$
$$x = \frac{12}{2}$$
$$x = 6$$

4. **(A)**
$$(10 + x)2 = 28$$
$$20 + 2x = 28$$
$$2x = 28 - 20$$
$$2x = 8$$
$$x = \frac{8}{2}$$
$$x = 4$$

5. **(A)** $2,000 x .35 = $700. The rest have wrong computations.

6. **(C)** Let x = length of time (# of mos) to recover cost.
$$3x = 24$$
$$x = \frac{24}{3}$$
$$x = 8 \text{ mos.}$$

7. **(C)** With one right angle (90°) and a given 30° angle, the missing angle,

therefore, is a 60° angle. (90° + 30° = 120°; 180° − 120° = 60°.)

8. (C) The perimeter is the distance around the triangle which is, therefore, *(a + b + c)* cm.

9. (D) The perimeter is the distance around the triangle. Therefore, 2 cm + 6 cm + 5 cm = 13 cm.

10. (E) The area of a parallelogram is base x height. Therefore, A = bh = (16 cm) x (4 cm) = 64 cm².

11. (B) Figure A has an area of about 9 square units while Figure B has an area of about 7 square units. Both Figures A and B have the same perimeter of about 12 units.

12. (E) Only E has an element (which is 5) not present in the given set of {1,2,3,4}.

13. (D) Nine is the square of an integer. 17, 11, and 15 are not squares of an integer, therefore, they are irrational numbers. 7 is not the cube of an integer, hence, it is an irrational number as well.

14. (A) 15 is used as a cardinal number. The rest are either ordinal (B) or nominal (C, D, E) numbers.

15. (A) Use Venn diagram (as shown below) with 3 circles to represent the set of students in each of the listed subject matter areas. Start with 4 students taking all 3 subjects. We write the number 4 in the region that is the intersection of all these circles. Then we work backward: Since 7 are taking math and English, and 4 of these have already been identified as also taking English, math, and science, there must be exactly 3 taking only math and English. That is, there must be 3 in the region representing math and English, but not science. Continuing in this manner, we enter the given data in the picture.

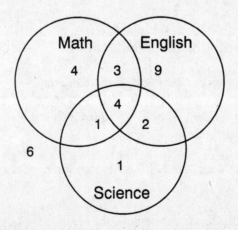

16. **(C)** There is one element in the intersection of all three sets. Thus, n (A ∩ B ∩ C) = 5.

17. **(D)** The sequence 1, 4, 9, 16 is the sum of the odd numbers.
    1. 1
    2. $1 + 3 = 4$
    3. $1 + 3 + 5 = 9$
    4. $1 + 3 + 5 + 7 = 16$

18. **(A)** Here one must use only needed information. Do not be distracted by superfluous data. Simple multiplication will do. If one pig eats four pounds of food per week, how much will 10 pigs eat in one week? 10 x 4 = 40 pounds. The problem intentionally contains superfluous data (52 weeks), which should not distract the reader from its easy solution. Ratio and proportion will also work here $\frac{1}{10} = \frac{4}{x}$, $x = 40$ pounds/week.

19. **(D)** Let the variable S stand for the cost of the shirt. Then the cost of the pair of pants is S + 25 and
    $S + (S + 25) = 65$
    $2S = 65 - 25$
    $2S = 40$
    $S = 20$
    $20 (cost of shirt)
    $20 + $25 = $45 (cost of pants)

20. **(D)** The possible handshakes are illustrated by listing all the possible pairs of letters, thus
    AB AC AD AE
    BC BD BE
    CD CE
    DE
    (a total of 10 handshakes)

21. **(C)** Only C involves a change by only translation.

22. **(A)** B is a rectangular prism. C is a square prism. D is a square pyramid. E is neither a prism nor a pyramid.

23. **(B)** If one continues lines AE and BF, they intersect at a common vertex. The rest do not.

24. **(C)** Points ABCDE are the vertices, thus 5.

25. (C) Let   D = down payment
         D = $20,000 x .20
         D = $4,000

26. (D) 20% of $3,200 = $640 amount price reduced
         $3,200 – $640 = $2,560 sale price

27. (E) Let x = 5th grade
         Average = $\dfrac{65 + 85 + 60 + 90 + x}{5}$

For Sue to obtain a C, her average must be greater than or equal to 70 but less than 80.

$$70 \leq \frac{65 + 85 + 60 + 90 + x}{5} < 80$$

$$70 \leq \frac{300 + x}{5} < 80$$

$$5(70) \leq 5(300 + x \div 5) < 5(80)$$

$$350 \leq 300 + x < 400$$

$$350 - 300 \leq x < 400 - 300$$

$$50 \leq x < 100$$

Thus, a grade of 50 up to but not including a grade of 100 will result in a C.

28. (D) All but D are constraints. The constraint for y is to at least make 2 mowers.

29. (A) The ratio 8:6:6:1 implies that for each $8 the wife received, each child received $6 and the foundation $1. The estate is divided into 8 + 6 + 6 + 1, or 21 equal shares. The wife received $\dfrac{8}{21}$ of $300,000 or $114,285.71, each child received $\dfrac{6}{21}$ of $300,000, or $85,714.29, and the foundation received $\dfrac{1}{21}$ of $300,000 or $14,285.71. As a check, $114,285.71 + $85,714.29 + $85,714.29 + $14,285.71 = $300,000.

30. (B) Simple division. $\dfrac{19}{9}$ = 2 whole hamburgers with one left over.

31. (C) Simple multiplication. 7 x 4 = 28.

32. (C) For a 15 ft. log, it will take 14 cuts to make 15 equal pieces. Therefore, 14 minutes for 14 cuts.

33. (E) Simple multiplication. 6 x 4 = 24.

34. **(D)** First find out how many shares of $1,000 there are in $50,000 ($50,000 ÷ 1,000 = 50). Then multiply the shares by the cost (50 x $32) and the answer is $1,600.

35. **(C)** Find the sum of the seven days. Thus: M = 25; T = 30; W = 20; Th = 25; F = 10; Sat = 40; Sun = 0, or a total of 150 minutes. Find the average by dividing 150 by 7 = 21.43 minutes.

36. **(B)** If each $\boxed{\$}$ stands for $12, only weeks 3 and 4 had a sale of $72 and $60, respectively. The rest are below $55.

37. **(C)** The volume of a pyramid is $V = \frac{1}{3} Bh$, where B is area of the base and h is height of the pyramid. Thus, $V = \frac{1}{3} (64)(6) = \frac{1}{3} (384) = 128$ m.

38. **(C)** Total the number of credits earned, (in this case = 16 credits). Multiply the credit and the weight for the earned grade per subject (e.g., biology = 5 x 4 = 20). Then add the total of the products of the credits and corresponding weights (in this case = 47). Then divide 47 by 16 to get the grade point average of 2.94. See table below.

$$
\begin{array}{rl}
\text{Biology} &= \quad 5 \times 4 = 20 \\
\text{English} &= \quad 3 \times 2 = 6 \qquad\qquad \text{GPA} = \dfrac{\text{total cr x wt}}{\text{total cr}} \\
\text{Math} &= \quad 3 \times 4 = 12 \\[4pt]
\text{French} &= \quad 3 \times 1 = 3 \qquad\qquad\qquad = \dfrac{47}{16} \\[4pt]
\text{P.E.} &= \quad \underline{2 \times 3 = 6} \qquad\qquad\qquad\quad = 2.94 \\
& \quad\;\; 16\text{ cr}\quad 47\text{ cr x gr wt}
\end{array}
$$

39. **(C)** Mode is the most frequent score. 81 appeared five times and is therefore the mode.

40. **(A)** Following the formula $(z = \dfrac{x - \bar{x}}{\text{s.d.}})$, thus

$$1.6 = x - \frac{190}{11}$$
$$17.60 = x - 190$$
$$x = 190 + 17.60$$
$$x = 207.60 \text{ cm (Glenn's height)}$$

41. **(A)** Multiply $1.83 by 145 and the answer is $265.35.

42. **(A)** By definition, a simple curve is a curve that can be traced in such a way that no point is traced more than once with the exception that the tracing may stop where it started. A closed curve is a curve that can be traced so that the starting and stopping points are the same. Therefore, a and b are simple closed curves. The rest are not.

43. **(C)** In a normal distribution half the data are always above the mean. Since 30,000 miles is the mean, half or 50% of the tires will last at least 30,000 miles.

44. **(D)** A line of symmetry for a figure is a line in which you can stand a mirror, so that the image you see in the mirror is just like the part of the figure that the mirror is hiding. In this case there are four lines.

45. **(D)** This can be solved using ratio and proportion, thus, 2 is to 1 as x is to 8. $\frac{2}{1} = \frac{x}{8}$, so $x = 16$ m.

46. **(E)** First find out how many ounces of orange juice is needed, so multiply 75 x 8 oz. = 600 oz. needed. Then divide 600 by 12 oz. = 50 12 oz. cans needed to serve 75 people with 8 oz. of juice each.

47. **(A)** m = number of miles you can travel
$0.08 m$ = amount spent for m miles travelled at 8 cents per mile,
rental fee + mileage charge = total amount spent
$139 + $0.08 m = 350
Solution: $139 - 139 + 0.08 m = 350 - 139$
$$0.08 m = 211$$
$$\frac{0.08m}{0.08} = \frac{211}{0.08}$$
$$m = 2,637.5$$
$$m = 2,637$$
Therefore, you can travel 2,637 miles (if you go 2,638 miles you have travelled too far).

48. **(A)** Let x = number of hours of overtime for the 1st worker,
x = number of hours of overtime for the 2nd worker,
x = number of hours of overtime for the 3rd worker,
$2x$ = number of hours of overtime for the 4th worker.
$$x + x + x + 2x = 50$$
$$5x = 50$$
$$x = \frac{50}{5}$$

x = 10 hrs of overtime for the 1st three workers

$2x$ = 20 hr of overtime for the 4th worker.

49. **(D)** Let m = number of miles covered the 1st day,

$m + 30$ = number of miles covered the 2nd day,

$m + 30 + 30$ = number of miles covered the 3rd day,

$m + 30 + 30 + 30$ = number of miles covered the 4th day,

$m + 30 + 30 + 30 + 30$ = number of miles covered the 5th day.

$m + m + 30$ and so on ... = 1,500

$5\,m + 30\,(10) = 1,500$

$5\,m + 300 = 1,500$

$5\,m = 1,500 - 300$

$5\,m = 1,200$

$$m = \frac{1,200}{5}$$

$m = 240$ mi

50. **(A)** Using the formula

$P = 2w + 2l$

$75 = 2w + 2(w + 5)$

$75 = 2w + 2w + 10$

$75 = 4w + 10$

$65 = 4w$

$16.25 = w$

The width is therefore 16.25 m and the length is w + 5 or 16.25 + 5 = 21.25 m.

CBEST Test 1

Section III: Essay Writing

TIME: 60 Minutes
          2 Essays

DIRECTIONS: Carefully read the two writing topics below. Plan and write an essay on each, being sure to cover all aspects of each essay. Allow approximately 30 minutes per essay.

Topic 1

There is a current trend in the United States toward smaller families. Sociologists attribute the decline in childbearing to many factors, including the dramatic rise of women in the work force, delayed marriage, divorce, and the high cost of raising and educating children. Discuss your view of smaller family size, and how it may affect future American society.

Topic 2

Write an essay in which you contrast your values and/or personality with the values and/or personality of some member of your family. Explain how two individuals from the same family could be different in the ways you and your relative are different.

SCORING THE ESSAY WRITING SECTION

Essay writing is a difficult section in which to predict your grade. There are no "right" and "wrong" answers since your grade will be decided by readers who are subjective.

Your essay is graded holistically, which means that your score is determined by grading the essay as a whole, not in parts. Your essay will receive one of four scores: Pass (4), Marginal Pass (3), Marginal Fail (2), or Fai l(1). The determination of each score is based on the following:

Pass (4) -

This score is achieved by writing an essay with the following characteristics:
1. Clear reasoning, good organization, clear development, and a thorough understanding of the assignment.
2. Minor flaws are acceptable, but the overall essay shows that the writer knows how to use language effectively.
3. The essay fully answers the essay question.

Marginal Pass (3) -

This score is achieved by writing an essay with the following characteristics:
1. Good reasoning, organization, and development of idea are present.
2. General statements are backed up by thorough, clear, and specific arguments.
3. Ability to use language effectively is demonstrated.
4. Writing errors are acceptable, but are not so serious that they deter the reader from understanding the main thrust of the essay.
5. Marginal Pass essays are often assigned this grade because although they successfully meet the other requirements of the assignment, they fail to answer the essay question completely.

Marginal Fail (2) -

This score is assigned by writing an essay with the following characteristics:
1. The essay is not organized clearly.
2. General statements are not backed up by specific pieces of information.
3. There are many generalizations or specific pieces of information which do not follow in a clear and organized way.
4. Serious grammatical errors and/or poor sentence construction.
5. There are major writing errors which distract the reader from understanding the essay.

Fail (1) -

This score is assigned by writing an essay with the following characteristics:
1. The essay is completely confusing to read.
2. No organization and/or no focus to the essay.
3. Ideas do not develop.
4. Writing errors are so severe that the reader cannot understand the essay.

Try to see if your essay falls into any of these categories by comparing its characteristics to the ones listed above. You may want to ask a teacher or a trusted friend to read your essay and grade it for you.

DETAILED EXPLANATIONS OF ANSWERS

Section III: Essay Writing

Topic 1 Sample Answer

Essay #1—Pass (Score = 4)

Although today people commonly complain about overcrowding and overpopulation, figures show that the average-sized family has dropped below the number needed for replacement of the population. I favor the trend toward smaller families. We need to move toward creating a world where children are guaranteed the simple things like food and shelter instead of giving birth to generations of starving and homeless people.

There are various reasons for such a steady decline in childbearing that are well worth taking note of. The high cost of raising and educating children, availability of birth control, the desire for greater freedom, and the realization that parenthood may well be a learned behavior rather than an instinct are a few examples.

The first of those points is the most obvious and rational explanation for not having children. The costs of pregnancy, and the first few years of the child's life alone can be staggering, assuming that it's a healthy child. Once you make it past that stage, parents are soon hit with the high cost of education, not to mention getting their child into the "right" school. Another factor to consider is birth control. In the past forty years we have gone from a period where sex was rarely discussed, to one where contraceptives are openly discussed, and distributed. The desire for greater freedom is another important consideration. People who grew up in large families, or whose jobs involve children, often desire the freedom of a marriage without kids. Having a family is quite obviously a lifetime commitment, and often by the time a parent may be ready to make it, it's too late. Last, but possibly the most important, is the growing belief that being a parent may be a learned behavior rather than an instinct. As I grew up I always figured that being a good parent was something that would "come to me" when the time is right. Judging by the high number of cases of abuse and abandonment, this is obviously not the case. It is true that being a good father or mother requires good instinct, but there is a bit more to it than that.

These are all issues worth considering, however they are concerned mostly with individuals, and not the "world family" in general. As I have said, I think we need to concentrate more on the kind of generations we are giving birth to, and the society they will live their lives in. It is ignorant to overlook the fact that we are giving birth to more children than we can possibly provide for. Even more importantly it is a cruel trick to play on something so young and innocent as a baby.

Scoring Explanation for Essay #1—Pass

Essay #1 is a clear pass because it offers lucid, well-reasoned arguments about smaller family size. The writer's position is clearly stated in the introduction, and several reasons for the steady decline in childbearing are then systematically explored.

The author's syntax and grammar are well under control. The text is nearly error-free and complex sentences are handled with ease. For example, embedded sentences like, "People who grew up in large families, or whose jobs involve children, often desire the freedom of a marriage without kids" occur often. In addition, the author goes beyond the obvious reactions to the issue of smaller families and draws more thoughtful conclusions, such as the point about good parenting being learned behavior rather than instinct. Finally, the essay addresses both crucial aspects the question requires, namely, to express a view on smaller family size and a speculation about how it may affect future society.

Essay #2—Marginal Pass (Score = 3)

According to sociologists, Americans are having fewer children. Possible reasons to account for this trend may be the increase of women in the work force and the strain of the many problems of adolescents as well as other factors. I feel the trend toward smaller families and childlessness is a definite result of these factors and predict that in the future less importance may be placed on raising a family as part of the "American dream".

To begin with, the norms of society used to reflect that the "woman's place is in the home". Yet, today women are taking charge of their lives, realizing their own ambitions and potential. Most of all they are seeing that children do not automatically have to be a part of their future. More and more women are placing their own ambitions do not include children, each generation is producing less offspring. I for example, intend to become a nurse and will probably postpone marriage and children. Secondly, people are realizing that there truly is a great deal involved in raising a family. Commitment to the responsibility of having children sometimes slacks when a family experiences difficulty during the child's adolescent years. It is hard enough to deal with the physical, emotional, and psychological changes of young adulthood yet a teenager must also face the pressures of society which may cause personal problems. This factor is one that many couples would rather avoid and, therefore, must refrain from having children altogether in order to do so.

Thirdly, this trend toward smaller family size will most likely continue in the future, affecting society in such a way that the term "family" may not necessarily include children. It seems that many people are living for today and are not concerned about carrying on the family name. Rather, they wish to live a life that is self-fulfilling. This attitude may affect future society in that it would project selfishness as a value on to future generations.

In essence, there is a definite trend toward smaller families and childlessness due to a greater concern for recognizing one's own personal ambitions and transforming them into a successful, fulfilling life. This is particularly true for women who are becoming increasingly active in the work force. Also, raising children is not easy and some couples would rather not deal with the difficulties. These and other factors will most likely result in a decrease in the importance of having children as a part of the "American dream."

Scoring Explanation for Essay #2—Marginal Pass

This essay shows adequate reasoning and organization. The introduction sets up a three-part discussion, and the ensuing paragraphs fulfill that commitment in the promised sequence. We read about (1) changing roles for women, (2) the problems involved in raising children (particularly adolescents), and (3) the resulting change in how we understand the concept of family. The first two of these issues are discussed in one paragraph, a departure from typical "5-paragraph theme" format.

There is both general ("More and more women are placing their own ambitions above what society dictates...") and specific information ("I plan to become a nurse...") offered in discussion. Generalizations, however, greatly outweigh the specifics offered.

The diction and syntax are generally adequate, though there are some errors in punctuation and a few awkward structures: "Commitment to the responsibility of having children sometimes slacks when a family experiences difficulty during the child's adolescent years."

The writer does address the question, predicting that smaller family size will affect the "American Dream," resulting in "living for today," a lack of concern for "carrying on the family name," and selfishness. Despite the over-generalization, the very typical strategy of restatement in the conclusion, and occasional errors in syntax and grammar, the essay deals with the question and is relatively easy to follow. It is a marginal pass.

Essay #3—Marginal Fail (Score = 2)

The trend toward smaller families and childlessness definitely makes our future society better. In the future, smaller family size will allow the people to live a more carefree and enjoyable lifestyle.

In the passage sociologists point out some good reasons for the decline in childbearing. In today's society the desire of the people to live affluently, the high divorce rates, and the high costs of raising and educating children makes the people to want fewer children or not at all. It may seem selfish but to enjoy oneself one needs to have a choice to not have babies or to have a few just to suit one's lifestyle. Some notices that having a large family give financial problem, the family cannot afford to send all the children to colleges. Also, since divorce rates is high few want to consider having children; they are afraid that it will give them troubles of settling child custody problem.

Because of this major reasons stated in the passage the future society seems to be moving toward a more pleasurable lifestyle. The people tend to look forward to delaying marriage and fulfilling one's desires. Then, of course, what is a bigger problem than childbearing? There is no surprise that a average- sized family is greatly reduced...it is necessary.

Scoring Explanation for Essay #3—Marginal Fail

The essay's introduction promises a discussion of smaller families resulting in a better society, more "carefree and enjoyable." The bulk of the essay, however, seeks to explain the reasons for the decline in childbearing. The writer has lost sight of his original focus or thesis, returning to it only briefly at the end of the essay.

There is a simplistic treatment of the topic; the writer primarily explains what is evident from the question and offers little new material. There is insufficient information to support the thesis, intriguing though it might be.

There are grammatical errors, several instances of awkward syntax ("… the high costs of raising and educating children make the people to want fewer children or not at all …"), and a few distracting punctuation problems. Still, the writer did attempt to address the question, though the essay lacks development. The essay is a marginal fail.

Essay #4—Fail (Score = 1)

Society in the United States has changed drastic in the ideas of family life. One can contribute this change through a various amount of reasons. One of the pertanent ideas revolve around society becoming more career oriented in their jobs they have been involved with. Another idea is the cost of raising a child and finally the knowledge that has developed over the centuries has played a factor in postponing child birth until later in life.

In the past, having a big family was the desired. Although a family struggled with the demands of raising a large family, they were able to prevale because as the children grew up they could also work with the father or mother, which resulted in an extra source of income. A college education was not a common option. That one could decide to do when they reached the age of 18. At many times a son or daughter would learn it and take over the business.

Today, that idea, has been altered. Couples or even individuals have become more career orientated in their jobs. This idea also stems with stress a greater freedom wanted, and less of a interest to family. The high cost of raising a family is also a factor in less child births. A family or couple can now wait until their late thirties to have a child. Medical advancement has helped in this area of having a family later in life. Through the use of medical procedures, a couple can conceive a child even when they are older in age. Statistics in conceiving a child in the forties age group has risen substantially because of medicine.

With less child births, cities such as Los Angeles won't be as crowded as it was before. Children can get a better education because teachers will be able to devote their attention to a smaller group of students, then a larger-sized group. Lower amounts of poverty striken families will exist. Because of the idea of couples waiting until they are financially stable before raising children. More jobs will also be available due to the decrease in child births. One can also say that the freeway system that people use everyday will in time get better, and more efficient. People today are now thinking twice about bringing up a family. Becoming financially secure first, is a good idea before deciding to have a child.

Scoring Explanation for Essay #4—Fail

Essay #4 fails on a number of counts. The writer's sentence structure shows a serious lack of focus and knowledge of proper syntax. Some sentences are simply awkward (such as the first: "Society in the United States has changed drastic in the ideas of family life."), while others are confused and exhibit missing elements or illogic (such as this sentence from paragraph three: "This idea also stems with stress a greater freedom wanted, and less of a interest to family.").

The writer does introduce an interesting idea relating medical advancement to childbearing later in life, but this idea is not explored, rather it is presented repetitively. Finally, the writer presents a list of benefits resulting from "less child births" that similarly go uninvestigated, and that rank serious issues ("poverty striken families") alongside trivial ones ("the freeway system will get more efficient"). This intellectual confusion, coupled with several kinds of errors in spelling, grammar, and punctuation, results in a failing score.

Topic 2 Sample Answer

Essay #1—Marginal Pass (Score = 3)

People tell me quite often that my brother and I look like twins. We both have brown hair, brown eyes, a fair complexion, and the same features. Though we look like each other, our personalities clash.

Alex is only sixteen years old, and he is very advanced for his age in school. He's intelligent, determined, confident, and always does what he says he's going to do. On my part, I can say that my intelligence is at the average level, and rather than being determined and confident about the things I do, I tend to be somewhat insecure about myself.

I've always wanted to be just like Alex. Throughout my life I've always looked up to him. He's outgoing and open, and I am the shy, quiet type. He's the one who always completes his work on time and never depends on anyone else but himself. I always procrastinate, and I'm lazy.

Also, Alex is the "outgoing" type who plays sports like tennis, football and baseball. Though I was on the tennis team in '88, I never continued to play on a regular basis. Alex likes to play sports, and I like to watch them on t.v.

My parents can similarly be compared to my brother and I. I share the same personality traits as my father, and Alex shares my mom's personality. My father is the introvert as I and we are both hesitant to get things done before the last minute. My mother is an open, confident woman and always trusts herself- which can similarly be compared to my brother. My father and I prefer to stay inside while my mom and brother are always on the go. When my mother was our age she was on a running team. She was involved in a lot of sports, and my father was always the one who liked to be alone.

As shown here, my brother and I are different in many ways, and so are my parents.

Scoring Explanation for Essay #1—Marginal Pass

The bulk of this marginally passing essay is spent providing the audience with a series of comparisons (ranging from physical differences to sports preferences) between the writer and his/her brother. These are offered in sentences that are readable and competent, though not terribly complex or sophisticated. There are very few grammatical errors and only minor punctuation problems.

The last major paragraph of the essay attempts to explain the differences between the siblings by offering corresponding differences between the parents. The author implies, but never clearly states, that the parental characteristics account for those of the children. Thus, there may be an attempt to address the question in its entirety, but the writer does not make the "explanation portion" explicit. The conclusion is brief and perfunctory, merely restating the general thrust of the previous paragraph. Because the essay only vaguely addresses the assignment in its entirety, though it is satisfactorily written, the essay is a marginal pass.

Essay #2—Marginal Fail (Score = 2)

Have you ever wondered if someone in your family could possibly be from the same family, do to the fact that you are so opposite? My sister Kate and I have to be one of the most opposite sisters in the world. Our likes, values, and personalities contrast terribly. At times I often ask myself: "How could we possibly be related?"

To begin with my sister has red hair, is two inches taller than me and two years younger than me. This is far different from me who is blonde, petite and older. Our looks are the outside appearance of how different we are in the inside.

When it comes to dating, Katie likes to date as many as possible, whereas I like to stick to just one. I am extremely competitive and hate to lose, especially in volleyball. Katie is more carefree and if her team loses it is not that big of a deal. Our bedrooms show a great deal of differences. Katie's room is piled with clothes and many unimportant things. She likes to save everything. On the other hand I am very metuculus, and I am annoyed if there is junk laying around. Even when it comes down to the "nitty gritty" of things such as music, clothes, or jewelry Katie and I have opposite taste.

Two individuals from the same family could be different in the ways my sister and me are different, possibly because of different genes in the family. Generations of a family consist of many genes from various relatives, and those genes are passed on contributing to the different personalities of a number of relatives. Every individual is his or her own person and just because people are from the same family, it does not mean that people can not have their own distinct values and personalities different than anyone else in the family.

Scoring Explanation for Essay #2—Marginal Fail

This essay provides a series of contrasts between the writer and her sister, beginning with physical characteristics and ending with tastes in clothing. None of the differences mentioned addresses a contrasting value system, though some minor personality differences are offered. Thus the question is partially, but not completely, answered in this essay.

There are several errors in grammar, syntax, and word choice. One example of an awkward construction appears in the first paragraph: "My sister Kate and I have to be one of the most opposite sisters in the world." Spelling and punctuation are similarly irregular.

The final paragraph of the essay offers genetic differences as an explanation for the contrasts between the sisters. The author relies on this biological explanation exclusively, though she is clearly only superficially familiar with genetics. The author concludes with a wordy restatement of her belief that despite blood ties, family members can differ. The writer is confused, therefore, about how genetics actually do or do not contribute to differences between siblings. This problem with reasoning contributes to the essay's marginally failing score.

Essay #3—Fail (Score = 1)

My uncle Gary and I are completely different peoples. First of all, my Uncle Gary is an atheist. I on the other hand am a religious person. I do not go to church every Sunday but I do believe in God. Secondly, my Uncle does not speak to anyone in the family. He has totally sheltered himself from everyone. I love to be with my family at family gatherings. I will admit they get on my nerves sometimes. But I would never want to lose contact with them. Last, but not least, my Uncle is a democrat. I am a Republican. This would be a good discussion topic. If my uncle would ever go to family gatherings. So there you have two completely different people. From the same family.

Scoring Explanation for Essay #3—Fail

This essay suffers from a serious lack of development. Its simplistic listing of differences between the author and his/her uncle only minimally addresses the question. No discussion of any difference is advanced, and the writer concludes without even attempting any explanation beyond: "So there you have two completely different people. From the same family."

Despite the essay's extreme brevity, the author also makes several errors in syntax. Sentence fragments appear regularly.

A lack of attention to the demands of the question, incomplete development, and errors in writing make this essay a clear fail.

California Basic Educational Skills Test

READING
COMPREHENSION
REVIEW

Overview

The reading comprehension segment of the CBEST measures your ability to understand information given through the written word and in charts and graphs. The emphasis is on comprehension of text materials, not on your knowledge of different topics. Test passages vary in difficulty and length. Long passages (up to 200 words) are mixed in with much shorter sections, which can be as brief as one or two lines.

The questions you must answer represent the three types of comprehension: literal (facts and figures), inferential (implied ideas), and critical (analysis and interpretation). Half of the questions are of the inferential type; the rest of the questions are equally divided between literal and critical comprehension.

1. Literal Comprehension

Questions in this category assess your ability to comprehend information explicitly stated in the text. The questions will be on the main idea in the section. You may have to identify specific facts about persons, places, events, or ideas included in the passage. Sometimes the question is based on a graph or chart.

Literal comprehension questions include:

- identifying the main idea or focus of a passage

- finding details or facts provided within the passage

- recognizing information provided in a graph or chart

2. Inferential Comprehension

Questions in this category require you to search for intended meanings or conclusions that can be appropriately drawn from, though not explicitly stated in, the information provided in the passage. Some questions may ask you to make comparisons, draw conclusions, or apply the information to other examples. You may have to identify statements that are implied or can be inferred from information given in a passage.

Specific inferential comprehension skills include:

- recognizing ideas or situations related to those presented in the passage

- identifying a logical conclusion based on facts or ideas provided in the passage or in illustrations

- applying ideas to problems or situations beyond the passage or charts

- recognizing ideas that are implied in the passage or in the illustrations or charts

- recognizing relationships that exist between ideas provided in the passage or in the illustrations

- finding generalizations that can be conducted from facts given in the passage

- comparing information, facts, or ideas given in various parts of the section

3. Critical Comprehension

The questions in this subsection refer to the organization or style of the selection. You may be asked to identify the author's point of view or reason for writing this piece, or to identify the writing style or tone of a selection. Some questions may require you to identify the implicit assumptions from a single statement or from the entire passage. You may be asked to select the appropriate definition of a word or phrase based upon the sentence or paragraph in which it appears, or to determine the meaning of a figure of speech, or to identify the organization of a passage.

Specific critical comprehension skills include:

- identifying the author's attitude or feelings about the subject of the passage
- identifying the author's primary purpose
- determining the author's tone in a passage
- identifying the organization of the selection
- selecting the best definition of a word or a figure of speech within the passage
- identifying the type of publication in which the passage would most likely appear
- identifying statements that tend to weaken or strengthen the points made in the selection

Following are general strategies for answering reading comprehension questions. These strategies apply to all text questions. Sample passages are given, along with an analysis and strategies for answering each type of reading section.

Key Strategies for Answering the Reading Comprehension Questions

1. **Read all directions through carefully.** Preview the questions before reading the passage so that you are acquainted with the subject.

2. **If possible, allocate your time for each question.** Do not spend too much time on any one question. If you can't answer the question easily after reading the passage twice, skip it and move on to the next item.

3. **Skim through the questions before reading each passage;** this will help you locate key words and ideas.

4. **Underline key words or sentences** and make any necessary notes in the margins.

5. **Be certain to mark each passage as you read.** Should you skip an answer to return to later, make a notation so that you do not mark an answer in the wrong place.

6. **If there are unfamiliar words, do not spend too much time attempting to define them until you have read through the entire passage.** Reading the phrase or sentence a couple of times and using the context (surrounding words) is valuable in determining meanings of vocabulary words.

7. **Always read all the answer choices before choosing the one best answer.**

8. **Decide whether the question asked is a literal, inferential, or critical comprehension question.**

9. **Choices of answers that are not relevant, reasonable, or that contradict the information in the passage should be eliminated at the beginning.**

The following directions are typical of those you will find on the CBEST.

> **DIRECTIONS:** One or more questions follow each statement or passage in this test. The question(s) are based on the content of the passage. After you have read a statement or passage, select the one best answer to each question from among the five possible choices. Your answers to the questions should be based on the stated (literal) or implied (inferential) information given in the statement or passage. Mark all answers on your answer sheet.

ANALYSIS

You are asked to select the one best answer from the five choices. In certain cases, the "best" answer will not be what you might believe is an ideal answer. Also, note that you must base your choice only on information given in the passage or implied by the information. Frequently, people who perform poorly on this test do so because they attempt to read more into the passage from their own experiences. Going with your first choice of answers is usually the best strategy.

SHORT PASSAGE SAMPLE

Experienced lawyers know that most lawsuits are won or lost before they are ever heard in court. Thus, successful lawyers prepare their cases carefully, undertaking exhaustive research and investigation prior to going to court. Interviews and statements taken from all available witnesses ascertain those who are likely to be called as witnesses for the other side. This is the time for strategy planning in the building of the case; decisions to be made about expert witnesses to be called (such as doctors, chemists, or others who have special knowledge of the subject matter); books and articles to be read pertaining to the subject matter of the case; and meetings with witnesses to prepare them for possible questions by the opposing lawyers and to review the case. Finally, in preparing the case, a trial memorandum of law is handed to the judge at the outset of the trial. As a result of this thorough preparation, experienced lawyers know their strong and weak points and can serve their clients well.

QUESTION

The main idea expressed in this passage is to

(A) describe the function of expert witnesses.

(B) explain the importance of pretrial preparation by lawyers.

(C)   warn persons who break the law.

(D)   verify the importance of the trial memorandum.

(E)   refute the belief that all lawyers are trial lawyers.

ANALYSIS

Passages such as this one are typically followed by one or two questions. Previewing the questions before reading the passage acquaints you with the overall writer's subject and possibly the author's approach or point of view to the subject. Usually the main idea of the reading passage is not explicitly stated but becomes apparent as you read. Always ask yourself: What was the most important thing that the author was trying to tell the reader in this passage?

It is important to read through the entire passage and to mark any key words and phrases that relate to the question. After you have read carefully and thoroughly one time, reread and consider each possible answer. Avoid marking an answer before you have read all of the choices. Frequently, there are two or more options that are very close, but one must be the best answer.

When considering a question that asks for the main idea, the reader should note the central theme or essential idea being developed in each sentence in the paragraph or paragraphs. It is also important to examine the first word of each of the answers for responses that can be eliminated. In the case of the above passage, choice (C), warn, and choice (E), refute, are not consistent with the rather objective nature of the passage; these two choices can therefore be eliminated. Also, these choices are irrelevant to the information in the passage, since the passage does not address people who break the law or the belief that all lawyers are trial lawyers. The remaining choices can be considered based on how central they are to the main idea or if they are subsidiary to the main idea. Choices (A), expert witnesses, and (D), importance of trial memorandum, are mentioned but are subsidiary to the overall theme of the passage. Choice (B) is the best choice. It discusses the preparation done by the lawyers before the trial begins (pretrial).

LONGER PASSAGE SAMPLE

Questions 1, 2, 3, 4, and 5 refer to the following passage:

Mark Twain has been characterized as "an authentic American author" and as "a representative American author." These descriptions seem to suit the man and his writings. He was born Samuel Clemens in 1835, when Missouri and Louisiana were the only states west of the Mississippi River. His birthplace was less than fifty miles from the river. His father, John Clemens, a lawyer and merchant, was rarely far from financial disaster. When Samuel Clemens was four, the family settled in Hannibal, Missouri, and it was there beside the great river that Samuel lived out the adventurous life he describes in his best-loved novels. Samuel traveled extensively and tasted life as no other author had done. He said of his life, "Now then: as the most valuable capital, or culture, or education usable in the building of novels is personal experience, I ought to be well equipped for that trade." He acquired a wealth of personal experiences for his novels. As a boy of twelve he was apprenticed to the printer of his brother's newspaper in Hannibal. Six years later, in 1853, he set out to see the world as a printer in St. Louis, then in Chicago, Philadelphia, Keokuk, and Cincinnati. In 1857 he impulsively apprenticed himself to Horace Bixby, a riverboat pilot, and traveled all 1,200 miles of the Mississippi River. He said of his years on the river, "I got personally and familiarly acquainted with all the different types of human nature that are to be found in fiction, biography, or history."

The Civil War ended his steamboating and he served briefly in a Confederate militia company. Following his stint in the military, he set out with his brother, Orion, by stagecoach over the Rockies. While in the West he tried prospecting and speculating, but found his true calling in journalism. He was greatly influenced by the literary comedians and local colorists of the period, Bret Harte and Artemus Ward. He became more skillful than his teachers in developing his rich characterizations. In 1865 he attained national fame using his pseudonym, Mark Twain, with his story "The Notorious Jumping Frog of Calaveras County." He also discovered a new vocation as a popular lecturer in San Francisco, keeping his audiences convulsed with tales of his adventures. Full public recognition came with the publishing of *Innocents Abroad* (1869) a wild and rollicking account of his invasion of the Old World, much of which would seem quite languid by today's standards. Some of his finest writings were three works filled with lively adventures on the Mississippi River and based on his boyhood, *Tom Sawyer* (1876), *Old Times on the Mississippi* (1883), and *Huckleberry Finn* (1884). Throughout his career Twain preferred to display his flair for journalistic improvisation rather than maintain the artist's concern for form. In his artfully told stories, Mark Twain conveyed his keen powers of observation and perception, his broad understanding of human nature, and his refreshing sense of humor.

QUESTIONS 1-5

1. The author's main purpose in writing this passage is to

    (A)   suggest when Samuel Clemens started writing.

    (B)   survey the variety of jobs Clemens held in his life.

    (C)   explain Clemens' philosophy of writing.

    (D)   argue that Clemens is one of the best American authors.

    (E)   discuss some of the major events that shaped Clemens' writing.

2. From the passage, the author's point of view regarding Clemens' writing is

    (A)   a literary criticism of his local color style.

    (B)   primarily one of extolling his writing.

    (C)   a defense of Clemens' journalistic style.

    (D)   indifferent to Clemens' writing style.

    (E)   a comparison of Clemens to other writers of the period.

3.   In the sentence about *Innocents Abroad,* "a wild and rollicking account of his travels through the Old World, much of which would seem quite languid by today's standards," languid probably means which of the following?

  (A) Similar to   (D) Impossible

  (B) Difficult   (E) Expensive

  (C) Tame

4.   The passage supports which of the following conclusions about Clemens' career as a writer?

  (A) Clemens acquired great personal wealth from his writing.

  (B) Clemens was a better journalist than novelist.

  (C) Clemens' lectures provided material for his writing.

  (D) Clemens' personal experiences shaped his writing.

  (E) Clemens' professional progress was aided by his associations with Bret Hart and Artemus Ward.

5.   According to the passage, which of the following best describes Clemens' appeal to his public?

  (A) His use of the humorous side of human nature

  (B) His descriptions of life on the Mississippi River

  (C) His tales of life in the West

  (D) Seeing him as the typical American writer

  (E) Viewing him as the impulsive world traveler

DETAILED EXPLANATIONS OF ANSWERS

1.   **(E)**   (E) is the correct answer. The passage mentions a variety of occupations Clemens held and travels he made, which provided the substance of many of his characterizations and settings. (A) is irrelevant to the question and choice (B) is a secondary purpose rather than the primary one because it digresses from the topic of Samuel Clemens' career as a writer. Choice (D) suggests the passage is an argument, which is not in keeping with the whole "discussion" tone, and choice (C) is information not given in the passage.

2.   **(B)**   This choice is supported in the passage with the statement, "He became more skillful than his teachers in developing his rich characterizations." It is also supported in the last sentence of the passage. Choices (A), a literary criticism, (C), a defense of journalistic style, and (E), a comparison, are not suggested by information in

the passage. Choice (D) can be eliminated because it contradicts the positive attitude of the passage towards Clemens' writing.

3.   **(C)**   When test questions involve the meaning of an unfamiliar word, definitions can frequently be determined from the context (surrounding words). Questions of this type are included to assess how well the reader can extract a word's meaning by looking within the passage for clues. Sometimes the opposite of the meaning is given somewhere in the text. The words "wild and rollicking" are being compared to traveling through Europe by today's standards. Choice (A), similar to today's standards, does not make sense when we compare traveling in the 1800s to today's standards. Choices (B), difficult, and (D), impossible, can be eliminated since they are contradictions; traveling is less difficult today, not impossible. Although choice (E), expensive, is a possible correct answer, the context of the passage should cause the reader to look for the opposite meaning of "wild and rollicking," which would be "tame."

4.   **(D)**   Choices (A), (B), and (C) contain information not given in the passage. These can therefore be eliminated as irrelevant. Choice (E) could be considered as a possible answer because Bret Hart and Artemus Ward were mentioned as having an influence on Clemens' writing style. However, it is important not to read into this that they assisted him professionally in the development of his writing career. The discussion that Clemens was a world traveler and experienced a wide variety of occupations which provided background for his writing supports choice (D).

5.   **(A)**   Choices (B) and (C) are possible correct answers because these settings provided the background for some of Clemens' most popular works, but these settings did not necessarily appeal to everyone. Choice (D) is not developed in the text as the reason for Clemens' public appeal. Choice (E) is irrelevant. Clemens' use of humor is discussed in relation to his becoming more skillful than the local colorists who influenced him and also in the last sentence of the passage. Choice (A) is the best answer since the passage ends by discussing Clemens' humor and gives examples throughout, and because his humor offered widespread appeal.

California Basic Educational Skills Test

MATHEMATICS
REVIEW

Overview

The following is intended as a *review* of the basic mathematical skills assessed on the mathematics section of the CBEST. It is not intended as a substitute for a comprehensive kindergarten-through-high-school mathematics curriculum. For a person taking the CBEST, this section should provide an efficient means of reviewing a wide range of mathematics topics developed during the individual's regular education, which will be assessed on the CBEST.

The mathematics portion of the CBEST assesses cumulative knowledge of the mathematics traditionally taught in elementary and high school and sometimes in college. Knowledge of this type of mathematics is needed by all teachers, whether or not they teach mathematics as an assigned class.

Three categories of mathematical ability are assessed:

1. Identifying Processes Used in Problem Solving

Questions in this category assess your ability to determine what is required to solve problems or "set up" problems. Questions in this category will not require you to actually solve the problem. Examples of tasks you may be required to perform include identifying an arithmetic operation (addition, subtraction, multiplication, division) that may be required to solve a problem, recognizing that sufficient information is or is not given to solve the problem, translating a word problem into mathematical symbols (or visa versa), or recognizing different ways of solving a problem. The problems in this section may require identifying arithmetic, geometric, logical, or graphic processes used in solving problems.

2. Solution of Word Problems

Questions in this category assess your ability to solve word or "story" problems. Mathematical topics included in this category are arithmetic, algebra, geometry, and statistics. You also may be asked to evaluate a given formula ("plug in" values and give an answer) or estimate the answer for a problem.

3. Demonstrating an Understanding of Mathematical Concepts and Relationships

Questions in this category assess your ability to understand basic mathematical concepts. Examples of the kinds of concept understanding that the test assesses include terms (e.g., area, perimeter, volume), order (greater than, less than, equal to), relationships demonstrated by a graph, and elementary probability. Concepts assessed in this category are from arithmetic, algebra, or geometry.

About 40% of the questions on the mathematics section of the CBEST are related to arithmetic. About 20% of the questions are related to elementary geometry. The remaining items are related to other mathematical concepts and skills. None of the questions strictly test computation as such; however, computational skill is required throughout the test.

Three basic categories of mathematical topics may appear on the mathematics section of the CBEST:

1. Arithmetic. Topics included in this category are: integers; prime and composite numbers; odd and even numbers; place value; powers and roots of whole numbers; addition, subtraction, multiplication and division of integers, common fractions, and decimal fractions; percents; and elementary statistics.

2. Algebra. Topics included in this category are: algebraic expressions; simplifying algebraic expressions; factoring; solving linear equations; solving inequalities; evaluating formulas; elementary probability; and algebra word problems.

3. Geometry and Measurement. Topics included in this category are: perimeter and area of rectangles, squares, and triangles; circumference and area of circles; volume of cubes and rectangular solids; angle measure; properties of triangles; the Pythagorean Theorem; properties of parallel and perpendicular lines; coordinate geometry; graphs; and the metric system.

Part I: Arithmetic

1.1 Integers

Natural or counting numbers are 1, 2, 3, ...
Whole numbers are 0, 1, 2, 3, ...
Integers are ...−2, −1, 0, 1, 2, ...
As shown below, a number line is often used to represent integers.

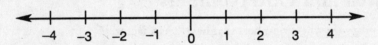

The following are properties of integers:

Commutative property: $a + b = b + a$.
Example: 2 + 3 = 3 + 2.

Associative property: $(a + b) + c = a + (b + c)$.
Example: (2 + 3) + 4 = 2 + (3 + 4).

Distributive property: $a(b + c) = ab + bc$.
Example: 2 (3 + 4)   =   (2 x 3) + (2 x 4)
                    2 x 7   =   6 + 8
                    14   =   14

Additive identity: $a + 0 = a$.
Example: 2 + 0 = 2.

Multiplicative identity: $a \times 1 = a$.
Example: 2 x 1 = 2.

1.2   Prime and Composite Numbers

When two whole numbers are multiplied, they yield a product. These two whole numbers can be called *factors* or *divisors* of the product. (An exception to this is 0. Zero can be a factor, but not a divisor, since division by 0 is undefined.)

Example: 2 x 3 = 6. 2 and 3 are factors or divisors of the product 6.

Example: 0 x 3 = 0. 3 is a factor and divisor of the product 0, but 0 is only a factor of the product 0, since 0 – 0 is undefined.

A *prime number* is a whole number that has only two different whole number factors, 1 and the number itself.

Example: 5 is a prime number, because it has only two different factors, 1 and 5.

A *composite number* is a whole number that has three or more whole number factors.

Example: 6 is a composite number, because it has four different factors, 1, 2, 3, and 6.

1.3   Even and Odd Numbers

Even numbers are whole numbers that have 2 as a factor.

Example: 6 is an even number, since 2 x 3 = 6.

Odd numbers are whole numbers that do not have 2 as a factor.

Example: 5 is an odd number, since 2 is not a factor of 5.

1.4   Place Value

Our numeration system uses the *Hindu-Arabic numerals* (0, 1, 2, 3, 4, 5, 6, 7, 8, 9) to represent numbers.

Our numeration system follows a *base 10 place-value scheme.* As we move to the left in any number, each place value is ten times the place value to the right. Similarly, as we move to the right, each place value is one-tenth the place value to the left.

Example: In the number 543.21, the place value of the 5 (100's) is ten times the place value of the 4 (10's). The place value of the 1 ($^1/_{100}$'s) is one-tenth the place value of the 2 ($^1/_{10}$'s).

The concept of place value will be discussed in section 1.8, Arithmetic Operations and Decimal Fractions.

1.5   Powers and Roots of Whole Numbers

1.5.1   Exponents and Bases

In the expression 5^3, 5 is called the *base* and 3 is called the *exponent.* The expression $5^3 = 5$ x 5 x 5. The base (5) gives the factor used in the expression and the exponent (3) gives the number of times the base is to be used as a factor.

Examples: $4^2 = 4 \times 4.$
$3^5 = 3 \times 3 \times 3 \times 3 \times 3.$

When the base has an exponent of 2, the base is said to be *squared*. When the base has an exponent of 3, the base is said to be *cubed*.

The Basic Laws of Exponents are

1) $b^m \times b^n = b^{m+n}.$
Example: $2^5 \times 2^3 = 2^{5+3} = 2^8.$

2) $b^m \div b^n = b^{m-n}.$
Example: $2^5 \div 2^3 = 2^{5-3} = 2^2.$

3) $(b^m)^n = b^{m \times n}.$
Example: $(2^5)^3 = 2^{5 \times 3} = 2^{15}.$

1.5.2   Roots

Consider again the expression 5^3. If we carry out the implied multiplication, we get $5^3 = 5 \times 5 \times 5 = 125.$ 5 is called the cube root of 125, since $5^3 = 125$. In general, when a base is raised to a power to produce a given result, the base is called the *root* of the given result.

If the power for the base is 2, the base is called the *square root*. If the power for the base is 3, the base is called the *cube root*. In general, if $b^n = p$, then b is the *nth root* of p.

Examples: Since $4^2 = 16$, 4 is the square root of 16.
Since $2^3 = 8$, 2 is the cube root of 8.
Since $3^5 = 243$, 3 is the 5th root of 243.

1.6   Arithmetic Operations and Integers

As illustrated in section 1.1, integers are *signed numbers* preceded by either a "+" or a "−" sign. If no sign is given for the integer, one should infer that the integer is positive (e.g., 3 means +3). As also illustrated in section 1.1, integers to the *left of zero are negative* and integers to the *right of zero are positive*.

The *absolute value* of an integer is the measure of the distance of the integer from zero. Since the measure of distance is always positive, absolute value is always positive (e.g., $|-3| = 3$, $|3| = 3$).

1.6.1   Addition

When two integers are added, the two integers are called *addends*, and the result is called the sum, as illustrated in the following:

$$5 \quad + \quad 3 \quad = \quad 8$$
$$\text{(addend)} \qquad \text{(addend)} \qquad \text{(sum)}$$

$$\text{or} \quad 5 \quad \text{(addend)}$$
$$\underline{+\,3} \quad \text{(addend)}$$
$$8 \quad \text{(sum)}$$

When adding two integers, one of the following two situations might occur:

Situation 1: Both integers have the same sign. In this case, add the absolute values of the two addends and give the sum the same sign as the addends.

Examples: 2 + 3 = 5, and

$$-2 + (-3) = -5.$$

Situation 2: The two integers have different signs. In this case, subtract the addend with the smaller absolute value from the addend with the larger absolute value. The sum gets the sign of the addend with the larger absolute value.

Examples: −2 + 5 = 3, but

$$2 + (-5) = -3.$$

1.6.2   Subtraction

In a subtraction sentence, the top or first number in the subtraction is the *minuend*, the bottom or second number is the *subtrahend*, and the result is the *remainder or difference*. These quantities are demonstrated in the following figure:

$$5 \quad - \quad 3 \quad = \quad 2$$
$$\text{(minuend)} \quad \text{(subtrahend)} \quad \text{(remainder)}$$

$$\text{or} \quad 5 \quad \text{(minuend)}$$
$$\underline{-\,3} \quad \text{(subtrahend)}$$
$$2 \quad \text{(remainder)}$$

When subtracting two integers, change the sign of the subtrahend and add the resulting two integers, following the procedures given in 1.6.1 above.

Examples: 5 − 3 = 2, but

$$5 - (-3) = 5 + (+3) = 5 + 3 = 8.$$

1.6.3   Multiplication

When multiplying two integers, the two integers are called *factors*, and the result is called the *product*, as illustrated in the following:

$$5 \quad \text{x} \quad 3 \quad = \quad 15$$
(factor)   (factor)   (product)

or   5   (factor)
x 3   (factor)
15   (product)

When multiplying two integers, multiply the absolute values of the factors. If the factors have the *same sign*, the product is *positive*; if the factors have *different signs*, the product is *negative*. If either factor is zero, the product is zero.

Examples: 3 x 5 = 15 and (–3) x (–5) = 15, but
(–3) x 5 = –15 and 3 x (–5) = –15.

1.6.4   Division

When dividing two integers, the number being divided is the *dividend*, the number being divided into another integer is the *divisor*, and the result is the *quotient*, as illustrated in the following:

$$10 \quad \div \quad 2 \quad = \quad 5$$
(dividend)   (divisor)   (quotient)

When dividing two integers, divide the absolute values of the dividend and divisor. The sign of the quotient can be obtained by following the same procedures given above in 1.6.3.

Examples: 10 ÷ 2 = 5 and (–10) ÷ (–2) = 5, but
(–10) ÷ 2 = (–5) and 10 + (–2) = (–5).

1.7   Arithmetic Operations and Common Fractions

A *common fraction* is a number that can be written in the form $\frac{a}{b}$, where a and b are whole numbers. In the expression $\frac{a}{b}$, the dividend a is called the *numerator* and the divisor b is called the *denominator*.

Example: In the expression $\frac{3}{4}$, 3 is the numerator and 4 is the denominator.

A common fraction may not have 0 as a denominator, since *division by 0 is undefined.*

A fraction is in *lowest terms* if the numerator and denominator have no common factors.

Examples: $\frac{1}{2}, \frac{3}{4}$, and $\frac{5}{6}$ are in lowest terms, since the numerator and denominator of each have no common factors.

$\frac{2}{4}, \frac{9}{12}$, and $\frac{20}{24}$ are *not* in lowest terms, since the numerator and denominator of each have common factors.

Fractions are *equivalent* if they represent the same number.

Example: $\frac{8}{16}, \frac{4}{8}, \frac{2}{4}$, and $\frac{5}{10}$ are equivalent fractions, since each represents $\frac{1}{2}$.

A *mixed numeral* is a number that consists of an integer and a common fraction.

Example: $5\frac{3}{4}$ is a mixed numeral since it consists of the integer 5 and the common fraction $\frac{3}{4}$.

An *improper fraction* is a common fraction whose numerator is larger than its denominator. A mixed numeral can be expressed as an improper fraction by multiplying the denominator of the common fraction part times the integer part and adding that product to the numerator of the common fraction part. The result is the numerator of the improper fraction. The denominator of the improper fraction is the same as the denominator in the mixed numeral.

Example: $5\frac{3}{4} = \frac{23}{4}$, since $(4 \times 5) + 3 = 23$, and 4 was the denominator of the common fraction part, $\frac{3}{4}$. $\frac{23}{4}$ is an improper fraction, since the numerator 23 is larger than the denominator 4.

1.7.1 Addition

In order to *add* two fractions, the denominators of the fractions must be the same;

when they are, they are called *common denominators.* The equivalent fractions with the smallest common denominator are said to have the *lowest common denominator.*

Examples: $\dfrac{3}{8}+\dfrac{2}{8}=\dfrac{5}{8}$, but

$\dfrac{3}{8}+\dfrac{1}{4}=\dfrac{3}{8}+\dfrac{2}{8}=\dfrac{5}{8}$. Note that while 16, 24, 32, and so forth, could have been used as common denominators to obtain equivalent fractions, the lowest common denominator, 8, was used to generate like denominators.

The procedures regarding the addition of signed numbers given in section 1.6.1 also apply for the addition of common fractions.

1.7.2   Subtraction

The procedures given for the addition of common fractions given in section 1.7.1, together with the procedures for subtraction of signed numbers given in section 1.6.2, form the basis for the subtraction of common fractions.

Examples: $\dfrac{3}{8}-\dfrac{2}{8}=\dfrac{1}{8}$, but

$\dfrac{3}{8}-\dfrac{1}{4}=\dfrac{3}{8}-\dfrac{2}{8}=\dfrac{1}{8}.$

As also suggested in section 1.7.1 and 1.6.2,

$\dfrac{3}{8}-\left(-\dfrac{2}{8}\right)=\dfrac{3}{8}+\dfrac{2}{8}=\dfrac{5}{8}$ and

$\dfrac{3}{8}-\left(-\dfrac{1}{4}\right)=\dfrac{3}{8}+\dfrac{1}{4}=\dfrac{3}{8}+\dfrac{2}{8}=\dfrac{5}{8}.$

1.7.3   Multiplication

To *multiply* two common fractions, simply find the product of the two numerators and divide it by the product of the two denominators. Reduce the resultant fraction to lowest terms (see 1.7).

Example: $\dfrac{2}{3}\times\dfrac{9}{11}=\dfrac{18}{33}=\dfrac{6}{11}.$

In addition, the procedures regarding the multiplication of integers give in section 1.6.3 apply for the multiplication of common fractions.

1.7.4 Division

To find the *reciprocal* of a common fraction, exchange the numerator and the denominator.

Examples: The reciprocal of $\dfrac{2}{3}$ is $\dfrac{3}{2}$.

The reciprocal of $\dfrac{21}{4}$ is $\dfrac{4}{21}$.

To *divide* two common fractions, multiply the fraction which is the dividend by the reciprocal of the fraction which is the divisor. Reduce the result to lowest terms.

Examples: $\dfrac{4}{9} \div \dfrac{2}{3} = \dfrac{4}{9} \times \dfrac{3}{2} = \dfrac{12}{18} = \dfrac{2}{3}$.

$\dfrac{7}{8} \div \dfrac{21}{4} = \dfrac{7}{8} \times \dfrac{4}{21} = \dfrac{28}{168} = \dfrac{1}{6}$.

In addition, the procedures regarding the division of integers given above in section 1.6.4 apply for the division of common fractions.

1.8 Arithmetic Operations and Decimal Fractions

As discussed above in section 1.4, our numeration system follows a base 10 place value scheme. Another way to represent a fractional number is to write the number to include integer powers of ten. This allows us to represent *decimal fractions* as follows:

$$\frac{1}{10} = 10^{-1} = 0.1 \text{ (said "one-tenth")}$$

$$\frac{1}{100} = 10^{-2} = 0.01 \text{ (said "one-hundredth")}$$

$$\frac{1}{1000} = 10^{-3} = 0.001 \text{ (said "one-thousandth"), and so forth.}$$

Examples: 3.14 is said "three and fourteen hundredths."
528.5 is said "five hundred twenty-eight and five-tenths."

1.8.1 Addition

To *add decimal fractions*, simply line up the decimal points for each decimal numeral to be added, and follow the procedures for the addition of integers given in section 1.6.1. Place the decimal point in the sum directly underneath the decimal point in the addends.

Examples:	89.8	32.456
	152.9	6561.22
	+7.21	+2.14
	249.91	6595.816

1.8.2 Subtraction

To *subtract decimal fractions*, place zeros as needed so that both the minuend and the subtrahend have a digit in each column. Follow the procedures for addition of decimal fractions given in section 1.8.1, and the procedures for the subtraction of integers given in section 1.6.2.

Examples: 152.9   →   152.90
             −7.21   −7.21
                            145.69

             32.456   →   32.456
             −2.14   −2.140
                            30.316

1.8.3 Multiplication

To *multiply decimal fractions*, follow the procedures for multiplying integers given in section 1.6.3, and then place the decimal point so that *the total number of decimal places in the product is equal to the sum of the decimal places in each factor.*

Examples: (3.14) (0.5) = 1.570, and
            (89.8) (152.9) = 13730.42

1.8.4 Division

To *divide decimal fractions,*

1) move the decimal point in the divisor to the right, until there are no decimal places in the divisor,

2) move the decimal point in the dividend the same number of decimal places to the right, and

3) divide the transformed dividend and divisor as given above in section 1.6.4.

4) The number of decimal places in the quotient should be the same as the number of decimal places in the transformed dividend.

Examples: 15.5 ÷ 0.5→ 155 ÷ 5 = 31, and
            32.436 ÷ 0.06 → 3243.6 ÷ 6 = 540.6

1.9 Percent

Percent is another way of expressing a fractional number. Percent always expresses a fractional number in terms of $\frac{1}{100}$'s or 0.01's. Percents use the "%" symbol.

Examples: $100\% = \frac{100}{100} = 1.00$, and

$25\% = \frac{25}{100} = 0.25$.

As shown in these examples, a percent is easily converted to a common fraction or a decimal fraction. To convert a decimal to a common fraction, place the percent in the numerator and use 100 as the denominator (reduce as necessary). To convert a percent to a decimal fraction, divide the percent by 100, or move the decimal point two places to the right.

Examples: $25\% = \frac{25}{100} = \frac{1}{4}$ and
$25\% = 0.25$.

Similarly, $125\% = \frac{125}{100} = 1\frac{25}{100} = 1\frac{1}{4}$ and

$125\% = 1.25$.

To convert a *common fraction to a percent,* carry out a division of the numerator by the denominator of the fraction out to three decimal places. Round the result to two places. To convert a *decimal fraction to a percent,* move the decimal point two places to the right (adding 0's as place holders, if needed) and round as necessary.

Examples: $\frac{1}{4} = 1 \div 4 = 0.25 = 25\%$, and

$\frac{2}{7} = 2 \div 7 \cong 0.28 = 28\%$.

If one wishes to find the *percentage* of a known quantity, change the percent to a common fraction or a decimal fraction, and multiply the fraction times the quantity. The percentage is expressed in the same units as the known quantity.

Example: To find 25% of 360 books, change 25% to 0.25 and
multiply times 360, as follows: 0.25 x 360 = 90.
The result is 90 books.

(Note: The known quantity is the *base,* the percent is the *rate,* and the result is the *percentage.*)

1.10 Elementary Statistics

1.10.1 Mean

The average, or *mean*, of a set of numbers can be found by adding the set of numbers and dividing by the total number of elements in the set.

Example: The mean of 15, 10, 25, 5, 40 is

$$\frac{15+10+25+5+40}{5} = \frac{95}{5} = 19.$$

1.10.2 Median

If a given set of numbers is ordered from smallest to largest, the *median* is the "middle" number; that is, half of the numbers in the set of numbers is below the median and half of the numbers in the set is above the median.

Example: To find the median of the set of whole numbers 15, 10, 25, 5, 40, first order the set of numbers to get 5, 10, 15, 25, 40. Since 15 is the middle number (half of the numbers are below 15, half are above 15), 15 is called the median of this set of whole numbers. If there is an even number of numbers in the set, the median is the mean of the middle two numbers.

1.10.3 Mode

The *mode* of a set of numbers is the number that appears most frequently in the set.

Example: In the set 15, 10, 25, 10, 5, 40, 10, 15, the number 10 appears most frequently (three times); therefore, 10 is the mode of the given set of numbers.

1.10.4 Range

The *range* of a set of numbers is obtained by subtracting the smallest number in the set from the largest number in the set.

Example: To find the range of 15, 10, 25, 5, 40, find the difference between the largest and the smallest elements of the set. This gives 40 − 5 = 35. The range of the given set is 35.

Part II: Algebra

2.1 Algebraic Expressions

An *algebraic expression* is an expression using letters, numbers, symbols, and arithmetic operations to represent a number or relationship among numbers.

A *variable*, or unknown, is a letter that stands for a number in an algebraic expression. *Coefficients* are the numbers that precede the variable to give the quantity of the variable in the expression.

Algebraic expressions are comprised of *terms*, or groupings of variables and numbers.

An algebraic expression with one term is called a *monomial*; with two terms, a *binomial*; with three terms, a *trinomial*; with more than one term, a *polynomial*.

Examples: $2ab - cd$ is a binomial algebraic expression with variables a, b, c, and d, and terms $2ab$ and $(-cd)$. 2 is the coefficient of ab and -1 is the coefficient of cd.

                $x^2 + 3y - 1$ is a trinomial algebraic expression using the variables x and y, and terms x^2, $3y$, and (-1);

                $z(x - 1) + uv - wy - 2$ is a polynomial with variables z, x, u, v, w, and y, and terms $z(x - 1)$, uv, $(-wy)$, and (-2).

As stated above, algebraic expressions can be used to represent the relationship among numbers. For example, if we know there are ten times as many students in a school as teachers, if S represents the number of students in the school and T represents the number of teachers, the total number of students and teachers in the school is $S + T$.

If we wished to form an algebraic sentence equating the number of students and teachers in the school, the sentence would be $S = 10T$. (Note that if either the number of students or the number of teachers were known, the other quantity could be found.)

2.2 Simplifying Algebraic Expressions

Like terms are terms in an algebraic expression that are exactly the same; that is, they contain the same variables and the same powers.

Examples: The following are pairs of like terms:
          x^2 and $(-3x^2)$, abc and $4abc$, $(x - 1)$
          and $(x - 1)^2$.

The following are not pairs of like terms:
x and $(-3x^2)$, abc and $4a^2bc$, $(x-1)$ and (x^2-1).

To simplify an algebraic expression, combine like terms in the following order:

1) simplify all expressions within symbols of inclusion (e.g., (), [], {}) using steps 2-4 below;

2) carry out all exponentiation;

3) carry out all multiplication and division from left to right in the order in which they occur;

4) carry out all addition and subtraction from left to right in the order in which they occur.

2.3   Factoring Algebraic Expressions

As noted in section 1.6.3, when two numbers are multiplied together, the numbers are called factors and their result is called the product. Similarly, algebraic expressions may be the product of other algebraic expressions.

In factoring algebraic expressions, first remove any monomial factors, then remove any binomial, trinomial, or other polynomial factors. Often one may find other polynomial factors by inspecting for the sum and difference of two squares; that is, $x^2 - y^2 = (x + y)(x - y)$.

Examples: $2a + 2b = 2(a + b)$
$4x^2y - 2xy^2 + 16x^2y^2 = 2xy(2x - y + 8xy)$
$x^2 - 4 = (x + 2)(x - 2)$
$4a^2 - 16b^2 = 4(a^2 - 4b^2) = 4(a + 2b)(a - 2b)$

In factoring polynomials, one often uses what is called the *"FOIL" method (First, Outside, Inside, Last)*.

Examples: $x^2 + 3x - 10 = (x - 2)(x + 5)$
$6y^2 - y - 2 = (2y + 1)(3y - 2)$
$ab^2 - 3ab - 10a = a(b^2 - 3b - 10) = a(b + 2)(b - 5)$

2.4   Solving Linear Equations

To solve a linear equation, use the following procedures:

1) isolate the variable; that is, group all the terms with the variable on one side of the equation (commonly the left side) and group all the constants on the other side of the equation (commonly the right side);

2) combine like terms on each side of the equation;

3) divide by the coefficient of the variable;

4) check the result in the original equation.

Problem: Solve $3x + 2 = 5$ for x.

Solution: $3x + 2 = 5$ (add -2 to both sides)

$3x = 3$ (multiply by $\frac{1}{3}$)

$x = 1$

Problem: Solve $a + 3a = 3a + 1$ for a.

Solution: $a + 3a = 3a + 1$ (add $-3a$ to both sides)

$a = 1$

Problem: Solve $3(y - 2) + 5 = 3 + 5y$ for y.

Solution: $3(y - 2) + 5 = 3 + 5y$ (simplify)

$3y - 6 + 5 = 3 + 5y$ (combine like terms)

$3y - 1 = 3 + 5y$ (add 1 to both sides)

$3y = 4 + 5y$ (add $- 5y$ to both sides)

$-2y = 4$ (multiply by $-\frac{1}{2}$)

$y = -2$

2.5   Solving Inequalities

The equivalence properties of integers given in section 1.1 and the procedures for solving linear equations given in section 2.4 are used *to solve inequalities*. In addition, the following properties of inequalities should be noted:

If $x < y$ and $z > 0$, then $zx < zy$.

If $x > y$ and $z > 0$, then $zx > zy$.

If $x < y$ and $z < 0$, then $zx > zy$.

If $x > y$ and $z < 0$, then $zx < zy$.

In other words, if both sides of an inequality are *multiplied by a positive number, the sense of the inequality remains the same.* If both sides of an inequality are *multiplied by a negative number, the sense of the inequality is reversed.*

Examples: Since $3 < 5$ and 2 is positive,

$(2)(3) < (2)(5)$ or $6 < 10$.

But since $3 < 5$ and -2 is negative,

$(-2)(3) > (-2)(5)$ or $-6 > -10$.

The above properties are also demonstrated in the following problems:

Problem: Find the values of y for which $2y > y - 3$.

Solution: $2y > y - 3$ (add $-y$ to both sides)

$y > -3$

Problem: Find the values of x for which $x > 4x + 1$.

Solution: $x > 4x + 1$ (add $-4x$ to both sides)

$-3x > 1$ (multiply by $-\dfrac{1}{3}$)

$x < -\dfrac{1}{3}$

2.6 Evaluating Formulas

Formulas are algebraic sentences that are frequently used in mathematics, science, or other fields. Examples of common formulas are $A = l \times w$, $d = r \times t$, and $C = \left(\dfrac{9}{5}\right)$ $(F - 32°)$. *To evaluate a formula,* replace each variable with the given values of the variables and solve for the unknown variable.

Example: Since $A = l \times w$, if $l = 2$ ft. and
$w = 3$ ft.,
then $A = 2$ ft. x 3 ft. = 6 sq. ft.

Example: Since $d = r \times t$, if $r = 32$ m/sec^2 and
$t = 5$ sec.,
then $d = (32$ m/sec$) \times 5$ sec. = 160 m.

Example: Since $C = \left(\dfrac{9}{5}\right)$ $(F - 32)$, if $F = 212°$,

then $C = \left(\dfrac{9}{5}\right)$ $(212° - 32°) = 100°$.

2.7 Elementary Probability

The likelihood or chance that an event will take place is called the *probability* of the event. The probability of an event is determined by dividing the number of ways the event could occur by the number of possible events in the given sample. In other words, if a sample space S has n possible outcomes, and an event E has m ways of occurring, then the probability of the event, denoted by $P(E)$, is given by

$$P(E) = \frac{m}{n}.$$

It should be noted that $0 \leq P(E) \leq 1$.

Problem: What is the probability of getting "heads" on the toss of a coin?

Solution: Since the number of possible outcomes in the toss of a coin is 2 and the number of ways of getting "heads" on a coin toss is 1,

$$P(\text{head}) = \frac{1}{2}.$$

Problem: What is the probability of drawing an ace from a standard deck of playing cards?

Solution: Since the number of aces in a standard deck is 4 and the number of cards in a standard deck is 52, $P(\text{ace}) = \frac{4}{52} = \frac{1}{13}$.

2.8   Algebra Word Problems

A general procedure for solving problems was suggested by Polya. His procedure can be summarized as follows:

1) Understand the problem.

2) Devise a plan for solving the problem.

3) Carry out the plan.

4) Look back on the solution to the problem.

When taking the mathematics section of the CBEST, you can use this procedure by translating the word problem into an algebraic sentence, then following the procedures for solving an algebraic sentence given in sections 2.4 or 2.6. Find a variable to represent the unknown in the problem. Look for key synonyms such as "is, are, were" for "=", "more, more than" for "+", "less, less than, fewer" for "−", and "of" for "x."

Problem: The sum of the ages of Bill and Paul is 32 years. Bill is 6 years older than Paul. Find the age of each.

Solution: If p = Paul's age, then Bill's age is $p + 6$. So that $p + (p + 6) = 32$. Applying the methods from above, we get $p = 13$. Therefore, Paul is 13 and Bill is 19.

Problem: Jose weighs twice as much as his brother Carlos. If together they weigh 225 pounds, how much does each weigh?

Solution: If c = Carlos' weight, then Jose's weight is $2c$. So $c + 2c = 225$ pounds. Applying the methods above, we get $c = 75$. Therefore, Carlos weighs 75 pounds and Jose weighs 150 pounds.

Problem: Julia drove from her home to her aunt's house in 3 hours and 30 minutes. If the distance between the houses is 175 miles, what was the car's average speed?

Solution: As noted in section 2.6, distance = rate x time. Since we know $d = 175$ mph and $t = 3\frac{1}{2}$ hr., then 175 mph = r x $3\frac{1}{2}$ hr. Solving for the rate (r), we get $r = 50$ mph.

(It is strongly suggested that individuals who feel they need additional practice in solving word problems using the above procedures seek out additional practice problems in a standard high school first-year algebra textbook.)

Part III: Measurement and Geometry

3.1 Perimeter and Area of Rectangles, Squares, and Triangles

Perimeter refers to the measure of the distance around a figure. Perimeter is measured in linear units (e.g., inches, feet, meters). *Area* refers to the measure of the interior of a figure. Area is measured in square units (e.g., square inches, square feet, square meters).

3.1.1 Perimeter of Rectangles, Squares, and Triangles

The *perimeter of a rectangle* is found by adding twice the length of the rectangle to twice the width of the rectangle. This relationship is commonly given by the formula $P = 2l + 2w$, where l is the measure of the length and w is the measure of the width.

Example: If a rectangle has $l = 10$ m and $w = 5$ m,
then the perimeter of the rectangle is given by
$P = 2(10$ m$) + 2(5$ m$) = 30$ m.

The *perimeter of a square* is found by multiplying four times the measure of a side of the square. This relationship is commonly given by the formula, $P = 4s$, where s is the measure of a side of the square.

Example: If a square has $s = 5$ feet,
then the perimeter of the square is given by
$P = 4(5$ feet $) = 20$ feet.

The *perimeter of a triangle* is found by adding the measures of the three sides of the triangle. This relationship can be represented by $P = s_1 + s_2 + s_3$, where s_1, s_2, and s_3 are the measures of the sides of the triangle.

Example: If a triangle has three sides measuring
3 inches, 4 inches, and 5 inches,
then the perimeter of the triangle is given by
$P = 3$ inches $+ 4$ inches $+ 5$ inches $= 12$ inches.

3.1.2 Area of Rectangles, Squares, and Triangles

The *area of a rectangle* is found by multiplying the measure of the length of the rectangle by the measure of the width of the triangle. This relationship is commonly given by $A = l \times w$, where l is the measure of the length and w is the measure of the width.

Example: If a rectangle has $l = 10$ m and $w = 5$ m,
then the area of the rectangle is given by
$A = 10$ m $\times 5$ m $= 50$ m^2.

The *area of a square* is found by squaring the measure of the side of the square. This relationship is commonly given by $A = s^2$, where s is the measure of a side.

Example: If a square has $s = 5$ ft.,
then the area of the square is given by
$A = (5$ ft$^2) = 25$ ft^2.

The *area of a right triangle* is found by multiplying $\frac{1}{2}$ times the product of the base and the height of the triangle. This relationship is commonly given by $A = \frac{1}{2} bh$, where b is the base and h is the height.

Example: If a triangle has a base of 3 in. and a height of 4 in.,
then the area of the triangle is given by

$$A = \frac{1}{2} (3 \text{ in.} \times 4 \text{ in.}) = \frac{1}{2} (12) = 6 \text{ in}^2.$$

3.2   Circumference and Area of Circles

The *radius of a circle* is the distance from the center of the circle to the circle itself. The *diameter of a circle* is a line segment that passes through the center of the circle, the end points of which lie on the circle. The *measure of the diameter of a circle* is twice the measure of the radius.

The number π (approximately 3.14 or $3\frac{1}{7}$) is often used in computations involving circles.

The *circumference of a circle* is found by multiplying π times the diameter (or twice the radius). This relationship is commonly given by $C = \pi \times d$, or $C = 2 \times \pi \times r$.

The *area of a circle* is found by multiplying π by the square of the radius of the circle. This relationship is commonly given by $A = \pi \times r^2$.

Example: If a circle has a radius of 5 cm, then
$C = \pi \times 10$ cm $= 3.14 \times 10$ cm ≈ 31.4 cm, and
$A = \pi \times 5^2 \approx 3.14 \times 5^2 = 78.50$ cm^2.

3.3 Volume of Cubes and Rectangular Solids

Volume refers to the measure of the interior of a three-dimensional figure.

A *rectangular solid* is a rectilinear (right-angled) figure that has length, width, and height. The volume of a rectangular solid is found by computing the product of the length, width, and height of the figure. This relationship is commonly expressed by $V = l \times w \times h$.

Example: The volume of a rectangular solid with
l = 5 cm, w = 4 cm, and h = 3 cm is given by
V = 5 cm x 4 cm x 3 cm = 60 cm³.

A *cube* is a rectangular solid, the length, width, and height of which have the same measure. This measure is called the *edge of the cube*. The volume of a cube is found by cubing the measure of the edge. This relationship is commonly expressed by $V = e^3$.

Example: The volume of a cube with e = 5 cm is given by V = (5 cm)³ = 125 cm³.

3.4 Angle Measure

An *angle* consists of all the points in two noncollinear rays that have the same vertex. An angle is commonly thought of as two "arrows" joined at their bases.

Two angles are *adjacent* if they share a common vertex, share only one side, and one angle does not lie in the interior of the other.

Angles are usually measured in *degrees*. A circle has a measure of 360°, a half circle 180°, a quarter circle 90°, and so forth. If the measures of two angles are the same, then the angles are said to be *congruent*.

An angle with a measure of 90° is called a *right angle*. Angles with measures less than 90° are called *acute*. Angles with measures more than 90° are called *obtuse*.

If the sum of the measures of two angles is 90°, the two angles are said to be *complementary*. If the sum of the measures of the two angles is 180°, the two angles are said to be *supplementary*.

If two lines intersect, they form two pairs of *vertical angles*. The measures of vertical angles are equivalent; that is, vertical angles are congruent.

3.5 Properties of Triangles

Triangles are three-sided polygons.

If the measures of two sides of a triangle are equal, then the triangle is called an *isosceles triangle*. If the measures of all sides of the triangle are equal, then the triangle is called an *equilateral triangle*. If no measures of the sides of a triangle are equal, then the triangle is called a *scalene triangle*.

The sum of the measures of the angles of a triangle is 180°.

Problem: Find the measures of the angles of a right triangle, if one of the angles measures 30°.

Solution: Since the triangle is a right triangle, a second angle of the triangle measures 90°. We know the sum of the measures of a triangle is 180°, so that, $90° + 30° + x° = 180°$. Solving for $x°$, we get $x° = 60°$. The measures of the angles of the triangle are 90°, 60°, and 30°.

The sum of the measures of any two sides of a triangle is greater than the measure of the third side.

If the measure of one angle of a triangle is greater than the measure of another angle of a triangle, then the measure of the side opposite the larger angle is greater than the side opposite the smaller angle. (A similar relationship holds for the measures of angles opposite larger sides.)

Related to the discussion of angles in section 3.4, if all of the angles of a triangle are acute, then the triangle is called an *acute triangle*. If one of the angles of a triangle is obtuse, then the triangle is called an *obtuse triangle*. If one of the angles of a triangle is a right angle, then the triangle is called a *right triangle*.

Two triangles are *congruent* if the measures of all corresponding sides and angles are equal. Two triangles are *similar* if the measures of all corresponding angles are equal.

3.6   The Pythagorean Theorem

In a right triangle, the side opposite the 90° angle is called the *hypotenuse* and the other two sides are called the *legs*. If the hypotenuse has measure c and the legs have measures a and b, the relationship among the measures, known as the *Pythagorean Theorem*, is given by

$$c^2 = a^2 + b^2.$$

Problem: Find the length of the hypotenuse of a triangle if the measure of one leg is 3 cm and the other leg is 4 cm.

Solution: By the Pythagorean Theorem, $c^2 = 3^2 + 4^2$, so that $c^2 = 9 + 16$, $c^2 = 25$. Taking the square root of both sides, we get $c = 5$ cm.

3.7   Properties of Parallel and Perpendicular Lines

If lines have a point or points in common, they are said to *intersect*.

Lines are *parallel* if they do not intersect.

Lines are *perpendicular* if they contain the sides of a right angle.

If a third line intersects two other lines, the intersecting line is called a *transversal*.

Two lines crossed by a transversal form eight angles. The four angles that lie between the two lines are called *interior angles*. The four angles that lie outside the two lines are called *exterior angles*.

The interior angles that lie on the same side of the transversal are called *consecutive interior angles.* The interior angles that lie on opposite sides of the transversal are called *alternate interior angles.* Similarly, exterior angles that lie on the same side of the transversal are called *consecutive exterior angles,* and those that lie on opposite sides of the transversal are called *alternate exterior angles.*

An interior angle and an exterior angle that have different vertices and have sides that are on the same side of the transversal are called *corresponding angles.*

3.7.1   Properties of Parallel Lines

The following are true for parallel lines:

Alternate interior angles are congruent. Conversely, if alternate interior angles are congruent, then the lines are parallel.

Interior angles on the same side of the transversal are supplementary. Conversely, if interior angles on the same side of the transversal are supplementary, then the lines are parallel.

Corresponding angles are congruent. Conversely, if corresponding angles are congruent, then the lines are parallel.

3.7.2   Properties of Perpendicular Lines

If two lines are perpendicular, the four angles they form are all right angles.

If two lines are perpendicular to a third line, the lines are parallel.

If one of two parallel lines is perpendicular to a third line, so is the other line.

3.8   Coordinate Geometry

The rectangular coordinate system is used as a basis for coordinate geometry. In this system, two perpendicular lines form a plane. The perpendicular lines are called the *x-axis* and the *y-axis.* The coordinate system assigns an *ordered pair of numbers* (x, y) to each point in the plane. The point of intersection of the two axes is called the origin, O, and has coordinates (0,0).

As shown in the figure below, the x-axis has positive integers to the right and negative integers to the left of the origin. Similarly, the y-axis has positive integers above and negative integers below the origin.

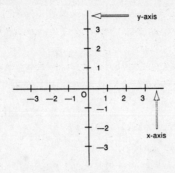

The distance between any two points in the coordinate plane can be found by using the *distance formula*. According to the distance formula, if P_1 and P_2 are two points with coordinates (x_1, y_1) and (x_2, y_2) respectively, then the distance between P_1 and P_2 is given by

$$P_1P_2 = \sqrt{\left(x_2 - x_1\right)^2 + \left(y_2 - y_1\right)^2}$$

Problem: Compute the distance between the points A and B with coordinates $(1,1)$ and $(4, 5)$ respectively.

Solution: Using the distance formula,

$$AB = \sqrt{\left(4 - 1\right)^2 + \left(5 - 1\right)^2}$$
$$= \sqrt{3^2 + 4^2}$$
$$= \sqrt{9 + 16}$$
$$= 5$$

3.9   Graphs

To *plot a point* on a graph, first plot the x-coordinate, then plot the y-coordinate from the given ordered pair.

Problem: Plot the following points on the coordinate plane: A (1, 2), B (2, 1), C (–2, –1).

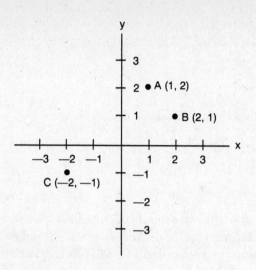

3.10   The Metric System

The *metric system of measurement* is closely related to the base 10 place value scheme discussed in section 1.4. The prefixes commonly used in the metric system are:

Prefix	Meaning
kilo-	thousand (1000)
deci-	tenth (0.1)
centi-	hundredth (0.01)
milli-	thousandth (0.001)

The basic unit of linear measure in the metric system is the *meter,* represented by m. The relationship among the commonly used linear units of measurement in the metric system is as follows:

1 kilometer (km)	=	1000 m
1 meter (m)	=	1.0 m
1 decimeter (dm)	=	0.1 m
1 centimeter (cm)	=	0.01 m
1 millimeter (mm)	=	0.001 m

The basic unit of measurement for mass (or weight) in the metric system is the *gram,* represented by g. The relationship among the commonly used units of measurement for mass in the metric system is as follows:

1 kilogram (kg)	=	1000 g
1 gram (g)	=	1.0 g
1 milligram (mg)	=	0.001 g

The basic unit of measurement for capacity (or volume) in the metric system is the *liter,* represented by L or l. The most commonly used relationship between two metric units of capacity is

1 liter (l) = 1000 ml.

Key Strategies for Answering the Mathematics Questions

1. **Make effective use of your time.** You will have seventy minutes to answer fifty questions on the mathematics section of the CBEST. This will allow you about a minute and a half to answer each question. If you find yourself taking longer than two minutes on a given question, mark the answer you think is most likely correct, circle the number of the item in the test booklet, and come back to it later if time allows.

2. **Answer all questions on this section of the test.** There is no penalty for guessing on this section of the CBEST, so do not leave any question unanswered. If you are not sure of the correct answer, narrow the choices to the two or three most likely, and choose one. Eliminate answers that could not possibly be correct before you choose.

3. **Read each question carefully.** Be sure you understand what the question is actually asking, not what a casual reading of the question might suggest. Be sure you have separated all the relevant information from the irrelevant information in the question.

4. **Devise a plan for answering the question.** This plan will be especially useful on the word problems and geometry items.

5. **Work the problem backwards to check your answer.** If time allows, check your work by substituting the answer into the original problem. Be certain that the answer meets all the conditions in the original question.

6. **Draw a diagram, sketch, or table to organize your work or to explain the question.** Not all questions that you need an illustration to understand will include an illustration, so make one yourself. This strategy may be especially useful in the geometry section.

7. **Write in the test booklet.** Mark up diagrams as needed. Write in the margins and other blank spaces. Write information directly into the statement of the problem, especially if you are having trouble setting up a solution.

8. **Look for similar questions.** Similar items may have appeared elsewhere on the test. You also may recall similar questions from classes you have taken previously. Apply suitable strategies from related work to the problem at hand.

Arithmetic

Practice Problems

1. $34 + 3 \times 2 - 25 \div 5 =$

   (A) 3
   (B) 13.8
   (C) 34
   (D) 35
   (E) 69

2. $\dfrac{4}{5} + \dfrac{6}{20} =$

   (A) $\dfrac{1}{2}$
   (B) $\dfrac{10}{25}$
   (C) $1\dfrac{1}{10}$
   (D) $1\dfrac{1}{20}$
   (E) $1\dfrac{1}{5}$

3. $.01 \times .4 =$

   (A) .4
   (B) .04
   (C) .004
   (D) .0004
   (E) 40

4. $\sqrt{100} =$

   (A) 10
   (B) 50
   (C) 200
   (D) 500
   (E) 10,000

5. $(2^2)^4 =$

   (A) $\sqrt{2}$
   (B) 2^6
   (C) 2^7
   (D) 2^8
   (E) 2^{16}

6. $\dfrac{3}{4} \times \dfrac{8}{9} =$

     (A) $\dfrac{24}{9}$ (D) $\dfrac{11}{13}$

     (B) $\dfrac{32}{3}$ (E) $\dfrac{5}{3}$

     (C) $\dfrac{2}{3}$

7. $146.1 - 8.07 =$

     (A)   6.54   (D)   138.03

     (B)   65.4   (E)   148.03

     (C)   137.04

8.   What is the mean of 25, 30, 25, 20, 35?

     (A)   25   (D)   33.75

     (B)   27   (E)   34

     (C)   27.5

9. $2(4 - 1) - (1 - 7) =$

     (A) -2 (D)   12

     (B)   0   (E)   18

     (C)   10

10. $11\dfrac{2}{3} - 2\dfrac{5}{6} =$

     (A) $9\dfrac{1}{2}$ (B) $8\dfrac{2}{3}$

     (C) $8\dfrac{5}{6}$ (D) $9\dfrac{5}{6}$

     (E) $9\dfrac{2}{3}$

Artithmetic

Practice Problem Answers

1.	(D)		6.	(C)
2.	(C)		7.	(D)
3.	(C)		8.	(B)
4.	(A)		9.	(D)
5.	(D)		10.	(C)

Algebra

Practice Problems

1. $x^2y + xy^2 - 2x^2y + 3xy^2 =$

    (A) $3x^2y$

    (B) $3xy^2$

    (C) $x^2y + 4xy^2$

    (D) $-x^2y + 4xy^2$

    (E) $4x^2y - xy^2$

2. $(x - 2)(x - 3) =$

    (A) $2x - 6$

    (B) $6x$

    (C) $x^2 - 2x - 6$

    (D) $x^2 + 5x + 6$

    (E) $x^2 - 5x + 6$

3. Solve $2x + 5 = 9$ for x.

    (A) -5

    (B) -2

    (C) 2

    (D) 7

    (E) 3

4. $5mn^2 \times 4mn^2 =$

    (A) $20m^2n^2$ (D) mn^2

    (B) $20m^2n^4$ (E) m^2n^4

    (C) $9mn^2$

5. $x^4 - 1 =$

    (A) $(x^2 + 1)(x^2)$ (D) $(x - 1)(x^3 + 1)$

    (B) $(x^2 - 1)(x^2)$ (E) $(x + 1)(x^3 - 1)$

    (C) $(x^2 + 1)(x - 1)(x + 1)$

6. $3m + 2 < 7$

    (A) $m \geq \dfrac{5}{3}$ (D) $m < \dfrac{5}{3}$

    (B) $m > 2$ (E) $m < 2$

    (C) $m \leq 2$

7. $2h^3 + 2h^2t - 4ht^2 =$

    (A) $2(h^3 - t)(h + t)$ (D) $2h(h + 2t)(h - t)$

    (B) $2h(h + t) - 4ht^2$ (E) $4h(ht - t^2)$

    (C) $2h(h - 2t)^2$

8. $0 < 2 - y < 6$

    (A) $-4 < y < 2$ (D) $0 < y < 4$

    (B) $-2 < y < 4$ (E) $-4 < y < -2$

    (C) $-4 < y < 0$

9. $7b^3 - 4c^2 - 6b^3 + 3c^2 =$

    (A) $b^3 - c^2$ (D) 0

    (B) $7b - c$ (E) $13b^3 - c$

    (C) $-11b^2 - 3c^2$

10. Solve $3x - 10 = 5 - 2x$ for x

    (A) −3   (D) 3

    (B) −2   (E) No solution

    (C) 2

Algebra

Practice Problem Answers

1.	(D)		6.	(D)
2.	(E)		7.	(D)
3.	(C)		8.	(A)
4.	(B)		9.	(A)
5.	(C)		10.	(D)

Measurement and Geometry

Practice Problems

1. Find the perimeter of a rectangle with $l = 3$ m and $w = 4$ m.

    (A) 12 m²   (D) 9 m

    (B) 14 m   (E) 16 m

    (C) 14 m²

2. Find the area of a circle with a diameter of 10 cm.

    (A) 10π cm   (D) 25π cm²

    (B) 20π cm²   (E) 100π cm²

    (C) 25π cm

3. Find the area of a square with a perimeter of 12 cm.

    (A) 9 cm²   (B) 12 cm²

(C)   48 cm²   (D)   96 cm²

(E)   144 cm²

4.   A triangle has angles = x, $2x$, and $3x$. Solve for x.

(A)   15°   (D)   45°

(B)   25°   (E)   90°

(C)   30°

5.   The circumference of a circle is 18π cm. Find the area of the circle.

(A) 18π cm²   (D) 36π cm²

(B)   81 cm²   (E) 81π cm²

(C)   36 cm²

6.   Find the volume of a solid with l = 4 cm, w = 3 cm, and h = 6 cm.

(A)   8 cm³   (D)   72 cm³

(B)   9 cm³   (E)   108 cm³

(C)   36 cm³

7. $\angle a$ and $\angle b$ are supplementary angles and $\angle a = 3\angle b$. Find $\angle b$.

(A)   22.5°   (D)   135°

(B)   45°   (E)   270°

(C)   90°

8.   Find the area of a triangle with b = 6 cm and h = 8 cm.

(A)   14 cm²   (D)   48 cm²

(B)   24 cm²   (E)   Not enough information given.

(C)   36 cm²

9.   Find the length of the hypotenuse of a triangle with one leg = 6 cm and the other leg = 8 cm.

(A) $\sqrt{28}$ cm   (D) $\sqrt{45}$ cm

(B)   7 cm   (E)   10 cm

(C) $\sqrt{70}$ cm

10. Find the perimeter of a square with $s = 8$ m.

   (A)   16 m   (D)   40 m

   (B)   24 m   (E)   Not enough information given

   (C)   32 m

Measurement and Geometry

Practice Problem Answers

1.	(B)	6.	(D)
2.	(D)	7.	(B)
3.	(A)	8.	(B)
4.	(C)	9.	(E)
5.	(E)	10.	(C)

CBEST
California Basic Educational Skills Test

ESSAY
WRITING
REVIEW

Overview

The writing portion of the CBEST assesses your ability to compose two effective essays within the one-hour time limit. You must write on two topics printed in the test booklet. In one essay you must analyze a given situation or a particular statement.

An example of this first type of essay topic is:

Topic 1

"Describing how individuals are different is the easier task; discovering how individuals are alike is the more important task."

On the basis of your own experience, explain why you agree or disagree with this idea.

In the other essay, you will be asked to write about a personal experience. An example of this second type of topic is:

Topic 2

Describe two incidents in your life that significantly influenced your decision to choose the career you are pursuing.

Essay writing demonstrates your ability to think critically and to use language logically and clearly. The 30-minute time limit for each essay allows you little time to rewrite and reflect on your writing. Therefore, your performance on the CBEST writing test will demonstrate your ability to quickly organize and support your ideas. This type of writing is illustrative of the kind of thinking all teachers need to do effectively in presenting concepts and ideas to their students.

Nine categories of writing ability are assessed:

1. **Quality of insight or central idea.** The evaluators will look at the premise or thesis statement you set forth in the opening paragraph and also how you support or develop your ideas in the succeeding paragraphs.

2. **Tone.** Do you write with the formality appropriate to an audience composed of teachers?

3. **Clarity.** Are your phrasing and your statements easy to understand.

4. **Consistent point of view.** Do your supporting statements maintain the point of view established in the opening paragraph or thesis statement?

5. **Cohesiveness.** How tightly do your supporting statements relate to the thesis statement of the opening paragraph and to the topic sentences of each succeeding paragraph?

6. **Strength and logic of supporting information.** Do your supporting statements include strong details to express your thinking?

7. **Rhetorical force.** Do you effectively use vocabulary and language to express your ideas and interest the reader?

8. **Diction and syntax.** Is your choice of words appropriate and your grammar correct when forming phrases, clauses, and sentences?

9. **Mechanics and usage.** Are your spelling, punctuation, verb tense agreement, and usage of parts of speech correct?

Review of Essay Writing Concepts and Skills

An essay is a group of related paragraphs organized around a single topic. This topic is fully developed, and all the sentences in each paragraph and all the paragraphs in the essay are tightly constructed around this topic. Essays that tend to receive the highest score on the CBEST, "a pass," have five or six short, well-focused paragraphs. The structure of a typical five-paragraph essay consists of an opening paragraph that contains a thesis statement, three supporting paragraphs, and a concluding paragraph.

The opening (introductory) paragraph performs three functions. First, the opening paragraph defines the audience. In other words, it sets the tone or style of your writing for the rest of the essay. Second, it attracts attention so that the reader will want to know what you have to say. Finally, it contains a thesis statement which is known as the main idea, purpose, or premise. This statement defines your opinion and predicts the direction or logic of your succeeding statements. The thesis statement is usually the final sentence of the essay.

The body of the essay follows the opening paragraph. Here you present several major points to support the thesis statement. Each major point is developed into a supporting paragraph. The number of supporting paragraphs will vary according to the nature of your topic and ideas, but three is a common number of major points in a test exercise of this type. Each supporting paragraph has a topic sentence and supporting information or statements that expand or explain the topic sentence of the paragraphs. Supporting paragraphs are important to the cohesiveness of your essay because they explain, narrate, describe, or argue the key points of the thesis statement in the opening paragraph.

The concluding paragraph of the essay summarizes the thesis statement and the topic sentences of the supporting paragraphs. You may rephrase your thesis statement and the three or so major supporting points. You may choose to summarize your essay to provide a logical conclusion. A summarization without restating is often more rhetorically forceful.

A chart of this multi-paragraph essay structure follows:

Opening Paragraph:	Includes the thesis statement, sets style or tone of writing appropriate for the audience, and captures the attention of the reader.
Supporting Paragraphs:	Includes a topic sentence, which is the first major point related to the thesis, and information that expands the topic sentence. (You may include as many supporting paragraphs as you need to set forth your major points. Three or four paragraphs are average. Fewer than three may also be acceptable, providing they are sufficiently developed.)
Concluding Paragraph:	Includes a restatement and/or summarization, and an appropriate logical conclusion.

Key Strategies for Answering the Essay Questions

You can use a number of strategies to increase the effectiveness of your writing on the essay section of the CBEST.

Before the Test (Preparation)

1. Practice writing essays about the example topics given in this book, and time yourself.

2. Practice making an outline in the form of the essay frame to help you structure your ideas.

3. Study a list of the most frequently misspelled words. This will aid you in proofreading your writing.

4. Review the basic rules for good grammar and mechanics. Many college handbooks or office references are good sources.

On the Day of the Test

1. **Wear a watch** so that you can keep track of the time. You have one hour to write two essays, so allow 30 minutes to write each essay. You will have to pace your own writing. No one will make time announcements during the test.

2. **Take two ballpoint pens in either blue or black ink and two No. 2 soft-lead pencils with good erasers.** You will need two ballpoints in case one fails. You will need two pencils in case one breaks. You are not allowed to have paper other than the test booklet during the test. However, you may take notes at the bottom of the test booklet page on which the assigned topic appears. Therefore, you may want to jot notes in the bottom margin so that you can erase while working with phrasing and wording before writing the essay. Once you know what to write, use either the ballpoint pen or the pencil to write the actual essay. An essay written in either pen or pencil is acceptable, and you should use whichever is more comfortable for you.

A number of strategies are helpful in writing a clearly reasoned, well-organized, well-developed essay that demonstrates an understanding of the assigned topic.

Writing Strategies

1. **Read the essay topic carefully.** Read it two or three times. Underline the key ideas and words so you know exactly what you are being asked to do. An essay on a topic other than the one assigned will not be accepted. Write only on the topic specified in the test booklet.

2. **Form a thesis statement.** Since this statement is crucial to the organization of the essay, write it down in rough form at the bottom of the test booklet page where you are allowed to make notes. Work with it until it is worded exactly as you want it, so you can develop the supporting paragraphs.

3. **Order your major supporting points.** Use the first five to ten minutes to make a list outline or diagram at the bottom margin of the test booklet. You can write the essay more easily if you first make an outline or diagram to keep your ideas on track.

4. **Take a stand and make all points relate to it.** Digressive information or contradictory statements will not help prove the thesis statement. If you do not stick to the thesis, the scorers will judge your writing as unorganized, lacking in focus, and confused. *You may fail if your essay is not well organized.*

5. **Write or print legibly.** Be as neat as possible. Readers like neat writing. Avoid using excessively large handwriting. Do not skip any lines in the test booklet. Do not leave margins wider than approximately an inch on either side. Indent approximately five spaces for each new paragraph.

6. **Proofread your writing** during the last five minutes for correct spelling, grammar, and punctuation. First, read quickly to check that what you have written makes sense and that you have not left out any words. Make sure there are no run-on sentences. Second, reread more slowly for spelling, grammar, and punctuation errors. *Correct errors as neatly as possible.*

There are several ways you can demonstrate your ability to use language effectively and construct good sentences. Most editors follow a handy rule that says "when in doubt (about what is written), cut it out" rather than leave it in and be in error. Although the appearance of your essay is not graded, too many crossed-out or squeezed-in words can be distracting and make it difficult for the evaluator to follow your train of thought. To keep from having to make too many messy corrections, the following "error avoidance" techniques are helpful.

The avoidance techniques help prevent you from making language errors that may cost you points. In a normal writing situation, you would have time to check references. In the absence of reference materials and when taking a timed test, make use of the editor's rule to leave it out when in doubt—find a better way that you know is correct.

Avoidance Techniques

Studying the following Avoidance Techniques will help you make fewer errors during timed writing.

1. **Avoid using words you do not know how to spell.** The *Oxford English Dictionary* lists approximately 500,000 words in the English language. This tremendous variety of words makes it possible to write with simple, easily spelled words which are synonyms to more complex words, which may be difficult to spell. When in doubt about the spelling of a difficult word, substitute a word that has the same meaning, but has a familiar spelling.

2. **Avoid contractions.** For example, write out the more formal *do not* instead of using the conversational contraction *don't*. A test situation like this requires a slightly more formal tone.

3. **Avoid the passive voice.** Use the active voice. Incorrect: A good time was had by everyone at the party. Correct: Everyone at the party had a good time.

4. **Avoid mixing verb tense.** If your topic sentence is in the present tense, then each sentence within the paragraph should also be in the present tense.

5. **Avoid using unfamiliar punctuation.** Colons, semicolons, dashes, parentheses or ellipsis points are confusing to most people who don't write professionally, so don't use them unless you're absolutely certain how to use them correctly.

6. **Avoid underlining, using all capital letters, or using quotation marks just to add emphasis.**

7. **Avoid overly long or complex, multiple-clause sentences.** Break the multiple clauses into separate sentences.

8. **Avoid beginning a sentence with conjunctions,** such as *and, but, or, so, nor, for,* and *yet.*

9. **Avoid ending a sentence with a preposition.** Say *of whom I spoke* instead of *whom I spoke of.*

10. **Avoid splitting infinitive verbs.** Say *to go slowly* instead of *to slowly go.*

11. **Avoid incorrect use of I/me, there/their/they're, to/two/too, its/it's.**

12. **Avoid constant repetition of the same transitional words.** Use transitional words for variety and a smooth flow of ideas. Instead of saying *first, second, third,* say *first, primary, following, subsequently.*

13. **Avoid using "ordinary" verbs.** Verbs are the key to presenting ideas forcefully and with variety. For example, instead of a simple verb such as "go," use *run, hurry, move,* or *stumble.*

14. **Avoid repeating words in close proximity.** *Next* is often overused in this way.

15. **Avoid all swear words, profanity, and derogatory or offensive language.**

Essay Scoring

The evaluators who will read and score your essays are experienced teachers. They will score your writing holistically; each of your essays will receive a single score based on their overall quality. Holistic scoring is similar to the scoring of individual ice skating competition in the Olympics. The skater's performance is ranked by the judges for its overall artistic appeal. However, the performance must also have technical merit. The overall score takes into account the skater's execution of certain prescribed skating techniques. Holistic scoring for writing means that the evaluators will judge not only the overall quality of your ideas, but also how well and correctly you use language. The organization of your ideas will receive the most weight, just as the judges in the skating competition give more weight to a skater's artistic performance. However, it is important to recognize that just as an excellent artistic performance by an Olympic skater can be hurt by executing techniques poorly, a writer with excellent organization and ideas can be hurt by not using language well and correctly. In other words, to receive the highest score on your writing you must demonstrate both good organization and ideas as well as correct and effective use of language.

Your essays will be read under very carefully controlled conditions to insure fairness and reliability. Two readers will score your first essay. Two different readers will score your second essay. The evaluators will rate you on the following points (mentioned earlier in this review):

• quality of insight or central idea

- tone

- clarity

- consistent point of view

- cohesiveness

- strength and logic of supporting information

- rhetorical force

- diction and syntax

- mechanics and usage

Each reader will give your writing a score. Individual readers will not see the other scores given to your writing. Pass (a score of 4) is the highest rating. Marginal Pass (a score of 3) is the second highest rating. Marginal Fail means a score of 2; fail means a score of 1 and is the lowest rating.

In order to receive a Pass you must meet three criteria. First, you must have excellent organization. Your writing must demonstrate clear reasoning or logic, must be well organized, and must be well developed so that your thesis statement is supported by subordinate paragraphs. Your writing must show a clear understanding of the assignment. Second, you must have excellent language use that is virtually free of errors. Minor flaws are acceptable. Your writing must show that you can use language effectively and that you know how to construct sentences that are grammatically correct, interesting, and good at conveying the power of your ideas. Finally, your writing must demonstrate that you followed instructions and completed all assigned tasks.

A Marginal Pass essay will evidence organization that is adequate but not as strong as in the Pass rating. The subordinate paragraphs and details will adequately support the thesis statement and topic sentences. The use of language is adequate. Writing errors in Marginal Pass essays are more frequent and noticeable than in Pass writing, and the essays may not complete all of the tasks or only vaguely addresses some of the tasks set forth in the assignment.

An essay will receive a Marginal Fail if the evaluators notice *one* or *more* of the following five weaknesses:

1. Poor organization or focus.
2. Weak supporting details, illustrations, paragraphs.
3. Stating the obvious, introducing new ideas with each sentence, writing too broadly so that little is said or listing meaningless details.
4. Problems with run-on sentences, misplaced clauses, lengthy multiple-clause sentences, or conversely, short choppy sentences with little variety.
5. Frequent or serious writing errors that distract or confuse the reader.

The essay will receive a Fail if the evaluators notice *one* or *more* of the following four serious weaknesses:

1 Confusion.
2. Lack of organization or focus.
3. No development of supporting illustrations.
4. Many severe writing errors.

In preparation for writing a Pass essay, you can analyze the essays that follow.

Topic 1

"Describing how individuals are different is the easier task; discovering how individuals are alike is the more important task."

On the basis of your own experience, explain why you agree or disagree with this idea.

Sample Essay on Topic 1:

When I am asked why Janet, my best friend, and I get along so well, I always tell people it is because we are so different. However, the more I think about our relationship, I realize our differences are not the only things that make our friendship so special. Beneath the obvious variations, there are many similarities which make us even more compatible.

In the middle of my sophomore year, my English teacher, Mrs. Estrada, changed the seating chart and I found myself sitting next to a quiet, but pretty black-haired girl named Janet. Being the loquacious person that I am, I immediately engaged her in a conversation. My lack of shyness, though I did not now it at the time, would create a beautiful friendship.

After I got to know Janet a little better, I became aware that we were very different. She was shy and pretty, and I was forward and gawky. She had a boyfriend and many friends, while I had not yet discovered boys and had few friends. She was from a lower socio-economic class, while I was from an upper socioeconomic class. With all of these differences, I wondered how we could be such good friends.

At first, I thought our friendship was as secure as it was because we contrasted so well. Yet, after we acknowledged that we were best friends and we began to spend more time together, I began to see many similarities. For instance, we both had the same goals and morals. We are both kind, compassionate, and sensitive people, and we both snort when we laugh.

It is very important for individuals to identify how they are different from others, but more difficult and more important is to discover how they are similar. By identifying how I am different from Janet, I was able to keep my individuality and learn about how another person operates, and by discovering our similarities, I was able to form a unbreakable bond with a unique and special individual who I can relate on terms that I understand. Now, when I am asked about why our relationship is so secure, I tell them it is because we are very different yet so very similar.

Analysis of the Essay

The essay above, which answers the first topic, fits the Pass criteria. The organization of the the essay is very strong. If you superimpose the chart or frame for multi-paragraph essays from earlier in this review, you see that the first topic essay is well structured. The opening paragraph includes the thesis statement: "Beneath the obvious variations, there are many similarities that make us even more compatible." This is an agreement statement, which fulfills the assignment of choosing to agree or disagree with the statement. The style and tone of the writing are appropriate for an audience of teachers. The illustrations from the areas of values, socioeconomics, physical appearances, and politics support the thesis statement and capture the attention of the reader. The three supporting paragraphs each expand on points first made in the opening paragraph. The first supporting paragraph tells how individuals are different. The second supporting paragraph elaborates on how characteristics of individuals differ. The third supporting paragraph emphasizes the importance of recognizing commonalities. The concluding paragraph summarizes the importance of similarities in relating to other people. It also brings in the uniqueness of individuals as a strong link to the mention of the topic sentence in the opening paragraph. Therefore, the first topic essay meets the criteria of a Pass score because it is "clearly reasoned, well organized, and well developed," and also demonstrates a clear understanding of the assignment.

The first topic also meets the second criteria for a Pass score. There are minor flaws such as over-using the word "friendship." These flaws do not take away from the fact that the overall language use is very good. The sentences are interesting and developed with variety. None of the sentences are too complex, although the sentences in the final paragraph are lengthy. The verb tense is active voice in primarily the present tense. There is variety in word use. The words are not so difficult that spelling errors are present. There are no run-on sentences. The punctuation is very simple and for the most part, correct. The first topic essay is writing that exhibits "the ability to use language effectively and to construct sentences of syntactic complexity and variety."

The first topic essay completes all the tasks set by the assignment. The writer took a stand. The writer used personal experience and observations to explain agreement with the quotation. It is important to notice that personal experience and observation are useful tools, but they do not preclude citing experience and observation gained from other sources.

Topic 2

Describe two incidents in your life that significantly influenced your decision to choose the career you are pursuing.

Sample Essay on Topic 2:

Throughout my life, I have made many decisions concerning my career goals. I wanted to do a variety of things, ranging from engineering to teaching, but certain circumstances and realizations discouraged me from carrying out those plans. My decision to be a psychologist was final after two incidents that occurred during high school.

During my sophomore year, my boyfriend was arrested and sent to a continuation high school. I was a sheltered girl with a high sense of values, and so this bewildered and angered me. Soon this anger was channeled into concern. We remained friends and I tried to be supportive. I discovered many reasons why he was delinquent, but I felt helpless because I couldn't do very much for him. I realized that many people have frustrations and other problems that drive them to hurt themselves. Recognizing this, I wanted to help others with their problems.

In the same year, my mother took me to a psychologist. I was going to see one because I have problems with my friends and I was very depressed and pessimistic about my life. Right away, I felt uncomfortable with the lady. When I explained the situations that were bothering me, she seemed to always tell me that I was feeling as all teenagers do. I felt as though she was citing from a textbook, readily willing to lump me into a stereotypical group. This made me more determined to counsel people. I am a person who can see others as individuals and I learned that this is necessary to work with people.

I have always had an awareness and concern for others and these incidents helped me realize my calling. I love talking and being with people but it is painful and confusing to see the strife people inflict upon themselves and on others. Psychology is a field where I will be working directly with people and actually help them; it also represents a continuing learning process for me and will encourage me to keep growing.

Analysis of the Essay

The essay above, which answers the second topic, also fits the Pass criteria.

The organization of the second topic essay is very strong. If you superimpose the chart or frame for multi-paragraph essays from earlier in this review, you see that this second topic essay is well structured. The opening paragraph includes the thesis statement: "My decision to be a psychologist was final after two incidents that occurred during high school." This sentence fulfills the assignment because it speaks of two experiences. It explains how the writer became a changed person because of the experiences. The two supporting paragraphs elaborate on the attitudes and events that supported the key statement in the opening paragraph. The second and third paragraphs describe the critical incidents and the impact on the writer's decision. The fourth paragraph addresses goals in life and finalizing a career choice. The concluding paragraph also summarizes the change that took place because of the two experiences and points out again their great influence. The second topic essay meets the criteria of a Pass score because it is "clearly reasoned, well organized, and well developed" and demonstrates a clear understanding of the assignment.

The second topic also meets the second criteria for a Pass score. There is use of a contraction, which could be easily avoided. However, this is not a serious flaw and does not detract from the fact that the overall language use is very good. The sentences are interesting and developed with variety. Some of the sentences have multiple clauses, which could be split into individual sentences. The verbs use active voice in the past tense. The writer uses a variety of words. The informal writing style holds the attention of the reader. If the style has been more casual or conversational, the writing would have been inappropriate for the audience. The words are not so difficult that spelling errors occur. There are no run-on sentences. The punctuation is simple and for the most part correct. The second topic essay writing exhibits "the ability to use language effectively and to construct sentences of syntactic complexity and variety."

The second topic essay completes all the tasks set by the assignment. The essay describes two experiences and shows how the writer changed. The content is based on early experiences that influenced career choice. You may want to practice some of the strategies and techniques described in this review. Compare your writing to the essays in this review, then analyze your own writing against the criteria set forth for the various scores.

Following is a practice topic.

Time yourself. Allow 30 minutes. Write on one piece of lined, 8 $\frac{1}{2}$ by 11 inch notebook paper. You may use the front and the back of the paper.

Sample Writing Topic

Describe the major qualities you feel have led to the success of the people you most admire.

Once you have completed this practice essay, ask another person, preferably an experienced teacher like the evaluators, to read and critique your work against the criteria in this review.

CBEST

California Basic Educational Skills Test

TEST 2

CBEST Test 2

Section I: Reading Comprehension
(Answer sheets appear in the back of this book.)

TIME: 65 Minutes
50 Questions

DIRECTIONS: One or more questions follow each statement or passage in this test. The question(s) are based on the content of the passage. After you have read a statement or passage, select the one best answer to each question from among the five possible choices. Your answers to the questions should be based on the stated or implied information given in the statement or passage. Mark all answers on your answer sheet.

Questions 1 and 2 refer to the following passage:

America's national bird, the mighty bald eagle, is being threatened by a new menace. Once decimated by hunters and loss of habitat, this newest danger is suspected to be from the intentional poisoning by livestock ranchers. Authorities have found animal carcasses injected with restricted pesticides. These carcasses are suspected to have been placed to attract and kill predators such as the bald eagle in an effort to preserve young grazing animals. It appears that the eagle is being threatened again by the consummate predator, humans.

1. One can conclude from this passage that

   (A) the pesticides used are detrimental to the environment.

   (B) the killing of eagles will protect the rancher's rangeland.

   (C) ranchers must obtain licenses to use the pesticides.

   (D) the poisoning could result in the extinction of the bald eagle.

   (E) pesticides have been obtained illegally.

2. The author's attitude is one of

   (A) detached observation.   (B) concerned interest.

(C)   informed acceptance.   (D)   suspicion.

(E)   unbridled anger.

Questions 3 and 4 refer to the graph below.

Number of Boys and Girls in Scouting in 1989 (in millions)

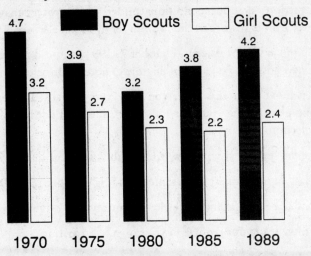

Source: 1991 Census Bureau's Statistical Abstract of the U.S.

3.   In what year was the involvement in scouting closest to being equal between girls and boys?

(A)   1970   (D)   1985

(B)   1975   (E)   1989

(C)   1980

4.   How much difference between the number of boys and the number of girls involved in scouting was there (in millions) in 1970?

(A)   1.6 million   (D)   2.4 million

(B)   .9 million   (E)   1 million

(C)   1.5 million

5.   The disparaging remarks about her performance on the job made Alice uncomfortable.

The word disparaging is closest in meaning to

(A)   complimentary.   (B)   evil.

(C) funny.   (D) technical.

(E) insulting.

Questions 6, 7 and 8 refer to the following passage:

INSTRUCTIONS FOR ABSENTEE VOTING

These instructions describe conditions under which voters may register for or request absentee ballots to vote in the November 5, 1991, election.

(1) If you moved on or prior to October 7, 1991, and did not register to vote at your new address, you are not eligible to vote in this election.

(2) If you move after this date, you may vote via absentee ballot or at your polling place, using your previous address as your address of registration for this election.

(3) You must register at your new address to vote in future elections.

(4) The last day to request an absentee ballot is October 29, 1991.

(5) You must be a registered voter in the county.

(6) You must sign your request in your own handwriting.

(7) You must make a separate request for each election.

(8) The absentee ballot shall be issued to the requesting voter in person or by mail.

6. A voter will be able to participate in the November 5, 1991, election as an absentee if he or she

(A) planned to register for the next election in 1992.

(B) requested an absentee ballot on November 1, 1991.

(C) voted absentee in the last election.

(D) moved as a registered voter on October 13, 1991.

(E) moved on October 7, 1991.

7. On October 15, 1991, Mr. Applebee requested an absentee ballot for his daughter, a registered voting college student, to enable her to participate in the election process. Mr. Applebee will most likely need clarification on which of the following instructions?

(A) 2   (D) 5

(B) 3   (E) 6

(C) 4

8. Which of the following best describes the most important piece of information for potential voters who want to participate in the election process, either in person or by absentee ballot?

    (A)   Do not change precincts.

    (B)   Do register to vote in the appropriate precinct.

    (C)   You may vote at your nearest polling place.

    (D)   The last day to register is always October 29.

    (E)   Your absentee ballot can be used for any election when you have to be out of town.

Questions 9 and 10 refer to the following statement:

The atrophy and incapacity which occur when a broken bone is encased in plaster and immobilized clearly demonstrate what a sedentary life-style can do to the human body.

9. In the passage above, "atrophy and incapacity" refer to

    (A)   a strengthened condition brought about by rest.

    (B)   a decrease in size and strength.

    (C)   a type of exercise.

    (D)   rest and recuperation.

    (E)   the effects of body building.

10. Which of the following statements does not reflect the author's view of sedentary living?

    (A)   If you don't use it, you lose it.

    (B)   Mobility is affected by life-style.

    (C)   A sedentary life-style is a healthy life-style.

    (D)   A body is as a body does.

    (E)   Exercise increases mobility.

Questions 11, 12, 13, 14 and 15 refer to the following passage:

Frederick Douglass was born Frederick Augustus Washington Bailey in 1817 to a white father and a slave mother. Frederick was raised by his grandmother on a Maryland plantation until he was eight. It was then that he was sent to Baltimore by his owner to be a servant to the Auld family. Mrs. Auld recognized Frederick's intellectual acumen and defied the law of the state by teaching him to read and write. When Mr. Auld warned that education would make the boy unfit for slavery, Frederick sought to continue his education in the streets. When his master died, Frederick was returned to the plantation to work in the fields at age sixteen. Later, he was hired out to work in the shipyards in Baltimore as a ship caulker. He plotted an escape but was discovered before he could get away. It took five years before he made his way to New York City and then to New Bedford, Massachusetts, eluding slave hunters by changing his name to Douglass.

At an 1841 anti-slavery meeting in Massachusetts, Douglass was invited to give a talk about his experiences under slavery. His impromptu speech was so powerful and so eloquent that it thrust him into a career as an agent for the Massachusetts Anti-Slavery Society.

Douglass wrote his autobiography in 1845 primarily to counter those who doubted his authenticity as a former slave. This work became a classic in American literature and a primary source about slavery from the point of view of a slave. Douglass went on a two-year speaking tour abroad to avoid recapture by his former owner and to win new friends for the abolition movement. He returned with funds to purchase his freedom and to start his own anti-slavery newspaper. He became a consultant to Abraham Lincoln and throughout Reconstruction fought doggedly for full civil rights for freedmen; he also supported the women's rights movement.

11. According to the passage, Douglass's autobiography was motivated by

   (A) the desire to make money for his anti-slavery movement.

   (B) the desire to start a newspaper.

   (C) his interest in authenticating his life as a slave.

   (D) his desire to educate people about slavery.

   (E) his desire to promote the Civil War.

12. The central idea of the passage is that Frederick Douglass

   (A) was influential in changing the laws regarding the education of slaves.

   (B) was one of the most eminent human rights leaders of the century.

   (C) was a personal friend and confidant to a president.

   (D) wrote a classic in American literature.

   (E) supported women's rights.

13. According to the author of this passage, Mrs. Auld taught Frederick to read because

   (A) Frederick wanted to learn like the other boys.

   (B) she recognized his natural ability.

    (C)   she wanted to comply with the laws of the state.

    (D)   he needed to read to work in the home.

    (E)   she obeyed her husband's wishes in the matter.

14.   The title that best expresses the ideas of this passage is

    (A)   The History of the Anti-Slavery Movement.

    (B)   The Dogged Determination of Frederick Douglass.

    (C)   Reading: Window to the World.

    (D)   Frederick Douglass's Contributions to Freedom.

    (E)   The Oratorical and Literary Brilliance of Frederick Douglass.

15.   In the context of the passage, "impromptu" is closest in meaning to

    (A)   unprepared.   (D)   loud and excited.

    (B)   a quiet manner.   (E)   elaborate.

    (C)   forceful.

Question 16 refers to the following passage:

Acupuncture practitioners, those who use the placement of needles at strategic locations under the skin to block pain, have been tolerated by American physicians since the 1930s. This form of Chinese treatment has been used for about 3,000 years and until recently has been viewed suspiciously by the West. New research indicates that acupuncture might provide relief for sufferers of chronic back pain, arthritis, and recently pain experienced by alcoholics and drug users as they kick the habit.

16.   According to the passage, acupuncture has been found to help people suffering from all of the following except

    (A)   arthritis.   (D)   liver disease.

    (B)   recurring back pain.   (E)   drug addicts in withdrawal.

    (C)   alcoholics in withdrawal.

Question 17 refers to the following passage:

Each time a person opens his or her mouth to eat, he or she makes a nutritional decision. These selections make a definitive difference in how an individual looks, feels, and performs at work or play. When a good assortment of food in appropriate amounts is selected and eaten, the consequences are likely to be desirable levels of health and energy to allow one to be as active as needed. Conversely, when choices are less than desirable, the consequences can be poor health or limited energy or both. Studies of American diets, particularly the diets of the very young, reveal unsatisfactory dietary habits as evidenced by the numbers of overweight and out-of-shape young children.

17.   The author's attitude toward American's dietary habits may be characterized as

    (A)   lacking in interest.   (D)   angry.

    (B)   concerned.   (E)   amused.

    (C)   informational.

Question 18 refers to the following passage:

Commercial enterprises frequently provide the backdrop for the birth of a new language. When members of different language communities need to communicate or wish to bargain with each other, they may develop a new language through a process called "pidginization." A pidgin language, or pidgin, never becomes a native language; rather, its use is limited to business transactions with members of other language communities. Pidgins consist of very simple grammatical structures and small vocabularies. They have tended to develop around coastal areas where seafarers first made contact with speakers of other languages.

18.   The passage suggests which of the following about pidgins?

    (A)   We could expect to hear pidgins along the west coast of Africa and in the Pacific islands.

    (B)   Pidgins are a complicated combination of two languages.

    (C)   Pidgins are located in inland mountain regions.

    (D)   Pidgins become the main language after several generations of use.

    (E)   Pidgins are the languages of seafarers.

Question 19 refers to the following passage:

There are two ways of measuring mass. One method to determine the mass of a body is to use a beam-balance. By this method, an unknown mass is placed on one pan at the end of a beam. The known masses are added to the pan at the other end of the beam until the pans are balanced. Since the force of gravity is the same on each pan, the masses must also be the same on each pan. When the mass of a body is measured by comparison with known masses on a beam-balance, it is called the gravitational mass of the body.

The second method to determine the mass of a body is distinctly different; this method uses the property of inertia. To determine mass in this way, a mass is placed on a frictionless horizontal surface. When a known force is applied to it, the magnitude of the mass is measured by the amount of acceleration produced upon it by the known force. Mass measured in this way is said to be the inertial mass of the body in question. This method is seldom used because it involves both a frictionless surface and a difficult measurement of acceleration.

19. Which of the following statements can best be supported from the passage?

(A) The gravitational and inertia mass methods measure different properties of the object.

(B) The masses are equal when the weights are equal and cause the beam to be balanced.

(C) Gravitational and inertial measurements do not give the same numerical value for mass.

(D) The same result for a beam-balance method cannot be obtained at higher altitudes.

(E) The mass of a body depends on where it is located in the universe.

Question 20 refers to the following statement:

Her introductory remarks provided a segue into the body of the speech.

20. In this context the word segue means

(A) delivery.   (D) credential.

(B) a pause.   (E) critique.

(C) direction.

Questions 21, 22, and 23 refer to the following passage:

One of the many tragedies of the Civil War was the housing and care of prisoners. The Andersonville prison, built by the Confederates in 1864 to accommodate 10,000 Union prisoners, was not completed when prisoners started arriving. Five months later the total number of men incarcerated there had risen to 31,678.

The sounds of death and dying were not diminished by surrender of weapons to a captor. Chances of survival for prisoners in Andersonville were not much better than in the throes of combat. Next to overcrowding, inadequate shelter caused unimaginable suffering. The Confederates were not equipped with the manpower, tools, or supplies necessary to house such a population of captives; prisoners themselves gathered lumber, logs, anything they could find to construct some sort of protection from the elements. Some prisoners dug holes in the ground, risking suffocation from cave-ins, but many hundreds were left exposed to the wind, rain, cold, and heat.

Daily food rations were exhausted by the sheer numbers they had to serve, and resulting in severe dietary deficiencies. The overcrowding, meager rations, and deplorable unsanitary conditions resulted in rampant disease and a high mortality rate. The consequences of a small scratch or wound could result in death in Andersonville. During the prison's thirteen-month existence, more than 12,000 prisoners died and were buried in the Andersonville cemetery. Most of the deaths were caused by diarrhea, dysentery, gangrene, and scurvy that could not be treated due to inadequate staff and supplies.

21. What is the central idea of the passage?

(A) The major problem for the Confederates was finding burial spaces in the cemetery.

(B) The prison was never fully completed.

(C) Prison doctors were ill-equipped to handle emergencies.

(D) Andersonville prison was not adequate to care for three times as many prisoners as it could hold.

(E) Many prisoners died as a result of shelter cave-ins.

22. From this passage the author's attitude toward the Confederates is one of

(A) approval.　　　　　　　(D) indifference.

(B) impartiality.　　　　　　(E) denial.

(C) contempt.

23. The first sentence of the second paragraph of this passage can best be described as

(A) a tribute.　　　　　　　(D) an exposé.

(B) a digression.　　　　　　(E) an irony.

(C) a hypothesis.

Question 24 refers to the following statement:

Maria commented to Joe, "Ted's nose is out of joint because he wasn't invited to the reception."

24. Someone hearing the conversation would most likely conclude that Ted

(A) had a swollen nose.

(B) does not have a large nose.

(C)   was upset about not being asked to the reception.

(D)   was not invited to the reception because his nose was hurt.

(E)   had a bandage on his nose at the reception.

Questions 25, 26, and 27 refer to the following passage:

To the Shakers, perfection was found in the creation of an object that was both useful and simple. Their Society was founded in 1774 by Ann Lee, an English-woman from the working classes who brought eight followers to New York with her. "Mother Ann" established her religious community on the belief that worldly interests were evil.

To gain entrance into the Society, believers had to remain celibate, have no private possessions, and avoid contact with outsiders. The order came to be called "Shakers" because of the feverish dance the group performed. Another characteristic of the group was the desire to seek perfection in their work.

Shaker furniture was created to exemplify specific characteristics: simplicity of design, quality of craftsmanship, harmony of proportion, and usefulness. While Shakers did not create any innovations in furniture designs, they were known for fine craftsmanship. The major emphasis was on function, and not on excessive or elaborate decorations that contributed nothing to the product's usefulness.

25.   The passage indicates that members of the religious order were called the Shakers because

(A)   they shook hands at their meetings.

(B)   they did a shaking dance at their meetings.

(C)   they took their name from the founder.

(D)   they were named after the township where they originated.

(E)   they developed a shaking disorder.

26.   Which of the following is the most appropriate substitute for the use of the term "innovative" in the second paragraph?

(A)   Corrections   (D)   Functions

(B)   Colors   (E)   Brocades

(C)   Changes

27.   The passage suggests which of the following about the Shakers?

(A)   Shaker furniture is well-proportioned and ornate in design.

(B)   Shakers believed in form over function in their designs.

    (C)   Shaker furniture has seen a surge in popularity.

    (D)   Shakers appeared to believe that form follows function.

    (E)   Shaker furniture is noted for the use of brass hardware.

Questions 28 and 29 refer to the following passage:

James Dean began his career as a stage actor, but in motion pictures he symbolized the confused, restless, and idealistic youth of the 1950s. He excelled at film parts that called for brooding, impulsive characterizations, the personification of frustrated youthful passion. Dean made three such movies: *East of Eden, Rebel Without a Cause,* and *Giant,* and established himself as a cult hero. Tragically, his career was cut short in an automobile crash before the release of *Giant.*

28.   One conclusion that could be drawn from this passage is that

    (A)   James Dean was not well regarded because of the kind of characters he portrayed.

    (B)   James Dean had to be replaced by another actor in *Giant* due to his death.

    (C)   James Dean was adept at portraying sensitive, youthful characters.

    (D)   James Dean had a long and distinguished career.

    (E)   James Dean was a promising stage actor.

29.   The author's attitude is one of

    (A)   regret.   (D)   pessimism.

    (B)   anger.   (E)   indifference.

    (C)   humor.

Questions 30, 31, and 32 refer to the following passage:

Benjamin Franklin began writing his autobiography in 1771, but he set it aside to assist the colonies in gaining independence from England. After a hiatus of thirteen years, he returned to chronicle his life, addressing his message to the younger generation. In this significant literary work of early United States, Franklin portrays himself as benign, kindhearted, practical, and hardworking. He established a list of ethical conduct and recorded his transgressions when he was unsuccessful in overcoming temptation. Franklin wrote that he was unable to arrive at perfection, "yet I was, by the endeavor, a better and happier man than I otherwise should have been if I had not attempted it."

30. Which of the following is the least appropriate substitute for the use of the term ethical near the end of the passage?

   (A) Moral

   (B) Depraved

   (C) Virtuous

   (D) Honorable

   (E) Qualifiable

31. The passage suggests which of the following about Franklin's *Autobiography?*

   (A) It was representative of early American literature.

   (B) It fell short of being a major work of literary quality.

   (C) It personified Franklin as a major political figure.

   (D) It was a notable work of early American literature.

   (E) It was directed toward his enemies.

32. Which of the following slogans best describes Franklin's assessment of the usefulness of attempting to achieve perfection?

   (A) Cleanliness is next to Godliness.

   (B) Nothing ventured, nothing gained.

   (C) Ambition is its own reward.

   (D) Time is money.

   (E) Humility is everything.

Questions 33, 34, and 35 refer to the graph below.

How the Average Consumer Spent Money in 1988
Total: $25,892

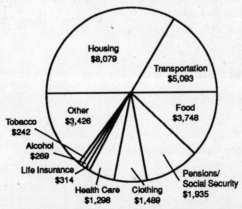

Source: 1991 Census Bureau's Statistical Abstract of the U.S.

33. According to the graph, the average consumer spent approximately 50% of her/his earnings on

    (A) housing and health care costs.   (D) none of the above.

    (B) transportation and housing.   (E) transportation and pensions.

    (C) leisure pursuits and food.

34. After transportation, the next greatest amount of money was spent on

    (A) clothing.   (D) health care.

    (B) other.   (E) pensions/social security.

    (C) food.

35. According to the graph, expenditure on health care was approximately equal to

    (A) clothing.   (D) food.

    (B) life insurance.   (E) other.

    (C) pensions.

Questions 36, 37, and 38 refer to the following passage:

The scarlet flamingo is practically a symbol of Florida. Once the West Indian flamingo population wintered in Florida Bay and as far north as St. John's River and Tampa Bay, but the brilliantly colored birds abandoned these grounds around 1885 due to the decimation of their numbers by feather hunters. The flock at Hialeah Race Track is descended from a handful of birds imported from Cuba in the 1930s. It took seven years before the first flamingo was born in captivity, but several thousand have since been hatched.

Flamingo raisers found that the birds require a highly specialized diet of shrimps and mollusks to maintain their attractive coloring. It is speculated that hunters as well as the birds' selective breeding habits perhaps caused the disappearance of these beautiful birds from the wild in North America.

36. The central idea of the passage is that the flamingos of Florida

    (A) are a symbol of Florida.

    (B) are hard to raise in captivity.

    (C) are no longer found in the wild in North America.

    (D) came from Cuba.

    (E) eat shrimps and mollusks.

37. The word decimation is closest in meaning to

    (A) destination.

    (B) desecration.

    (C) restoration.

    (D) eradication.

    (E) appeasement.

38. According to the passage, which of the following is responsible for the flamingo's brilliant plumage?

    (A) Warm waters off the coast of Florida

    (B) Selective breeding

    (C) Their diet of marine organisms

    (D) Shallow water plants

    (E) Fish and water snakes

Questions 39, 40, and 41 refer to the following passage:

Teachers should be cognizant of the responsibility they have for the development of children's competencies in basic concepts and principles of free speech. Freedom of speech is not merely the utterance of sounds into the air, rather, it is couched in a set of values and legislative processes that have developed over time. These values and processes are a part of our political conscience as Americans. Teachers must provide ample opportunities for children to express themselves effectively in an environment where their opinions are valued. Children should have ownership in the decision-making process in the classroom and should be engaged in activities where alternative resolutions to problems can be explored. Because teachers have such tremendous power to influence in the classroom, they must be careful to refrain from presenting their own values and biases that could "color" their students' belief systems. If we want children to develop their own voices in a free society, then teachers must support participatory democratic experiences in the daily workings of the classroom.

39. The title that best expresses the ideas in the passage is

    (A) The Nature of the Authoritarian Classroom.

    (B) Concepts and Principles of Free Speech.

    (C) Management Practices that Work.

    (D) Exploring Freedom in American Classrooms.

    (E) Developing Children's Citizenship Competencies.

40. It can be inferred from the passage that instructional strategies that assist children in the development of citizenship competencies include all of the following except

    (A) children participation in rule making.

    (B) fostering self-esteem.

    (C) indoctrination in principles of society.

    (D) consideration of cultural and gender differences.

    (E) conflict management skills taught.

41. It can be inferred from the passage that "color" refers to

    (A) remove.

    (D) disintegrate.

    (B) influence.

    (E) embellish.

    (C) stipulate.

Question 42 refers to the following statement:

The funnel cloud appeared capricious with its destruction, darting from one street to another, obliterating any object in its path.

42. In this context the word capricious means

    (A) unpredictable.

    (D) adaptable.

    (B) intense.

    (E) belligerent.

    (C) threatening.

Questions 43 and 44 refer to the following passage:

Many times different animal species can inhabit the same environment and share a common food supply without conflict, because each species occupies a separate niche defined by its specific physical adaptations and habits. For example, the little green heron, equipped with legs too short to do much wading, fishes from shore for its food. The Louisiana heron wades out a little further into the shallows during the daytime hours, while the yellow-crowned night heron stalks the same shallows after dark. Diet also varies in size and amount, according to the size of the bird.

43. According to the passage, which one of the following basic assumptions can be made about how a bird's diet varies according to size?

    (A) Small birds can eat twice their weight.

    (B) The larger birds can swallow larger fish and water snakes.

(C)   Birds have to adapt their diets according to what is available within their environment.

(D)   Fishing from shore is difficult for smaller birds.

(E)   The type of bill is an adaptation for the type of food the animal eats.

44.   The title that best expresses the ideas of this passage is

(A)   The Heron Family.

(B)   Diet Variations of Birds.

(C)   A Separate Niche at the Same Pond.

(D)   Long-Legged Fishing.

(E)   Fishing Habits of the Heron.

Questions 45 and 46 refer to the following passage:

Most Americans assume that English is the language of the United States, but they are naive to imagine that every American speaks it fluently. According to the 1980 U.S. Census, 11 percent of Americans come from non-English-speaking homes. Over one percent of the U.S. population speaks English not well or not at all.

Non-English speakers reside in all 50 states. In some 23 states, the non-English speaking minority makes up 10 percent or more of the total population. All of American history is characterized by this language phenomenon. For those misguided Americans who believe that their country is and always has been a monolingual country, the facts just do not support their claim.

45.   This selection implies that the author's attitude toward a belief that America is a monolingual country is one of

(A)   impartiality.   (D)   anger.

(B)   indifference.   (E)   optimism.

(C)   criticism.

46.   Which of the following statements can best be inferred from the information given?

(A)   Non-English languages are found primarily along the East and West Coast areas.

(B)   No indicators suggest that the percentages of non-English speaking populations will decrease.

(C)   This language situation is relatively new to the United States.

(D)   In the next decade the United States should become primarily monolingual.

(E)   The United States is comparable to Great Britain in percentages of non-English speakers.

Questions 47, 48, and 49 refer to the following passage:

The Indians of California had five varieties of acorn which they used as their principal source of food. This was a noteworthy accomplishment in technology since they first had to make the acorn edible. A process had to be developed for leaching out the poisonous tannic acid. They ground the acorns into a meal and then filtered it many times with water. This had to be done through sand or through tightly woven baskets. Early Indian campsites reveal the evidence of the acorn-processing labor necessary to provide enough food for their subsistence. The women patiently ground acorns into meal with stone pestles. The result, a pinkish flour that was cooked into a mush or thin soup, formed the bulk of their diet.

47.   The central idea of the passage is the early Indians of California

(A)   had ample food sources.

(B)   left evidence of their meal processing at ancient campsites.

(C)   differed from other Indians in their use of natural resources.

(D)   contributed distinctive talents and technological expertise in providing food sources.

(E)   produced finely crafted woven baskets.

48.   According to the passage, which of the following was a technological innovation developed by the early California Indians in the production of food?

(A)   Irrigation of crops   (D)   Dams

(B)   Grinding meal   (E)   Removal of tannic acid

(C)   Filtration system

49.   It can be inferred from the passage that the early Indians faced a major problem in their production of food. What was it?

(A)   They needed many pounds of acorns to produce enough meal.

(B)   Acorns had to be carried a great distance to their campsites for grinding.

(C)   The acorn grinding took many hours of hard labor.

(D)   Acorns were scarce.

(E)   It was difficult to filter the meal without losing it.

Question 50 refers to the following statement:

There was a vestige of the original manuscript for us to review.

50. In the context of the passage, vestige means

(A) reproduction.   (D) engraving.

(B) cartoon.   (E) trace.

(C) counterfeit.

Section II: Mathematics

TIME: 70 Minutes
50 Questions

DIRECTIONS: Each of the questions or incomplete statements below is followed by five suggested answers or completions. Select the one that is best in each case.

---

1. Simplify the following expression: $6 + 2(x - 4)$

   (A) $4x - 16$ (D) $-24x$

   (B) $2x - 14$ (E) $4x$

   (C) $2x - 2$

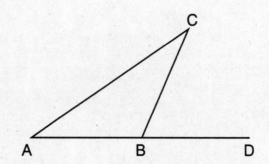

2. Referring to the figure above, if the measure of $\angle C$ is 20° and the measure of $\angle CBD$ is 36°, then what is the measure of $\angle A$?

   (A) 16°   (D) 56°

   (B) 20°   (E) 144°

   (C) 36°

3. If six cans of beans cost $1.50, what is the price of eight cans of beans?

   (A) $.90   (D) $2.00

   (B) $1.00   (E) $9.60

   (C) $1.60

4. Bonnie's average score on three tests is 71. Her first two test scores are 64 and 87. What is her score on test three?

(A) 62   (D) 151

(B) 71   (E) 222

(C) 74

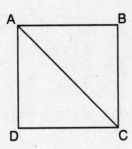

5. In the figure above, what is the perimeter of square ABCD if diagonal AC = 8?

(A) 32   (D) $16\sqrt{2}$

(B) 64   (E) $8\sqrt{3}$

(C) $4\sqrt{2}$

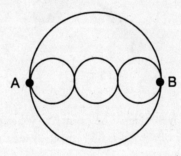

6. Three small circles, all the same size, lie inside a large circle as shown above. The diameter AB of the large circle passes through the centers of the three small circles. If each of the smaller circles has area 9π, what is the circumference of the large circle?

(A) 9   (D) 27π

(B) 18   (E) 54π

(C) 18π

7.　A jar contains 20 balls. These balls are labeled 1 through 20. What is the probability that a ball chosen from the jar has a number on it which is divisible by 4?

(A) $\dfrac{1}{20}$　　　　　　　　　(D)　4

(B) $\dfrac{1}{5}$　　　　　　　　　(E)　5

(C) $\dfrac{1}{4}$

8.　If $2x^2 + 5x - 3 = 0$ and $x > 0$, then what is the value of x?

(A) $-\dfrac{1}{2}$　　　　　　　　　(D)　$\dfrac{3}{2}$

(B) $\dfrac{1}{2}$　　　　　　　　　(E)　3

(C)　1

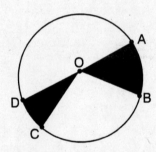

9.　The center of the above circle is the point O. What percentage of the circle is shaded if the measure of arc AB is 65° and the measure of arc CD is 21.4°?

(A)　86.4%　　　　　　　　(D)　27.4%

(B)　50%　　　　　　　　　(E)　24%

(C)　43.6%

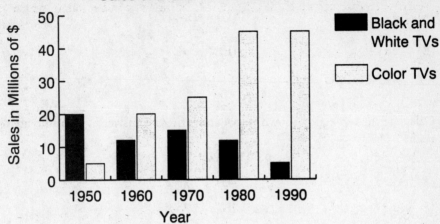

Sales of Brand X Televisions

■ Black and White TVs

□ Color TVs

Sales in Millions of $

10. According to the above chart, in what year was the total sales of Brand X televisions the greatest?

(A) 1950   (D) 1980

(B) 1960   (E) 1990

(C) 1970

11. How many odd prime numbers are there between 1 and 20?

(A) 7   (D) 10

(B) 8   (E) 11

(C) 9

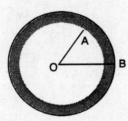

12. Two concentric circles are shown in the figure above. The smaller circle has radius OA = 4 and the larger circle has radius OB = 6. Find the area of the shaded region.

(A) 4π   (D) 36π

(B) 16π   (E) 100π

(C) 20π

13. Solve the following inequality for x: $8 - 2x \leq 10$

(A) $x \leq 1$

(D) $x \geq -1$

(B) $x \geq -9$

(E) $x = \leq \dfrac{5}{3}$

(C) $x \leq -1$

14. Calculate the expression shown below and write the answer in scientific notation.

$$0.003 \times 1.25$$

(A) 3.75

(D) 3.75×10^{-3}

(B) 0.375×10^{-2}

(E) 3.75×10^3

(C) 0.375×10^2

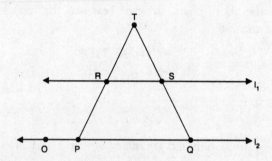

15. In the figure above $l_1 \parallel l_2$, ΔRTS is an isosceles triangle, and the measure of $\angle T = 80°$. Find the measure of $\angle OPR$.

(A) 50°

(D) 105°

(B) 80°

(E) 130°

(C) 100°

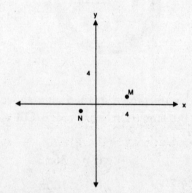

16. What is the midpoint of $\overline{MN}$ in the figure above?

(A)   (–4, 2)   (D)   (1, 0)

(B)   (0, 0)   (E) $\left(-\frac{1}{2}, 1\right)$

(C) $\left(-\frac{3}{2}, 1\right)$

17.   The ratio of men to women at University X is 3:7. If there are 6,153 women
      at University X, how many men are at University X?

(A)   879   (D)   2,637

(B)   1,895   (E)   14,357

(C)   2,051

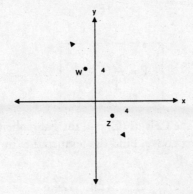

18.   Find the slope of the line passing through the points W and Z in the figure
      above.

(A) $-\frac{1}{2}$ (D)   –2

(B) $\frac{1}{2}$ (E)   2

(C) $\frac{1}{4}$

19.   Linda bought a jacket on sale at a 25% discount. If she paid $54 for the
      jacket, what was the original price of the jacket?

(A) $72.00   (D) $40.50

(B) $67.50   (E) $36.00

(C) $54.00

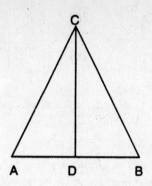

20. Assume that $\triangle ABC$ above is an equilateral triangle. If $CD \perp AB$ and $CD = 6$, what is the area of $\triangle ABC$?

(A) $3\sqrt{3}$ (D) 18

(B) 12   (E) 36

(C) $12\sqrt{3}$

$$F = \frac{9}{5}C + 32$$

21. The formula relating the Celsius (C) and the Fahrenheit (F) scales of temperature is given in the box above. Find the temperature in the Celsius scale when the temperature is 86° F.

(A) 25°   (D) 124.6°

(B) 30°   (E) 188.6°

(C) 105°

22. In the number 72104.58, what is the place value of the 2?

(A) Thousands   (D) Tenths

(B) Millions   (E) Thousandths

(C) Ten thousands

23. Mrs. Wall has $300,000. She wishes to give each of her six children an equal amount of her money. Which of the following methods will result in the amount that each child is to receive?

(A) 6 x 300,000   (D) 6 – 300,000

(B) 6 + 300,000   (E) 300,000 – 6

(C) 300,000 ÷ 6

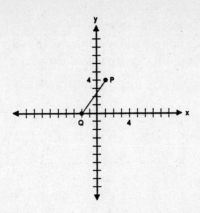

24. Referring to the figure above, what is the length of $\overline{PQ}$?

(A) $2\sqrt{5}$ (D) 7

(B) $5\sqrt{2}$ (E) 25

(C) 5

25. Bob wants to bake some cupcakes. His recipe uses $2\frac{2}{3}$ cups of flour to produce 36 cupcakes. How many cups of flour should Bob use to bake 12 cupcakes?

(A) $\frac{1}{3}$ (D) $1\frac{2}{9}$

(B) $\frac{8}{9}$ (E) $1\frac{2}{3}$

(C) 1

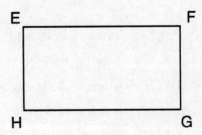

26. The area of rectangle EFGH above is 120 and EF is twice as long as EH. Which of the following is the best approximation of the length of EH?

(A) 7   (D) 12

(B) 8   (E) 15

(C) 10

27. Ricky drove from Town A to Town B in 3 hours. His return trip from Town B to Town A took 5 hours because he drove 15 miles per hour slower on the return trip. How fast did Ricky drive on the trip from Town A to Town B?

    (A) 25.5

    (D) 45

    (B) 32

    (E) 52

    (C) 37.5

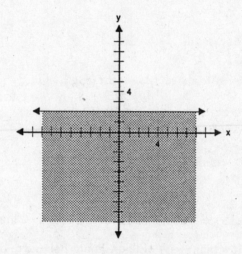

28. Which of the following inequalities represents the shaded region in the figure above?

    (A) $x \geq 2$

    (D) $y \leq 2$

    (B) $x \leq 2$

    (E) $x + y \geq 2$

    (C) $y \geq 2$

    I.   If $x > y$ then $x^2 > y^2$.

    II. If $x > y$ then $x + z > y + z$.

    III. If $x > y$ then $x - y > 0$.

    IV. If $x > y$ then $xz > yz$.

29. Given that x, y, and z are any real numbers, which of the above statements are true?

    (A) I and II only

    (D) I, II, and III only

    (B) II and III only

    (E) II, III, and IV only

    (C) II and IV only

30. Round the following number to the nearest hundredths place: 287.416

    (A) 300   (D) 287.41

    (B) 290   (E) 287.42

    (C) 287.4

31. Simplify the above expression.

    (A) x^6 (D) x^{10}

    (B) x^7 (E) x^{13}

    (C) x^8

$$\frac{1}{9}, \frac{2}{15}, \frac{3}{21}$$

32. List the fractions shown above from least to greatest.

    (A) $\dfrac{1}{9}, \dfrac{2}{15}, \dfrac{3}{21}$ (D) $\dfrac{1}{9}, \dfrac{3}{21}, \dfrac{2}{15}$

    (B) $\dfrac{2}{15}, \dfrac{3}{21}, \dfrac{1}{9}$ (E) $\dfrac{2}{15}, \dfrac{1}{9}, \dfrac{3}{21}$

    (C) $\dfrac{3}{21}, \dfrac{1}{9}, \dfrac{2}{15}$

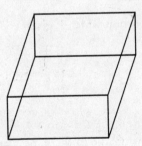

33. A rectangular box with a square base is shown above. If the volume of the box is 256 cubic feet and the height of the box is one-half the length of a side of the base, find the height of the box.

    (A) 4 feet   (D) 10 feet

    (B) 6 feet   (E) 12 feet

    (C) 8 feet

34. If $x - 3$ then find the value of $-x^2 + 2x$.

    (A) −15

    (B) −3

    (C) 3

    (D) 6

    (E) 15

35. If $a = b^3$ and $a = \dfrac{1}{8}$, what is the value of b?

    (A) $\dfrac{1}{512}$

    (B) $\dfrac{1}{8}$

    (C) $\dfrac{3}{8}$

    (D) $\dfrac{1}{2}$

    (E) $\dfrac{3}{2}$

36. In a barn there were cows and people. If we counted 30 heads and 104 legs in the barn, how many cows and how many people were in the barn?

    (A) 10 cows and 20 people

    (B) 16 cows and 14 people

    (C) 18 cows and 16 people

    (D) 22 cows and 8 people

    (E) 24 cows and 4 people

$$\boxed{\dfrac{12}{x-1} = \dfrac{5}{6}}$$

37. Solve for x in the proportion which is given above.

    (A) 14.6

    (B) 15.4

    (C) 16

    (D) 16.6

    (E) 16.8

38. If two lines, l_1 and l_2, which lie in the same plane, are both perpendicular to a third line, l_3, in the same plane as the first two, what do you definitely know about l_1 and l_2?

    (A) l_1 and l_2 are perpendicular.

    (B) l_1 and l_2 are parallel.

    (C) l_1 and l_2 intersect.

    (D) l_1 and l_2 are skew.

    (E) l_1 and l_2 are the same line.

39. What is $\frac{1}{2} + \frac{1}{3}$?

(A) $\frac{1}{5}$

(D) $\frac{2}{6}$

(B) $\frac{2}{5}$

(E) $\frac{5}{6}$

(C) $\frac{1}{6}$

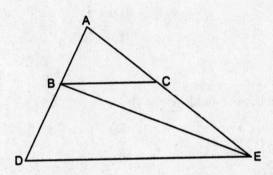

40. Given that BC ‖ DE in the above figure, write down the pair of similar (~) triangles.

(A) $\triangle ABC \sim \triangle ADE$

(D) $\triangle BCE \sim \triangle BAC$

(B) $\triangle ABC \sim \triangle ABE$

(E) $\triangle ADE \sim \triangle CBE$

(C) $\triangle ABC \sim \triangle AED$

41. Which of the following sets is graphed above?

(A) $\{x \mid x \geq -1\}$

(D) $\{x \mid x < -1\}$

(B) $\{x \mid x > -1\}$

(E) $\{x \mid x \neq -1\}$

(C) $\{x \mid x \leq -1\}$

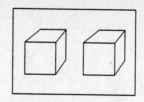

42. Sal has a set of blocks. If 8% of this collection is shown in the box above, how many blocks did Sal have?

(A) 8   (D) 64

(B) 16   (E) 100

(C) 25

43. Solve the following problem: $|x - 3| < 2$

(A) $-5 < x < 5$ (D) $1 < x < 5$

(B) $x = -5$ or 5 (E) $x = 5$

(C) $x < 5$

44. In the above figure, a semicircle is attached to the top of rectangle ABCD. If AB = 4 and AC = 6, what is the total area enclosed by the above figure?

(A) 26π (D) $24 + 16\pi$

(B) 40π (E) $24 + 2\pi$

(C) $20 + 4\pi$

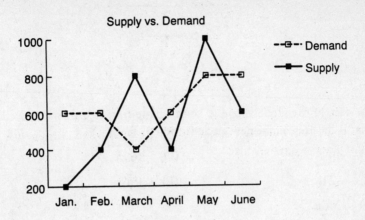

Supply vs. Demand

45. According to the graph above, during how many months was supply greater than demand?

(A) 0   (D) 3

(B) 1   (E) 4

(C) 2

46. What is the greatest common divisor of 120 and 252?

(A) 2   (D) 12

(B) 3   (E) 2,520

(C) 6

47. How many negative integers are between −9 and 5?

(A) 13   (D) 8

(B) 10   (E) 6

(C) 9

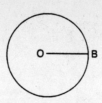

48. The area of the circle above is 144π square feet. If $\overline{OB}$ is increased by 2 feet, what is the area of the new circle (in square feet)?

   (A) 4π   (D) 169π

   (B) 121π   (E) 196π

   (C) 146π

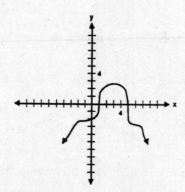

49. On what interval is the above function positive?

   (A) [0, 2]   (D) [1, 5]

   (B) (0, 2)   (E) (1, 5)

   (C) (0, 2]

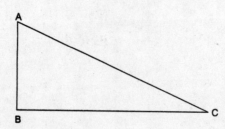

50. In the above figure, AB⊥BC, AC = 10, and AB = 6. What is the area of △ABC?

   (A) 24   (D) 240

   (B) 48   (E) 480

   (C) 121

Section III: Essay Writing

TIME: 60 Minutes
2 Essays

DIRECTIONS: Carefully read the two writing topics below. Plan and write an essay on each, being sure to cover all aspects of each essay. Allow approximately 30 minutes per essay.

Topic 1

The minimum wage in America has been the subject of debate for many years. Many people argue we should be careful about sharp increases in the minimum wage because of the resulting inflation (higher labor costs equal higher consumer prices) and layoffs. Others believe the minimum wage is too low to support a family and should be raised to keep up with the cost of living.

Write an essay analyzing and evaluating these opposing views on the minimum wage. You may include personal experience, knowledge, or observations.

Topic 2

Popular psychology tells us that "habit" is a powerful force, compelling us to live out our lives with basically the same behaviors we learned as we grew up. Write an essay in which you discuss a significant habit of yours that you'd like to change. Speculate on why this may be difficult for you.

CBEST TEST 2 – ANSWER KEY

Section I: Reading Comprehension

1.	(D)	14.	(D)	27.	(D)	40.	(C)
2.	(B)	15.	(A)	28.	(C)	41.	(B)
3.	(C)	16.	(D)	29.	(A)	42.	(A)
4.	(C)	17.	(B)	30.	(B)	43.	(B)
5.	(E)	18.	(A)	31.	(D)	44.	(C)
6.	(D)	19.	(B)	32.	(B)	45.	(C)
7.	(E)	20.	(C)	33.	(B)	46.	(B)
8.	(B)	21.	(D)	34.	(C)	47.	(D)
9.	(B)	22.	(B)	35.	(A)	48.	(C)
10.	(C)	23.	(E)	36.	(C)	49.	(E)
11.	(C)	24.	(C)	37.	(D)	50.	(E)
12.	(B)	25.	(B)	38.	(C)		
13.	(B)	26.	(C)	39.	(E)		

Section II: Mathematics

1.	(C)	14.	(D)	27.	(C)	40.	(A)
2.	(A)	15.	(E)	28.	(D)	41.	(A)
3.	(D)	16.	(D)	29.	(B)	42.	(C)
4.	(A)	17.	(D)	30.	(E)	43.	(D)
5.	(D)	18.	(D)	31.	(C)	44.	(E)
6.	(C)	19.	(A)	32.	(A)	45.	(C)
7.	(C)	20.	(C)	33.	(A)	46.	(D)
8.	(B)	21.	(B)	34.	(A)	47.	(D)
9.	(E)	22.	(A)	35.	(D)	48.	(E)
10.	(D)	23.	(C)	36.	(D)	49.	(E)
11.	(A)	24.	(C)	37.	(B)	50.	(A)
12.	(C)	25.	(B)	38.	(B)		
13.	(D)	26.	(B)	39.	(E)		

DETAILED EXPLANATIONS OF ANSWERS

Section I: Reading Comprehension

1.   (D)   It is implied that the poisoning of animal carcasses in the habitat of bald eagles presents a new danger of extinction for America's symbol. Answers (A), (C), and (E) are not mentioned in the passage. Answer (B) suggests a reason for the poisoning; however, the overall focus of the passage does not support this.

2.   (B)   The author's use of words such as "mighty bald eagle" and "threatened by a new menace" supports concern for the topic. Therefore, answers (A) and (C) are not applicable. The author appears, for the most part, to be objective. Answers (D) and (E) are too strong to be correct.

3.   (C)   In 1980, the difference between the numbers of boys and girls in scouting was .9 million. This represents the closest margin, the largest being 1.6 in 1985.

4.   (C)   In 1970, the difference between the numbers of boys and girls in scouting was 1.5 million.

5.   (E)   If Alice is uncomfortable with remarks about her performance on the job, it could mean either that the remarks were unkind or that compliments might lead to embarrassment. However, the prefix "dis" means to take away or not. In this instance then, we can assume that the remarks were not complimentary or funny, answers (A) and (C). Nothing in the text indicates that the remarks were technical or menacing, responses (B) and (D).

6.   (D)   Answer (D) fulfills requirements stated in rules 2 and 4 of the instructions for absentee voting. All other choices do not.

7.   (E)   Mr. Applebee's daughter must sign her own request for an absentee ballot. Since the passage indicates that she is registered, the most important instruction for her is number 6 (E).

8.   (B)   Answers (A), (D), and (E) are not stated in the passage. Answer (C) is not true unless voters have registered, answer (B).

9.   (B)   Atrophy and incapacity mean to experience a decrease in size and strength.

10. **(C)** The passage associates loss of mobility with a sedentary life-style.

11. **(C)** Douglass was interested in raising social consciousness about slavery. The passage stresses his interest in refuting those who doubted his claim to have been a slave.

12. **(B)** Answer (A) is not supported by the text. All other choices, while true, are irrelevant to the question.

13. **(B)** This choice is supported by the statement, "Mrs. Auld recognized Frederick's intellectual acumen." Choices (C) and (E) contradict information in the passage. The passage does not support choices (A) and (D).

14. **(D)** Choices (A), (B), and (C) are either too broad or too general. Choice (E) is too specific and limited to cover the information in the passage.

15. **(A)** An "impromptu" speech is one given suddenly without preparation.

16. **(D)** All other choices are mentioned as providing relief from pain.

17. **(B)** Use of terms "good," "consequences," and "desirable" indicate a concern for a healthy diet. Choices (A) and (C) contradict the author's attitude. Choices (D) and (E) are not supported by the text.

18. **(A)** Choices (B), (C), and (D) are contradicted in the passage, and choice (E) is not relevant.

19. **(B)** All other choices are not supported in the text.

20. **(C)** A "segue" provides a direction or lead into the speech.

21. **(D)** The passage states that housing of prisoners was "one of many tragedies of the Civil War," and that "overcrowding, meager rations ... resulted in high mortality," implying that the prison facility was inadequate for the number of prisoners. All other choices are discussed, but the main issue was overcrowded conditions.

22. **(B)** The author emphasizes a lack of supplies and manpower to care for the prisoners, not a lack of interest in doing so by the Confederates. Hence, answers (C), (D), and (E) are not appropriate. Answer (A) is not suggested by the text.

23. **(E)** An irony is a result that is the opposite of what might be expected or appropriate. The passage implies that being captured was not a guarantee of survival in Andersonville. This choice is supported by the second sentence of the second paragraph.

24. **(C)** The figure of speech "his or her nose is out of joint" is an expression used to indicate that someone feels slighted. It has nothing to do with the condition of someone's nose.

25. **(B)** This choice is supported by the first paragraph of the passage. All other choices are irrelevant to information in the passage.

26. **(C)** Innovative means to introduce something new or make changes.

27. **(D)** The passage discusses the importance of usefulness as well as simplicity to the Shakers; therefore, the function of the piece of furniture would be more important than the particular form. Answers (A), (B), and (E) are contradictory to the information given, while choice (C) is beyond information given in the text.

28. **(C)** The passage states that Dean "symbolized the confused, restless, and idealistic youth," which implies that he was adept at portraying sensitive youthful characters. Choices (A), (B), and (D) are contradictory to information in the text. Choice (E) is a conclusion not supported by the text.

29. **(A)** The author's use of the word "tragically" in reference to Dean's death indicates a feeling of regret.

30. **(B)** Depraved means corrupted or perverted. All other choices have to do with accepted standards of conduct.

31. **(D)** The author states that Franklin's work was a "significant work of early United States." Each of the other choices are not supported by the text.

32. **(B)** The final sentence of the paragraph supports this choice. Choice (C) might apply, but choice (B) is closest to the overall mood of the passage. Choices (A), (D), and (E) are not relevant to the question.

33. **(B)** Transportation and housing total about half of the $25,892.

34. **(C)** According to the graph, food is next after transportation in amount of expense paid by the consumer.

35. **(A)** According to the graph, health care was closest to clothing in total amount spent.

36. **(C)** The author's use of the word "decimation" as well as the last sentence in the second paragraph supports this choice. All other choices are secondary to the central idea of the passage.

37. **(D)**   To decimate is to eradicate or destroy a large part of something.

38. **(C)**   This choice is supported by the first sentence of the second paragraph. All other choices are irrelevant to the discussion of the flamingo's plumage.

39. **(E)**   The first and last sentences of the passage support this choice. Choice (A) contradicts information in the passage, and choices (B), (C), and (D) are too broad in nature and go beyond the scope of the passage.

40. **(C)**   Reviewing the author's discussion of developing children's citizenship competencies, we may conclude that indoctrination is contradictory to information given in the passage.

41. **(B)**   In the context of the passage, to "color" means to influence.

42. **(A)**   Capricious means unpredictable.

43. **(B)**   This choice is supported by the last sentence in the passage.

44. **(C)**   The author discusses how the birds share the same food supply but occupy different areas of the pond. Each of the other choices is too broad and general.

45. **(C)**   The author's terms "misguided" and "facts do not support this claim" indicate more than impartiality, answer (A), or indifference, answer (B), for those who believe that America is or ever was a monolingual country. Nothing in the passage characterizes anger, answer (D), or an optimistic nature, answer (E).

46. **(B)**   Choices (A), (D), and (E) generalize beyond information in the passage. Choice (C) contradicts information given in the passage.

47. **(D)**   This choice is supported in the second sentence. All other choices are secondary to the central idea.

48. **(C)**   The passage states that this was a "noteworthy accomplishment in technology."

49. **(E)**   The passage emphasizes the complicated process of filtering the meal through sand or tightly woven baskets. Choices (A), (B), and (C), while true, are not the most difficult problem. Choice (D) is contradictory to information given in the text.

50. **(E)**   In the context of the passage, vestige means a small remaining amount.

Section II: Mathematics

NOTATION: m $\angle$ PQR will represent "the measure of angle PQR."

1.   (C)   When simplifying algebraic expressions, always work from left to right. First perform all multiplications and divisions then once this is done, start again from the left and do all additions and subtractions.

SUGGESTION: It can be helpful to translate the algebraic statement to English. For example, $6 + 2(x - 4)$ is "six plus two *times* the quantity x minus 4." The word *times* indicates multiplication, so we must first perform $2(x - 4)$ by using the *distributive property a(b − c) = ab − ac:*

$$6 + 2(x - 4) = 6 + 2 \times x - 2 \times 4 = 6 + 2x - 8.$$

Then we perform the subtraction to combine the terms 6 and 8:

$$6 + 2x - 8 = 2x + (6 - 8) = 2x - 2.$$

Note that we did not combine the $2x$ term with the other terms. This is because they are not *like terms*. Like terms are terms which have the same variables (with the same exponents). Since the terms 6 and 8 have no variable x, they are not like terms with $2x$.

2.   (A)   The sum of the measures of the interior angles of a triangle is 180° therefore;

$$\angle A + m \angle ABC + m\angle C = 180°.$$

We also know that $m\angle C = 20°$, so if we substitute this into the previous equation we have

$$m\angle A + m\angle ABC + 20° = 180°.$$

Subtracting 20° from both sides of this equation gives us

$$m\angle A + m\angle ABC = 160° \text{ or } m\angle A = 160° - m\angle ABC.$$

Therefore, if we know $m\angle ABC$, we are done! To find $m\angle ABC$, notice that $\angle ABD$ is a straight angle and, thus, $m\angle ABD = 180°$. But

$$m\angle ABC + m\angle CBD = m\angle ABD.$$

So, using the facts that

$$m\angle CBD = 36° \text{ and } m\angle ABD = 180°, \text{ and substituting, we have}$$

$$m\angle ABC + 36° = 180° \text{ or } m\angle ABC = 180° - 36° = 144°. \text{ Hence,}$$

$$m\angle A = 160° - m\angle ABC = 160° - 144° = 16°.$$

3.   (D)   Let x be the cost of one can of beans. Then $6x$ is the cost of six cans of beans. So $6x = \$1.50$. Dividing both sides of the equation by 6, we get $x = \$.25$ and, hence, since

$8x$ is the cost of eight cans of beans, we have $8x = 8 \times \$.25 = \$2.00$.

4.   (A)   Let t_1, t_2, t_3 represent Bonnie's scores on tests one, two, and three, respectively. Then the equation representing Bonnie's average score is

$$\frac{t_1 + t_2 + t_3}{3} = 71.$$

We know that $t_1 = 64$ and $t_2 = 87$. Substitute this information into the equation above:

$$\frac{64 + 87 + t_3}{3} = 71$$

Combining 64 and 87 and then multiplying both sides of the equation by 3 gives us

$$3 \times \frac{151 + t_3}{3} = 3 \times 71 \text{ or } 151 + t_3 = 213.$$

Now subtract 151 from both sides of the equation so that

$$t_3 = 213 - 151 = 62.$$

5.   (D)   Let s be the length of each side of square ABCD. Since triangle ADC is a right triangle, we can use the Pythagorean Theorem to solve for s. We have $AD^2 + DC^2 = AC^2$ or $s^2 + s^2 = 8^2$. Simplifying the equation, we get: $2s^2 = 64$. Now divide both sides of the equation by two:

$$s^2 = 32 \text{ so } s = \sqrt{32} = \sqrt{16} \times \sqrt{2} = 4\sqrt{2}.$$

Therefore, the perimeter of square ABCD is

$$P = 4s = 4 \times 4\sqrt{2} = 16\sqrt{2}.$$

6.   (C)   Let r be the length of the radius of each of the small circles and let R be the length of the radius of the large circle. Then, $R = 3r$. The area of each of the small circles is $\pi r^2 = 9\pi$. Now divide both sides of the equation by π:

$$r^2 = 9 \rightarrow r = 3. \text{ Then,}$$

$$R = 3r = 3 \times 3 = 9.$$

Therefore, the circumference of the large circle is

$$C = 2\pi R = 2\pi \times 9 = 18\pi.$$

7.   (C)   Note that the numbers 4, 8, 12, 16, and 20 are the only numbers from 1 through 20 that are divisible by 4. The probability that a ball chosen from the jar has a number on it which is divisible by 4 is given by

$$\frac{\text{total number of balls with numbers that are divisible by 4}}{\text{total number of possible outcomes}} = \frac{5}{20} = \frac{1}{4}.$$

8.   **(B)**   To solve the equation $2x^2 + 5x - 3 = 0$, we can factor the left side of the equation to get $(2x - 1)(x + 3) = 0$. Then use the following rule (this rule is sometimes called the Zero Product Property): If $a \times b = 0$ then either $a = 0$ or $b = 0$. Applying this to our problem gives us

$$2x - 1 = 0 \text{ or } x + 3 = 0.$$

Solve these two equations:

$$2x - 1 = 0 \rightarrow 2x = 1 \rightarrow \frac{1}{2} \text{ or } x + 3 = 0 \rightarrow x = -3.$$

But $x > 0$, so $x = \frac{1}{2}$.

9.   **(E)** $\angle$AOB and $\angle$COD are central angles, meaning that their vertices are at the center of a circle. The measure of a central angle is equal to the measure of its intercepted arc. Hence, since arc AB and arc CD are the intercepted arcs of $\angle$AOB and $\angle$COD, respectively, $m\angle$AOB = 65° and $m\angle$COD = 21.4°. So,

$$m\angle\text{AOB} + m\angle\text{COD} = 86.4°.$$

Therefore, since one revolution of a circle is 360°, the shaded portion of the circle is represented by the following:

$$\frac{86.4}{360} = 0.24 = 24\%.$$

10.   **(D)**   First find the total sales for each year by reading the graph for the sales of (i) black and white televisions and (ii) color televisions. Then combine these numbers:

1950	$20,000,000	+	$5,000,000	=	$25,000,000
1960	$10,000,000	+	$20,000,000	=	$30,000,000
1970	$15,000,000	+	$25,000,000	=	$40,000,000
1980	$10,000,000	+	$45,000,000	=	$55,000,000
1990	$5,000,000	+	$45,000,000	=	$50,000,000

The greatest total sales occurred in 1980.

11.   **(A)**   A prime number is an integer which is greater than one and which has no integer divisors other than 1 and itself. So, the prime numbers between 1 and 20 (not including 1 and 20) are: 2, 3, 5, 7, 11, 13, 17, 19. But 2 is not an odd number, so the odd primes between 1 and 20 are: 3, 5, 7, 11, 13, 17, 19. Hence, there are seven odd primes between 1 and 20.

12. __(C)__ The area of the shaded region is equal to the area of the large circle (which has $\overline{OB}$ as a radius), minus the area of the smaller circle (which has $\overline{OA}$ as a radius). Since the area of a circle with radius r is $A = \pi r^2$, the area of the shaded region is:

$$\pi\,(OB)^2 - \pi\,(OA)^2 = 36\pi - 16\pi = 20\pi.$$

13. __(D)__ To solve this inequality, we shall use the following rules:

(i) If $a \le b$ and c is any number then $a + c \le b + c$.

(ii) If $a \le b$ and $c < 0$ then $ca \ge cb$.

The goal in solving inequalities, as in solving equalities, is to change the inequality so that the variable is isolated (i.e., by itself on one side). So, in the equation $8 - 2x \le 10$, we want the term $-2x$ by itself. To achieve this, use rule (i) above and add -8 to both sides obtaining $8 - 2x + (-8) \le 10 + (-8)$ or $-2x \le 2$. Now we use rule (ii) and multiply both sides of the inequality by $-\dfrac{1}{2}$ as follows: $-\dfrac{1}{2} \times 2x \ge -\dfrac{1}{2} \times 2$ or $x \ge -1$.

14. __(D)__ Since 0.003 has three numbers to the right of the decimal point and 1.25 has two numbers to the right of the decimal point, our answer will have (three plus two) or five numbers to the right of the decimal point. Multiplying 0.003 and 1.25 we get 0.00375, since 3 times 125 is 375. Numbers of the form $A \times 10^n$, where A is a number between 0 and 1 inclusive, and n is an integer, are in scientific notation. Thus, 0.00375 in scientific notation is 3.75×10^{-3}. Notice that when the exponent $n < 0$, the original number is smaller than A.

15. __(E)__ Since $\angle OPQ$ is a straight angle, $m\angle OPQ = 180°$. But

$$m\angle OPQ = m\angle OPR + m\angle RPQ,\ \text{so}$$

$$m\angle OPR + m\angle RPQ = 180° \ \text{or} \ m\angle OPR = 180° - m\angle RPQ.$$

Thus, we need to find $m\angle RPQ$. Now, $l_1 \parallel l_2$, therefore, $mRPQ = m\angle TRS$ since $\angle RPQ$ and $\angle TRS$ are corresponding angles. Recall that corresponding angles are two angles which lie on the same side of the transversal (i.e., a line intersecting other lines, in this case line TP is a transversal since it intersects both line l_1 and l_2), are not adjacent, and one is interior ($\angle RPQ$ in this problem) while the other is exterior ($\angle TRS$). Also, we know that the sum of the measures of the interior angles of a triangle is $180°$ and

$$m\angle T = 80°,\ \text{so}\ m\angle TRS + m\angle RST = 180° - m\angle T = 100°.$$

But $m\angle TRS = m\angle RST$ since $\triangle RTS$ is isosceles. Thus, $m\angle TRS = 50°$. Thus,

$$m\angle RPQ = 50°\ \text{and}\ m\angle OPR = 180° - m\angle RPQ = 180° - 50° = 130°.$$

16. __(D)__ The midpoint of a segment with endpoints (x_1, y_1) and (x_2, y_2) is

$$\left(\frac{x_1 + x_2}{2}, \frac{y_1 + y_2}{2}\right).$$

Our endpoints are M = (4,1) and N = (–2, –1), so the midpoint of $\overline{MN}$ is

$$\left(\frac{4 + (-2)}{2}, \frac{1 + (-1)}{2}\right) = (1,0).$$

17. **(D)**   Let m = the number of men at University X. Then we have the following proportion:

$$\frac{3}{7} = \frac{m}{6153}.$$

To solve this equation, we isolate the variable (i.e., get m by itself) by multiplying both sides of the equation by 6153 to get

$$\left(\frac{3}{7}\right) 6153 = \left(\frac{m}{6153}\right) 6153 \text{ or } m = 2637.$$

18. **(D)**   Note that the line passing through W and Z slants downward as we look at it from left to right. This means our slope should be a negative number! To find the slope of the line passing through the points (x_1, y_1) and (x_2, y_2) we use the following formula:

$$\text{slope} = \frac{y_2 - y_1}{x_2 - x_1}.$$

Our points are W = (–1, 4) and Z = (2, –2) and so our slope is

$$\frac{(-2) - 4}{2 - (-1)} = \frac{-6}{3} = -2.$$

19. **(A)**   Let p be the original price of the jacket. Linda received a 25% discount so she paid 75% of the original price. Thus, 75% of p equals 54. Writing this in an equation, we get:

$$0.75p = 54 \text{ or } \frac{3}{4}p = 54.$$

To solve this equation, multiply both sides of the equation by the reciprocal of $\frac{3}{4}$ which is $\frac{4}{3}$. This will isolate the variable p.

$$\frac{4}{3}\left(\frac{3}{4}p\right) = \left(\frac{4}{3}\right)54 \text{ or } p = \frac{216}{3} = 72.$$

20. **(C)** The area of $\triangle ABC = \frac{1}{2}$ (base)(height) $= \frac{1}{2}$ (AB)(CD) $= \frac{1}{2}$ (AB)(6) $= 3$(AB). So we need to find AB. Let $s = $ AB. Then since $\triangle ABC$ is equilateral (i.e., all the sides have the same length) BC $= s$. Also, since $\triangle ABC$ is equilateral, D is the midpoint of AB so DB $= \frac{s}{2}$. Now CD$\perp$AB so $\triangle CDB$ is a right triangle and we can use the Pythagorean Theorem: $(CD)^2 + (DB)^2 = (BC)^2$. As CD $= 6$, this equation becomes $6^2 + \left(\frac{s}{2}\right)^2 = s^2$, or $36 + \frac{s^2}{4} = s^2$. To solve for s, subtract $\frac{s^2}{4}$ from both sides:

$$36 = s^2 - \frac{s^2}{4} = \frac{3}{4}s^2.$$

Now multiply both sides of the equation by the reciprocal of $\frac{3}{4}$ which is $\frac{4}{3}$: $\frac{4}{3}(36) = s^2$ or $s^2 = 48$. Hence, $s = \sqrt{48} = \sqrt{16} = \sqrt{3} = 4\sqrt{3}$. The area of $\triangle ABC = 3s$ $= 3\left(4\sqrt{3}\right) = 12\sqrt{3}$.

21. **(B)** Substituting F $= 86$ into the formula $F = \frac{9}{5}C + 32$ we get: $86 = \frac{9}{5}C + 32$. To solve for C, first subtract 32 from both sides:

$$86 - 32 + \frac{9}{5}C + 32 - 32 \text{ or } 54 = \frac{9}{5}C.$$

Now multiply both sides of this equation by the reciprocal of $\frac{9}{5}$ which is $\frac{5}{9}$:

$$\left(\frac{5}{9}\right)54 = \left(\frac{5}{9}\right)\frac{9}{5}C \text{ or } \frac{270}{9} = C \text{ or } C = 30.$$

22. **(A)** 72104.58 is read "seventy-two thousand, one hundred four and fifty-eight hundredths."

23. **(C)** Another way to phrase the second sentence is: She wants to divide her money equally among her six children. Therefore, each child is to receive $300,000 \div 6$.

24. **(C)** To find the distance between two points (x_1, y_1) and (x_2, y_2), we may use the following formula:

$$d = \sqrt{(x_2 - x_1)^2 + (y_2 - y_1)^2}$$

For our two points, P = (1,4) and Q = (–2,0), the above formula gives us the length of segment PQ:

$$d = \sqrt{\left(-2-1\right)^2 + \left(0-4\right)^2} = \sqrt{\left(-3\right)^2 + \left(4\right)^2} = \sqrt{9+16} = \sqrt{25} = 5.$$

25. **(B)**   Bob wants to bake 12 cupcakes. The recipe is for 36 cupcakes. Therefore, Bob wants to make $\frac{12}{36}$ or $\frac{1}{3}$ of the usual amount of cupcakes. Thus, Bob should use $\frac{1}{3}$ of the recipe's flour or $\left(\frac{1}{3}\right)\left(\frac{8}{3}\right) = \frac{8}{9}$. Note we used $\frac{8}{3}$ since $2\frac{2}{3} = \frac{8}{3}$.

26. **(B)**   Let x be the length of EH, then the length of EF is $2x$. The area of a rectangle is length (EF) times width (EH). So we have

$$(2x)(x) = 120 \text{ or } 2x^2 = 120.$$

To solve for x divide both sides of the equation by 2 to get $x^2 = 60$. Note that $49 < x^2 < 64$, so $\sqrt{49} < \sqrt{x^2} < \sqrt{64}$ or $7 < x < 8$. But 60 is closer to 64 than it is to 49, so 8 is the best approximation of x which represents the length of EH.

27. **(C)**   Let s_1 and s_2 be Ricky's speed (rate) on the trip from A to B and the return trip from B to A, respectively. Then, since he drove 15 miles per hour slower on the return trip, $s_2 = s_1 - 15$. Recall that rate times time equals distance. So the distance from A to B is $(s_1)3 = 3s_1$ and the distance from B to A is $(s_2)5 = 5s_2 = 5(s_1 - 15) = 5s_1 - 75$. But the distance from Town A to Town B is the same as the distance from Town B to Town A so we have the following equation:

$3s_1 = 5s_1 - 75$. To solve this equation, first add 75 to both sides of the equation:

$$3s_1 + 75 = 5s_1 - 75 + 75 \text{ or } 3s_1 + 75 = 5s_1.$$

Now to isolate the variable, subtract $3s_1$ from both sides:

$$3s_1 + 75 - 3s_1 = 5s_1 - 3s_1 \text{ or } 75 = 2s_1.$$

To finish the problem, divide both sides of the equation by 2:

$$s_1 = \frac{75}{2} = 37.5.$$

Thus, Ricky drove 37.5 miles per hour on his trip from Town A to Town B.

28. **(D)**   The shaded region consists of all the points on the horizontal line passing through the point (0, 2) and those below the line. All of these points have y = coordinate less than or equal to 2: Thus, our answer is $y \leq 2$.

29. **(B)** Statement I is not always true. For example, let $x = 2$ and $y = -3$. Then $x > y$ but $x^2 = 4$ and $y^2 = 9$ so $x^2 < y^2$. Statement IV is not always true. For example, let $x = 5$, $y = 1$, and $z = -2$. Then $xz = -10$ and $yz = -2$ so that $xz < yz$. Statements II and III are true.

30. **(E)** The 1 is in the hundredths place. If the number to the immediate right of the 1 (i.e., the number in the thousandths place) is greater than or equal to 5 we increase 1 to 2, otherwise do not change the 1. Then we leave off all numbers to the right of the 1. In our problem a 6 is in the thousandths place so we change the 1 to a 2 to get 287.42 as our answer.

31. **(C)** Recall the following Laws of Exponents:

$$x^p \times x^q = x^{p+q} \text{ and } \frac{x^p}{x^q} = x^{p-q}.$$

So, $x^2 \times x^7 = x^{2+7} = x^9$. Hence, $\dfrac{x^2 \times x^7}{x} = \dfrac{x^9}{x^1} = x^{9-1} = x^8$.

32. **(A)** We need to write the three fractions with the same denominator. So, find the least common multiple (LCM) of 9, 15, and 21. $9 = 3^2$, $15 = 3 \cdot 5$, and $21 = 3 \cdot 7$ therefore, the LCM is $3^2 \times 5 \times 7 = 315$. Then $\dfrac{1}{9} = \dfrac{5 \times 7}{5 \times 7} \times \dfrac{1}{9} = \dfrac{35}{315}$, $\dfrac{2}{15} = \dfrac{3 \times 7}{3 \times 7} \times \dfrac{2}{15} = \dfrac{42}{315}$, and $\dfrac{3}{21} = \dfrac{3 \times 5}{3 \times 5} \times \dfrac{3}{21} = \dfrac{45}{315}$. Clearly, $\dfrac{35}{315} < \dfrac{42}{315} < \dfrac{45}{315}$ and hence, in order, from least to greatest we have: $\dfrac{1}{9}, \dfrac{2}{15}, \dfrac{3}{21}$.

33. **(A)** The volume of a rectangular box is the area of the base times the height. So if we let s be the length of each side of the base (it is a square), the area of the base is s^2.

The height of the box is one-half the length of a side of the base, thus, the height is $\dfrac{1}{2}s$.

The volume is then $V = s^2 \times \dfrac{1}{2}s = \dfrac{1}{2}s^3$. But the volume is given as 256. Substituting this into the equation $V = \dfrac{1}{2}s^3$ gives us:

$$256 = \frac{1}{2}s^3.$$

Now multiply both sides of the equation by 2 to get: $2 \times 256 = 2\dfrac{1}{2}s^3$ or $512 = s^3$. But,

$512 = 8^3$ so that we have $8^3 = s^3$ or $s^3 = 8$. The height of the box is $\frac{1}{2}s = \frac{1}{2} \times 8 = 4$ feet.

34. **(A)**   If $x = -3$ then $-x^2 + 2x = -(-3)^2 + 2(-3) = -(9) + (-6) = -15$.

35. **(D)**   If $a = b^3$ and $a = \frac{1}{8}$, then substituting into the first equation we have:

$$\frac{1}{8} = b^3 \text{ or } \left(\frac{1}{2}\right)^3 = b^3 \text{ so } b = \frac{1}{2}.$$

36. **(D)**   Let x be the number of people in the barn. Then, since each person and cow has only one head, the number of cows must be $30 - x$. Since people have two legs, the number of human legs totals $2x$. Similarly, since the number of legs each cow has is 4, the total number of cow legs in the barn is $4(30 - x)$. Thus, we have this equation:
$$2x + 4(30 - x) = 104.$$

To solve this equation, use the distributive property: $a(b - c) = ab - ac$. We get:

$$4(30 - x) = (4 \times 30) - (4 \times x) = 120 - 4x.$$

Our equation reduces to:

$$2x + 120 - 4x = 104 \text{ or } 120 - 2x = 104.$$

Now subtract 120 from both sides or the equation to get $-2x = 104 - 120 = -16$. Dividing both sides of the equation by -2: $x = 8$. Therefore, there were 8 people and $30 - 8 = 22$ cows in the barn.

37. **(B)**   To solve the proportion $\frac{12}{x-1} = \frac{5}{6}$, multiply both sides of the equation by 6 and by $(x - 1)$ so that we have:

$$6(x - 1) \times \frac{12}{x-1} = 6(x - 1) \text{ or } 72 = 5(x - 1).$$

Now, use the distributive property: $a(b - c) = ab - ac$ to get $72 = 5x - 5$. Add 5 to both sides of the equation: $77 = 5x$ and then divide both sides by 5:

$$x = \frac{77}{5} = 15.4.$$

38. **(B)**   If two lines, l_1 and l_2 which lie in the same plane, are both perpendicular to a third line, l_3, l_1 and l_2 are parallel.

39. **(E)**   First of all the least common multiple (LCM) of 2 and 3 is $2 \times 3 = 6$, so let's rewrite the expression so that both fractions have 6 as a common denominator:

$$\frac{1}{2} + \frac{1}{3} = \frac{3}{3} x \frac{1}{2} + \frac{2}{2} x \frac{1}{3} = \frac{3}{6} + \frac{2}{6} = \frac{5}{6}.$$

40. **(A)** Two triangles are similar if we can find two pairs of angles, one in each triangle, that are congruent. Given that BC ‖ DE we know that ($\angle$ABC, $\angle$BDE) and ($\angle$ACB, $\angle$CED) are two pairs of corresponding and hence congruent angles. Thus, taking care in the order that we write the angles so that we match the correct angles, $\triangle$ABC ~ $\triangle$ADE.

41. **(A)** Note that there is a solid dot on –1 which means to include –1 in the set. The numbers to the right of –1 are shaded; this means to include these numbers also. Hence, this is the graph of all numbers greater than or equal to –1 ($\{x \mid x \geq -1\}$).

42. **(C)** Let 2 be the number of blocks that Sal has. Then, 8% of x is 2 according to the given figure. Thus, we have the equation:

$$.08x = 2 \text{ or, dividing both sides by } .08, \ x = \frac{2}{.08} = \frac{2}{.08} x \frac{100}{100} = \frac{200}{8} = 25.$$

43. **(D)** $|x - 3| < 2$ is equivalent to $-2 < x - 3 < 2$. To solve this double inequality we must add 3 to all three sides: $3 + -2 < x - 3 + 3 < 2 + 3$ or $1 < x < 5$.

44. **(E)** We must find the area of the rectangle and of the semicircle. The area of the rectangle is length times width or 6 x 4 = 24. The area the semicircle is one-half the area of a circle with diameter AB or $\frac{1}{2}$ x πr^2 where r is one-half the length of the diameter AB. So $r = 2$ and the area of the semicircle is $\frac{1}{2}\pi(2)^2 = 2\pi.$ Thus, the total area is 24

+ 2π.

45. **(C)** According to the graph, the supply was greater than the demand in March and May only.

46. **(D)** The greatest common divisor (GCD) is the greatest integer which divides both 120 and 252. To find the GCD, factor both numbers and look for common factors. $120 = 2^3$ x 3 x 5 and $252 = 2^2$ x 3^2 x 7, so the GCD = 2^2 x 3 = 12.

47. **(D)** The list of all the negative integers between –9 and 5 is: –8, –7, –6, –5, –4, –3, –2, –1.

48. **(E)** The area of a circle is πr^2 where r is the radius. In the given circle, $\overline{OB}$ is the radius and A = 144π. So, 144π = πr^2 so that $r = 12$. If we increased the radius by 2 feet

so that now $r = 16$, the area of the new circle is $A = \pi (16)^2 = 196\pi$.

49.   (E)   A function is positive when the points on its graph lie above the x-axis. In our graph this occurs when x is between 1 and 5 or (1, 5).

50.   (A)   Since $AB \perp BC$, we know that $\triangle ABC$ is a right triangle and thus we may use the Pythagorean Theorem to find the length of BC (let x be the length of BC): $AC^2 = AB^2 + BC^2$ or $(10)^2 = 6^2 + x^2$ or $100 = 36 + x^2$. To solve this, subtract 36 from both sides of the equation to get: $64 = x^2$ so that $x = 8$. The area of $\triangle ABC =$

$$\frac{1}{2}(AB)(BC) = \frac{1}{2}(6)(8) = 24.$$

Section III: Writing

Topic 1 Sample Answer

Essay #1—Pass (Score = 4)

There is no doubt that minimum wage laws are necessary for the well being of workers and their families. It had always been the policy for most businesses to pay laborers less than they deserve. Minimum wage laws are one of the only ways workers can be protected from management; without them they are fair game to whatever exploitation the employer can manage.

Many argue against the minimum wage, protesting that it is too high. The fact is, even with raises in the rate, it still does not meet the needs of the laborers because of the increases in inflation and the basic cost of living. At present, it would be extremely difficult, or even impossible, to support a family on a salary as low as $5.00 an hour. There is no person (or family) in my experience who survives on minimum wage; teenagers who have financial help from their parents, might find a minimum wage adequate, but no "head of a household" would. If anything, the current minimum wage rate is too low.

Another argument against minimum wage, especially sharp increases, is the possibility of inflation due to higher labor costs which might cause higher consumer prices. The problem with this is management. Workers do not cause inflation, businesses and corporations do. If the leaders of these companies were not so money hungry, workers could have higher salaries without causing an increase in the price of goods and services. It is quite possible to do this because products are extremely overpriced. Most businesses, however, look to short-term, easy money instead of long term stability. A raise in the minimum wage would actually help the business in the long-run because workers would be happier and thus, productivity would be increased. The only way a raise in the minimum wage would cause inflation would be if the companies themselves let it.

The final point made by those opposed to minimum wage is the possibility of inflationary pressures resulting in worker lay-offs. As was discussed earlier, inflation in this situation is not a given. For the moment however, let's just theorize on the possibilities of workers being fired. Those most likely to be laid off are the teenagers, minorities, seniors, and the disabled. Although this seems like the course of action many businesses would take, it is not if the companies are smart. First, firing workers would not be tolerated by unions. Next, even in non-union companies, laying off workers would cost the business money in the long run; with less workers, productivity is diminished and when there is a need for more workers they will have to be paid at the same wage as were the ones who were fired. There is little chance that businesses would make decisions that would cost them money.

It would be ridiculous to say that minimum wage is a panacea for the laborers of the world. It barely makes a dent, even with the recent increases in their bills. What it does do, though, is give the worker a guarantee that he will get paid no less than is mandated; this, in many cases, is enough.

Scoring Explanation for Essay #1—Pass

This essay is thoughtful and well-organized, introducing several interesting arguments supporting the minimum wage. The author obviously has some knowledge and experience about the effect of minimum wage legislation on businesses and tries to debunk arguments that a minimum wage necessarily means inflation, higher costs and layoffs. The writer presents his/her views straightforwardly and clearly, although the opinions expressed may not be popular (or accurate) from an employer's point of view.

Still, the author systematically addresses the most typical arguments against the minimum wage and reaches a realistic conclusion. In other words, he/she doesn't argue that minimum wage is a panacea, but merely a help. In addition, the syntax is quite readable, there are few errors of any kind and the text is easy to follow. The essay is very well-developed considering the writing time allotted.

Essay#2—Marginal Pass (Score = 3)

The issue of minimum wage for American workers is definitely a controversial one. Since there are so many aspects of this issue, many conflicting opinions are held concerning what constitutes a fair minimum wage. Because the cost of living changes so frequently in society, minimum wage should definitely change with it.

Some people argue that raising minimum wage constantly will harm, rather than benefit society. They believe that "higher labor costs would be reflected in higher consumer prices," thereby causing unnecessary inflation. They feel that many workers would be needlessly laid off, due to the fact that their employers would not be able to pay higher wages to many workers. Consequently, there are some people who vehemently oppose the raising of minimum wage and cannot see how it would benefit society.

While these arguments are somewhat understandable, the fact still remains that living conditions change over the years, and the average cost of living only continues to grow.

Although people may have survived on a lower salary many years ago, it is entirely unrealistic to think that this same salary will be adequate for those living in the 1990's. For those who are raising a family, it is crucial that they receive a reasonable salary so that their family can function and survive today's standards. Minimum wage should be raised whenever necessary, for people cannot be expected to manage properly unless they are receiving wages which reflect the current cost of living.

The present minimum wage for American workers is $4.25, so it is evident that Congress had seen the changes in society and raised the minimum wage accordingly. It becomes more expensive daily to live comfortably by today's standards. It is obvious that many people feel the need to earn more money, since the cost of living today is so high.

In order for society to continue functioning efficiently, it must adequately meet the growing needs of its people. One such need is to provide a fair minimum wage for workers which coincides with their cost of living.

Scoring Explanation for Essay #2—Marginal Pass

This essay is generally coherent and satisfactorily written. It has much less specific information than a passing essay typically has, and relies on repetition of a couple of key points rather than thorough investigation.

The writer concludes, in reasonable fashion, that the cost of living continues to rise and that the minimum wage should correspondingly increase. But rather than present specific evidence that it is difficult for workers to keep up with inflation or demonstrate that the minimum wage should periodically increase, the writer merely asserts that these things are true. Still, the essay reads well and shows an adequate command of the language. In short, the essay does more asserting than analyzing and assumes the reader will accept, without question, its assertions.

Essay #3—Marginal Fail (Score = 2)

The baby begins to cry as the father enters the run-down apartment. He dodges the dripping ceiling and proceeds over to help his wife who is caught between the bargain dinner and the crying child. After soothes the child he goes onto explain that on account of his low wage, there will not be any hot water for a while. We can't have everything, it was either that or the streets.

I don't believe that the minimum wage is high. It is not fair, some people should be expected to live such a low standard. The Adult work force should be given a more fair and reliable wage to support themselves. Then they would gain a better self esteem and, in turn, give their children a better outlook on life.

The minimum wage does not have to be raised for the teenagers. I believe there should be separate minimums for minors and adults. This way a business owner does not have to pay extra for a teenagers incompetence, and the adult worker who is struggling to support a family is much better.

The poverty levels of this country is increasing more and more. If the minimum wages would be lifted for adults it may aliviate some of the poverty. It may also solve some problems for many struggling families who are going homeless, and once your homeless, the minimum wage doesn't matter any more.

Scoring Explanation for Essay #3—Marginal Fail

This essay begins with a rather interesting and compelling vignette describing the effects of a "non-living" wage. Unfortunately, this is the only real positive aspect of the essay.

There are several errors in punctuation and syntax. A good example is the comma splice in the first paragraph: "We can't have everything, it was either that or the streets." The author does, however, take a clear stand on the issue of the minimum wage, and presents an alternative solution to the problem. He/she suggests that teenagers be paid a lower minimum wage than adults, but fails to explore the potential difficulties with such a proposal.

The essay concludes with a grim reminder of the effects of insufficient pay—poverty and homelessness—and ends the essay where it began. Though the writer clearly has a sense of style, the essay loses its power due to its inadequate development and frequent writing errors.

Essay #4—Fail (Score = 1)

Todays american economy and cost of-living index has change dramatically within the past years. For the value of the dollar has weaken compared to what it was worth in the early 1900's; thus making the cost of living for low income and disabled people much more difficult than what it was already. Minimum wage law was created to prevent Americans form becoming poor and homeless by raising the minimum wage for to coincid with todays living standards. But now, the standards of living are very difficult and the minimum wage law has become controversial. People feel the law might enuse inflation and consumer prices. But this is not so.

The minimum wage does not pose a threat and should be raise. We live in a low income society. But since minimum wage was raised in early of 1988 more have a chance for college.

Minimum wage gives us americans a chance to live a better and enjoyible life; one of the things that makes this country so great. It makes us americans feel as though we are here to live a life, not just survive and never expand beyond what our life could be.

Many people claim that the raise in minimum wage might cause inflation. But before the minimum increased the prices and inflation were at a high. That is why many of us americans demanded a increase. We cannot live at a pay of $3.25 an hour.

Scoring Explanation for Essay #4—Fail

This essay is fraught with grammatical and syntactic errors, which cause considerable distraction for the reader. One of the most common problems is a difficulty with proper tense endings, especially in past tense (i.e., "has change," "has weaken" in the first paragraph). The writer also has no control over possessives and there are several dramatic spelling errors.

The analysis of the issue is simplistic, alluding to the "better life" afforded by a minimum wage, but never demonstrating what this consists of. Further, the essay ends with a brief comment on inflation and the impossibility of "americans" surviving on $3.25 an hour. Thus, the essay merely stops rather than effectively summarizing its claims. Unfortunately, many of these claims are awkward and/or confusing, such as the author's prediction that we might "never expand beyond what our life could be." The essay, therefore, fails.

Topic 2 Sample Answer

Essay #1—Pass (Score = 4)

As people grow older, they begin to look at themselves and examine who they are. They look at their life and how they go about living it. These introspections can be very reassuring for a person, revealing many strong qualities that provide them with much comfort. However, some people are able to go further and examine every aspect of their lives—including the things they are uncomfortable with.

As I reflect on my life, I am able to discover many positive qualities which I can be very proud of. On the other hand, I am also able to realize some things about myself which I am not comfortable with and would like to change. One such thing is a bad habit I developed in my youth. Ever since I can remember, I've had trouble letting people know what it is I want to do.

Many times I've let people get away with things just because I'm afraid to tell them how I feel or what I want. For some reason, it's always been hard for me to speak my mind. This inability to communicate my inner feelings has led to many difficulties. In many situations I have wanted to tell someone how I feel but was afraid to. For example, I ended up attending a party where drugs were being used because I wasn't strong enough to tell my friends I didn't want to go. I didn't want to be thought of as a "nerd." Fortunately, I was able to leave the party without incident.

At times dealing with my parents has been difficult because I won't always let them know what I'm thinking. The same thing occurs in relations with teachers, friends and members of the opposite sex. Perhaps if I could be more open, future difficulties could be avoided.

It's difficult to ascertain the source of this problem. Maybe it's because I grew up under the impression that "real men" don't show emotions. Maybe it's just because I'm a quiet person. Whatever the reason, I'd like to change it, and I have been trying. Lately, I've been more able to tell people how I feel and not hold back. I may have finally realized that people aren't going to laugh at me when I tell them how I feel. It's becoming easier to express myself, but it's still difficult. Perhaps as I grow older the problem will disappear. That is my hope, but I intend to continue my periodic, introspective self-analysis to make sure I don't slip.

Scoring Explanation for Essay #1—Pass

The writer begins this essay on "habit" by speculating about the value of self-examination and concludes on a similar note. In the body of the essay the writer explores a habit he/she is uncomfortable with and would like to change. The discussion of this problematic habit is well developed and specific, offering both generalizations and illustrations of how the habit is manifested.

The writer also attempts to address the origin of the habit, providing several possible rationales for its existence. The aspect of the question regarding speculation on why it may be difficult to change habitual behavior is also addressed in the concluding paragraph. All in all, the writer offers a reasonable, well-written response that is also a sincere investigation of a personal issue. There are few errors of any kind, and the syntax is competent, also contributing to the essay's passing score.

Essay #2—Marginal Pass (Score = 3)

In developing habitual behaviors or tendencies one may find himself limited or restrained. One's habits limit the diversity he is able to experience and develop. They, habits, limit your ability to change, learn and experience novelties by always acting in one particular manner.

I find I have various habits that limit my growth as an individual. One specific habit is that of not speaking my thoughts or opinions amongst family and friends. This habit, although its seemingly minor, often limits the capacity and development of a relationship.

All the burdens and pressures of planning, "what we should do," are thrown on the shoulders of the individual. The burdens I create can easily be eased by my own input or opinion. No matter how insignificant the input may be, it still causes more of a "mutual agreement."

This habit will be difficult to break since it takes all the pressure off me. Forcing another to decide everything may make my part of the relationship easier. I have grown so accustomed to not giving input that it will be hard for me to start deciding because of the added pressure. However, I believe if I take some pressure, my relationships will develop fully and concretely.

Scoring Explanation for Essay #2—Marginal Pass

This essay contains elevated diction and usually sophisticated, complex sentences. These features are often characteristic of good writing. The absence of error, however, is shadowed by the writer's reliance on pompous phrases and abstract discussion.

The author's implied promise to discuss his habit of "not speaking [his/her] thoughts or opinions amongst family and friends" is never completely fulfilled. The reader is offered few specific examples of the habit "in action," so the writer's speculations about the burdens he/she creates for himself/herself are less powerful. The reader is left wondering what, precisely, is meant by "the burdens and pressures of planning."

Similarly, the writer mentions the difficulty involved in altering the habit (because it's easier not to), but this section is obtuse and generalized. In short, the writer is clearly syntactically competent, but the ideas are difficult to digest because they are buried in verbose abstraction.

Essay #3—Marginal Fail (Score = 2)

Popular Psychology tell us that "habit" is a powerful force, compelling us to live out our lives with basically the some behaviors we learned as we grew up. Reassurance in decision making is a significant habit, I'd like to change. In this essay, I will discuss why this may be difficult.

Since the time I could remember, I would always ask my mother or sister, Alex, to help me. In making a decision; For example, clothes I bought, the University I wanted to attend or whether to cut my hair or not. Some of these decision makings, life did not depended on, but asking for their advice–in trying to make my decision—I was assured that I was right.

I know I need to break this habit, but it is difficult for me. Many times I tell myself that I need to make my own decisions. Because Alex and my mother are not going to be there all the time. One of the reasons it is difficult for me is because I always need someone to approve. Someone to say, "yes, you're making the right choice."

Now in college I am begin to make my own decisions without their consents; but I still need to work on it. I am beginning to force myself to do what I want to do whether someone likes it or not. Although I am trying to break away from this habit, it will take a long time to break completely from it. This is because, although I am making some decisions with out their consent, there are other decisions I make in which I feel I need reassurance.

Scoring Explanation for Essay #3—Marginal Fail

The writer reiterates the question to open this rather ordinary response. A specific example is offered to illustrate the difficulty the writer has in decision making, but it appears in the midst of sentences lush with errors of various kinds.

The writer has difficulty with punctuation and syntax, creating some awkward, incomplete sentences. In paragraph two, the reader is presented with: "In making a decision; for example, clothes I bought, the University I wanted to attend or whether to cut my hair or not." Still, the writer does attempt to address the question and mentions needing approval as the impediment to change. Rather than exploring this issue, however, the writer merely reasserts it in the conclusion. The combination of a superficial response and several errors results in a less than successful essay.

Essay #4—Fail (Score = 1)

A habit becomes a heartbeat that lets us live on. By this, I mean, that it becomes voluntary; once we start that habit until we end it. A habit that I have and I would like to change is massaging and "cracking my nuckles when I am nervous.

It is a significant habit because I start massaging my hand and once I finished, it feels relaxed, but what I realized is that it makes my hand shake more. Sometimes I am so nervous, for example when I am about to give speech in Public Speaking class, that I massage my hand so hard - it turns red and swollen. I cause myself a lot of pain!

I finished massaging my hand, Well, what can I do now? I then start cracking my nuckles(fingers). I know one day I am going to end up with arthritus if I keep on doing this! Sometimes when I do it, it feels good, but other times I over do it. I usually over do it by cracking my fingers so much that they don't want to crack no more. Then they start hurting very much.

I guess I don't realize what pain I am causing myself with this habit. For me it has become a heartbeat. I can't stop it This is how this habit works. Maybe I forget about being nervous. Because I am feeling pain - That is what I think, maybe.

Somehow I think it will be difficult to stop this habit. I don't think when I massage and crack my fingers It just happens. It became - something to do when I am nervous. A painful Heartbeat that will probably go on forever until I die. By then the doctors would of cut of my hands or maybe I cut them of. Who knows what will happen with this habit of mine.

Scoring Explanation for Essay #4—Fail

This confusing piece of writing seeks to liken the habit of knuckle-cracking to a life-sustaining heartbeat. This melodramatic metaphor is one example of the author's difficulty in effectively dealing with the question.

The first problem is perhaps found in the author's insistence upon the significance of the habit, despite its apparently minor importance. (The writer says it *may* help with nervousness.) Furthermore, the syntax and diction are very poor. Frequent mistakes cause the reader considerable distraction. For example, "By then the doctors would of cut of my hands or maybe I cut them of." The writer's hyperbole is only outdistanced by the many different types of writing errors.

CBEST

California Basic Educational Skills Test

TEST 3

CBEST Test 3

Section I: Reading Comprehension
(Answer sheets appear in the back of this book.)

TIME: 65 Minutes
50 Questions

DIRECTIONS: One or more questions follow each statement or passage in this test. The questions are based on the content of the passage. After you have read a statement or passage, select the one best answer to each question from among the five possible choices. Your answer to the questions should be based on the stated or implied information given in the statement or passage. Mark all answers on your answer sheet.

Questions 1, 2, and 3 refer to the following passage:

Representatives of the world's seven richest and most industrialized nations held a three-day economic summit in London on July 14-16, 1991. On the second day of the summit, Mikhail Gorbachev, who appealed for help, was offered support by the seven leaders for his economic reforms and his "new thinking" regarding political reforms. However, because the allies were split on giving a big aid package to Gorbachev, the seven leaders decided to provide help in the form of technical assistance in fields such as banking and energy, rather than in hard cash.

1. Which of the following statements best synthesizes what the passage is about?

    (A) A seven-nation economic summit was held in London in July 1991.

    (B) An economic summit of the world's richest nations was held in London in July.

    (C) Mikhail Gorbachev appealed for help and the seven leaders agreed to support his economic reforms.

    (D) At a three-day economic summit held in London in July 1991, leaders of the world's seven richest and most industrialized nations agreed to provide technical assistance to Gorbachev.

    (E) Representatives of the world's seven most industrialized nations, at a summit conference in London, were split on giving Gorbachev assistance in the form of hard cash.

2.   The passage implies

(A)   that, under the leadership of Gorbachev, the Soviet Union is faced with a financial crisis.

(B)   that Gorbachev's "new thinking" on democratic reforms needs support from the seven nations meeting in London.

(C)   that the seven leaders meeting in London were split on giving Gorbachev economic and political support.

(D)   that with only technical assistance from the seven nations that met in London, the Soviet Union under the leadership of Gorbachev is heading for economic disaster.

(E)   that with the support of political and economic reforms along with provisions for technical assistance from the seven nations that met in London, the Soviet Union under the leadership of Gorbachev can achieve political and economic stability.

3.   The passage suggests that technical assistance will be provided to the Soviet Union

(A)   only in the fields of banking and energy.

(B)   in the fields of banking and energy and possibly other fields also.

(C)   by the U.S. in the fields of banking and energy.

(D)   by any of the seven nations that met at a summit in London.

(E)   by all seven nations—U.S., Great Britain, France, Germany, Italy, Canada, and Japan.

Questions 4, 5, and 6 refer to the following passage:

A follow-up survey of the 1990 census showed an estimated undercount of 5.2 million people nationwide. This "undercount" was greatest in California where approximately 1.1 million people were not recorded. This estimated undercount was based on a post-census survey of 171,390 households nationwide. Failure to achieve an accurate count would affect federal funding and political representation. If the higher numbers were used, California would gain eight congressional seats instead of seven and about $1 billion in federal funds. Last July 14, 1991, however, Commerce Secretary Robert Mosbacher decided to stick to the original figures of the 1990 census.

4.   Which of the following statements gives the main idea of the passage you just read?

(A)   California will gain an additional congressional seat and more federal money if the 1.1 million people undercounted in the census are included.

(B) The population in a state is the basis for determining the political representation for that state.

(C) An undercount in the census, if not considered, will be a disadvantage to any state.

(D) A post-census survey is necessary in getting to a more accurate population figure for the states.

(E) California will suffer the most because of the 1.1 million undercount in the 1990 census.

5. If the 1.1 million undercount was considered for California

(A) it would settle any political dispute arising from the undercount.

(B) it would give California eight congressional seats and $1 billion in federal funds.

(C) it would discourage the practice of a post-census survey.

(D) it would create political unrest for other states.

(E) it would reverse the decision made by Commerce Secretary Mosbacher.

6. What would it mean for California if the original figures of the 1990 Census were to remain the same?

(A) No additional federal funding will be given.

(B) There will be no additional political representation.

(C) The amount of federal funding and number of congressional seats will remain the same.

(D) The census undercount will not make a difference.

(E) The results of the follow-up survey of the 1990 census will be meaningless.

Questions 7, 8, 9, and 10 refer to the following passage:

A big toxic spill took place on the upper Sacramento River in California on July 13, 1991 about 10 P.M. when a slow moving Southern Pacific train derailed north of the town of Dansmuir. A tank car containing 19,500 gallons of pesticide broke open and spilled into the river. This pesticide is used to kill soil pests. Since the spill, thousands of trout and other fish were poisoned along a 45-mile stretch of river. In addition, 190 people were treated at a local hospital for respiratory and related illnesses. Residents along the river have been warned to stay away from the tainted water. Once this water reaches Lake Shasta, a source of water for millions of Californians, samples will be taken to assess the quality of the water.

7. Which of the following statements conveys the message in the passage?

    (A) Pesticides intended to kill soil pests can be dangerous to all living things.

    (B) Water uncontaminated by pesticides is safe to drink.

    (C) Take every precaution not to come in contact with the pesticide-infected water.

    (D) Pesticides that killed thousands of trout and other fish will not necessarily kill human beings.

    (E) Only residents along the tainted river need worry.

8. The Southern Pacific train that derailed was

    (A) a passenger train.   (D) a cargo and passenger train.

    (B) a cargo train.   (E) a special train.

    (C) a commuter train.

9. The most serious problem that can come about as a result of the toxic spill is

    (A) possible movement of residents in Dansmuir to another place of residence.

    (B) reduction in tourism attraction for Dansmuir and other nearby areas.

    (C) the negative effects on those whose livelihood depends on the fishing industry.

    (D) when the tainted water reaches Lake Shasta, which is a source of water supply for millions of Californians.

    (E) the uncertain length of time it will take to make the tainted water safe and healthy again.

10. This unfortunate incident of toxic spill resulting from train derailment implies

    (A) the need for more environmental protection.

    (B) other means for transporting pesticides need to be considered.

    (C) that there should be more precaution for trains running by nighttime.

    (D) that there should be an investigation as to the cause of the train derailment and effective measures to prevent its occurrence again should be applied.

(E)   that there should be research on how to expedite making infected water safe and healthy again.

Questions 11, 12, and 13 refer to the following passage:

Labor Day, a national holiday observed in the United States, is really a day we should remember to give thanks to the labor unions. In the days before the unions became effective, a holiday meant a day off, but the loss of a day's pay to working people. It was not until World War II that unions succeeded, through negotiations with the federal government, in making paid holidays a common practice.

11.   The main idea in the passage you just read is

(A)   the role labor unions played in employer-employee relations.

(B)   Labor Day as a national holiday in the U.S.

(C)   the role labor unions played in effecting paid holidays.

(D)   the dispute between paid and unpaid holidays.

(E)   Labor Day before World War II.

12.   The passage implies that before World War II

(A)   a holiday gave working people a chance to rest from work.

(B)   Labor Day meant losing a day's pay.

(C)   a holiday was a day to make up for upon returning to work.

(D)   labor unions were ineffective.

(E)   taking off from work set a worker one day behind in his or her work.

13.   As a national holiday, Labor Day should really be a day to remember and be thankful for

(A)   working people.

(B)   help from the federal government.

(C)   paid holidays.

(D)   labor unions.

(E)   a free day.

Question 14 refers to the following passage:

President Bush's proposed educational "program of choice" will give parents more say in choosing schools for their children. This will encourage states and local districts to change their laws so that parents can apply their tax dollars toward the public or private school to which they choose to send their children, rather than be forced to send their child to the public school in their district or pay for private school tuition.

14. President Bush's proposed educational program implies

   (A)   the freedom to choose.

   (B)   competition among schools.

   (C)   school standards need to be raised.

   (D)   more money is needed.

   (E)   curricula should be improved.

Questions 15, 16, and 17 refer to the following passage:

Ash from Mt. Pinatubo in the Philippines has been found to contain gold and other precious metals. However, officials warned against any hopes of a new "gold rush." They found gold content of only 20 parts per billion, which is far below commercial levels. Other metals found were chromium, copper, and lithium.

15. The passage indicates

   (A)   the possibility of existing gold mines beneath Mt. Pinatubo.

   (B)   the need for further exploration of what else lies beneath the volcano.

   (C)   that there is a new resource for boosting the economy of the Philippines.

   (D)   other active volcanoes might be worth exploring as possible gold resources.

   (E)   that the gold content of the ash from Mt. Pinatubo does not warrant a commercial level.

16. Which of the following makes a good title for the passage you just read?

   (A)   A New Gold Rush

   (B)   Mt. Pinatubo's Gold Mine

   (C)   Ash Content from Mt. Pinatubo

   (D)   A Philippine Discovery

   (E)   Precious Metals

17. What might be a possible research project resulting from the ash content finding of Mt. Pinatubo?

   (A) Research on the ash content from the eruption of Mt. Fujiyama in Japan

   (B) Potential market value of the gold and other metals content in the volcanic ash from Mt. Pinatubo

   (C) Further excavation into possible gold underneath Mt. Pinatubo

   (D) Research on what lies underneath active volcanoes

   (E) Compare volcanic ash content with what lies underneath the same volcano when it is inactive

Questions 18, 19, and 20 refer to the following passage:

Gary Harris, a farmer from Conrad, Montana, has invented and patented a motorcycle helmet. It provides a brake light which can signal traffic intentions to other drivers behind. In the U.S., all cars sold are now required to carry a third, high-mounted brake light. Harris' helmet will meet this requirement for motorcyclists.

18. The passage tells about

   (A) a new invention for motorcyclists.

   (B) a requirement for all cars in the U.S.

   (C) a brake light for motorcyclists.

   (D) Harris' helmet.

   (E) Gary Harris, inventor.

19. An implication regarding the new invention is

   (A) any farmer can come up with a similar traffic invention.

   (B) the new brake light requirement for cars should likewise apply to motorcycles.

   (C) the new brake light requirement for cars cannot apply to motorcycles.

   (D) if you buy a car from outside of the U.S., you are exempted from the brake light requirement.

   (E) as an inventor, Gary Harris can make more money if he leaves farming.

20. Because of the new brake light requirement for cars

   (A) drivers can readily see the traffic signals of car drivers ahead of them.

(B)   less accidents can happen on the road.

(C)   car prices will go up and will be less affordable to buy.

(D)   more lights on the road can be hazardous.

(E)   more traffic policemen will be needed.

Questions 21, 22, 23, and 24 refer to the following passage:

Lead poisoning is considered by health authorities to be the most common and devastating environmental disease of young children. According to studies made, it affects 15% to 20% of urban children and from 50% to 75% of inner-city, poor children. As a result of a legal settlement in July 1991, all of California's Medical-eligible children, ages one through five, will now be routinely screened annually for lead poisoning. Experts estimate that more than 50,000 cases will be detected in California because of the newly mandated tests. This will halt at an early stage a disease that leads to learning disabilities and life-threatening disorders.

21.   Lead poisoning among young children, if not detected early, can lead to

(A)   physical disabilities.   (D)   heart disease.

(B)   mental disabilities.   (E)   death.

(C)   learning disabilities.

22.   The new mandate to screen all young children for lead poisoning is required of

(A)   all young children in California.

(B)   all children with learning disabilities.

(C)   all Medical-eligible children, ages one through five, in California.

(D)   all minority children in California.

(E)   all school-age children in California.

23.   According to findings, more cases of lead poisoning are found among

(A)   urban children.   (D)   children in rural areas.

(B)   inner-city poor children.   (E)   middle-class children.

(C)   immigrant children.

24.   The implication of this new mandate in California regarding lead poisoning is

(A)   non-eligible children will not be screened.

(B)   children older than five years will not be screened.

(C)   middle-class children will not be screened.

(D)   new immigrant children will not be screened.

(E)   thousands of young children in California will remain at risk for lead poisoning.

Question 25 refers to the following passage:

As millions of children returned to school in the year 1991-1992, teachers in California had to face the reality of what many consider as the worst fiscal crisis to hit the schools in more than a decade. This crisis caused reductions in teaching positions, increases in class sizes, cuts in teacher paychecks in some school districts, reductions in special programs, reductions in school supplies, etc.

25.   Those who will be most affected by the effects of the financial crisis in California schools are

(A)   the teachers.   (D)   the paraprofessionals.

(B)   the parents.   (E)   the students.

(C)   the school administrators.

Questions 26, 27, and 28 refer to the following passage:

The U.S. Postal Service issued a 50-cent stamp in Anchorage, Alaska on October 12, 1991 to commemorate the 500th anniversary of the arrival of the Italian explorer Christopher Columbus in the New World. The stamp depicts how Americans may have appeared to Asians crossing the Bering Strait. The stamp series will show the pre-Columbian voyages of discovery.

26.   Which of the following makes an appropriate title for the passage?

(A)   The Discovery of the Americas

(B)   500th Anniversary of the Discovery of America

(C)   The Significance of the Bering Strait

(D)   A Commemorative New U.S. Postal Stamp

(E)   A Tribute to Asians

27.   The passage implies that

(A)   historical facts need to be verified.

(B)   Christopher Columbus was not the first to arrive in the New World.

(C)   Asians discovered America.

(D)   native Americans came from Asia.

(E)   history books need to be rewritten.

28.   Which of the following would you consider as the most historically signifi-cant?

(A)   Asians crossed over the Bering Strait to the New World before Colum-bus came.

(B)   It has been 500 years since Christopher Columbus arrived in the New World.

(C)   A tribute to Christopher Columbus was held on October 12, 1991.

(D)   Native Americans are of Asian origin.

(E)   There were other voyages undertaken before Christopher Columbus'.

Questions 29 and 30 refer to the following passage:

A 150 million-year-old allosaurus skeleton which appears to be intact was found on September 9, 1991 by a Swiss team in north-central Wyoming. This Zurich-based company sells fossils to museums. They were digging on private property, but the fossil actually showed up on federal land.

Immediately, the federal government sealed off the site along the foot of Big Horn Mountains in Wyoming and deployed rangers from the Bureau of Land Management to prevent vandalism. Paleontologists believe that this discovery could lead them to a vast dinosaur graveyard.

29.   The passage you just read can best be utilized by a classroom teacher in

(A)   reading.   (D)   zoology.

(B)   mathematics.   (E)   history.

(C)   biology.

30.   A teaching strategy that the classroom teacher can use appropriately with the students regarding the allosaurus fossil discovery is

(A)   the problem-solving approach.

(B)   the survey approach.

(C)   the deductive approach.

(D)   the comparative study approach.

(E)   the historical approach.

Questions 31, 32, and 33 refer to the following passage:

Popular U.S. attractions such as Disneyland, the Golden Gate Bridge, Las Vegas, and the Statue of Liberty have attracted millions of foreign tourists whose spending helped the U.S. post a $31.7 billion service trade surplus in 1990 compared with a $101 billion merchandise trade deficit in the same year. The heavy-spending Japanese tourists accounted for the biggest portion of the tourism trade surplus, spending $5.5 billion more touring the U.S than U.S. tourists spent visiting Japan. Canadians also outspent American tourists to Canada by $2.2 billion.

31.   The main idea in the foregoing passage is

(A)   foreign tourists in the U.S. spend more than American tourists spend abroad.

(B)   there are more tourist attractions in the U.S. than any foreign country.

(C)   Japanese tourists are the biggest spenders among tourists to the U.S.

(D)   Canadians rank second to Japan in tourism spending in the U.S.

(E)   tourism is very important to the economy of the U.S.

32.   A significant implication of the passage is

(A)   that Japan will have to reduce its tourist spending in U.S.

(B)   that the U.S. should increase its tourist spending in Japan.

(C)   that tourist spending in the U.S. reduces its trade deficit.

(D)   that Canada needs to improve its tourism attractions.

(E)   that Japan has more money on which to spend on tourism than any other country.

33.   Based on the passage, which of the following would be an appropriate topic of discussion with students?

(A)   International relations

(B)   Global relations

(C)   Balance in global tourism industry

(D)   Interdependency of nations

(E)   Global competition

Questions 34 and 35 refer to the following passage:

San Francisco was named the world's favorite travel destination in the prestigious 1991 Conde Nast Traveler magazine poll. It was considered the best city in the world that year, beating out Florence, Italy, (No. 2) and London and Vienna which tied for No. 3. A red-carpet gala in the City Hall rotunda is planned in which Mayor Agnos will laud the city's 60,000 tourism industry workers including hotel maids, taxi drivers, bellhops, and others in the local hospitality industry.

34. An appropriate title for the foregoing passage is

   (A) San Francisco: World's Favorite Travel Destination.

   (B) A Gala for San Francisco's Tourism Workers.

   (C) San Francisco: Top in Ranking.

   (D) Best City in the World.

   (E) Top City in 1991.

35. The prestigious citation for the city of San Francisco could mean in practical terms

   (A) increasing tourism attractions for city runner-ups in the poll.

   (B) more openings for tourism industry workers.

   (C) higher pay demands from hotel maids, bellhops, and other workers.

   (D) more tourists will come to the city.

   (E) more money coming to the city from its tourism industry.

Questions 36, 37, and 38 refer to the following passage:

Results of a study released by the College Board and the Western Interstate Commission for Higher Education shows that by 1994, the majority of California's high school graduates will be non-white and that by 1995, one-third of all the nation's students will be from minority groups. It is also predicted that, nationally, the total non-white and Hispanic student population for all grade levels will increase from 10.4 million in 1985-1986 to 13.7 million in 1994-1995. The figures suggest that now, more than ever, equal educational opportunity for all students must be our nation's Number one priority.

36. The foregoing passage suggests

   (A) that this nation is, educationally, at risk.

   (B) that something needs to be done to reduce the growing numbers of minority students in the school system.

   (C) that urgent educational reforms are needed to provide equal opportunity for all students.

   (D) that a Spanish bilingual system be endorsed.

(E)   that immigration laws be strictly enforced to balance the numbers of white and non-white student populations.

37.   Because of changes in demographics, what preparation is needed in California in the area of teacher preparation?

(A)   Recruitment of more minority teachers

(B)   Increase budget appropriation for schools

(C)   Enforce school desegregation

(D)   Encourage non-Hispanic, white students to enroll in private schools

(E)   Revise teacher preparation programs to reflect appropriate preparation for multicultural classrooms

38.   What problem could result from the increasing minority population in the nation?

(A)   Strong resentment from mainstream whites towards the school system.

(B)   Increase in enrollment in private and parochial schools.

(C)   "White flight" to the suburbs where minorities are not yet the majority.

(D)   School budget crisis

(E)   Inappropriate and inadequate school curriculum and teacher preparation to meet the needs in multicultural classrooms.

Questions 39, 40, and 41 refer to the following passage:

The United States' final offer on a lease agreement for the Subic Bay Naval Base in the Philippines was rejected by the Philippine Senate. Hence, for the first time in nearly a century, U.S. military strategy for the Asia-Pacific region will no longer be centered on the Philippines, and the nation's economic survival and development will no longer rely on U.S. dependency. Somehow, this dependency on the U.S. has served as an impediment to the Philippines' ability to join East Asia's economic boom.

39.   Which of the following best summarizes what the passage is about?

(A)   Philippine-U.S. military relations have come to an end.

(B)   The Philippines' economic dependency on the U.S. ended with its Senate's rejection of the U.S. lease offer.

(C)   The U.S. lease offer for the Subic Naval Base was rejected by the Philippine Senate, hence the U.S. will no longer have its military base in the Asia-Pacific region.

(D)   The Philippines is now on its own in its economic survival and development.

(E)   The U.S. military strategy for the Asia-Pacific Region will no longer be on the Philippines following the Philippine Senate's rejection of the U.S. lease offer.

40.   The U.S. military's pullout from Subic Bay would mean

(A)   less jobs for Filipinos.

(B)   less Americans in the Philippines.

(C)   a chance for the Philippines to survive on its own.

(D)   weakening of U.S.-Philippine relations.

(E)   less protection for the Philippines.

41.   What could be the reason that the Philippine Senate rejected the U.S. lease offer?

(A)   Filipinos are getting more nationalistic.

(B)   It will be an opportunity for the Philippines to survive and develop on its own economically.

(C)   Less money was offered by the U.S.

(D)   The U.S. would be better off somewhere else.

(E)   To defeat President Aquino's stand on the issue

Questions 42, 43, and 44 refer to the following passage:

The Matsushita Electric Industrial Co. in Japan has developed a computer program that can use photographs of faces to predict the aging process and, also, how an unborn child will look. The system can show how a couple will look after 40 years of marriage and how newlyweds' future children will look. The computer analyzes facial characteristics from a photograph based on shading and color differences, and then creates a three-dimensional model in its memory. The system consists of a personal computer with a program and circuit board and will be marketed by the Matsushita Company soon.

42.   The main idea in the passage you just read is about

(A)   a computer that shows the aging process.

(B)   a computer that chooses the right mate.

(C)   a computer that predicts the number of children for newlyweds.

(D)   a computer that predicts the looks of future children as well as their parents.

(E)   a computer that analyzes photographs.

43.   The new computer program developed in Japan uses

(A)   a three-dimensional face model.

(B)   photographs of faces to predict the aging process and looks of an un-born child.

(C)   shading and color differences in photographs.

(D)   a personal computer and circuit board.

(E)   facial characteristics from a photograph.

44.   What might result from this new computer system developed in Japan?

(A)   The U.S. will develop an even more sophisticated computer system.

(B)   Competition among trading partners of Japan will be keener.

(C)   Japan's economy will skyrocket.

(D)   The trade imbalance between Japan and the U.S. will increase.

(E)   The next computer system Japan will develop will be even more refined and sophisticated.

Questions 45 and 46 refer to the following passage:

On September 17, 1991, a communications power failure brought New York's three big airports to a virtual stop for several hours. Air traffic control centers communicate with planes through a network of radio towers linked to them by phone. Due to this power failure, local air traffic centers could not communicate properly amongst themselves or with other U.S. airports.

45.   What could have happened to airplanes en route to New York when the power failure took place?

(A)   They could have turned back from where they came.

(B)   They could have encircled New York until the control towers were able to communicate with the pilots.

(C)   They could have been diverted to other airports by other air control centers.

(D)   They could have slowed down their speed while waiting for the power failure to be corrected.

(E)   They could have landed, as usual, at the New York airports.

46.   What can air travelers learn from this power failure incident?

(A)   Expect delays or being diverted to other airports for landing.

(B)   Take the train instead.

(C)   Prepare for the unexpected each time you fly.

(D)   A power failure in New York can happen again.

(E)   Flight delays are due to failure in communications systems.

Questions 47, 48, 49, and 50 refer to the following passage:

New health research shows that regular vigorous exercise during the middle and late years of life not only keep the heart healthy, but also may protect against colon cancer, one of the major killers in the U.S. The researchers in the study compared the rate of colon cancer among those who were physically inactive with those who were either active or highly active. Seventeen thousand one hundred forty eight men, ages 30 to 79, were covered in the study. Among men judged to be inactive there were 55 cases of colon cancer; among those moderately active, there were 11; and only 10 cases of colon cancer were found among the very active ones.

47.   Which of the following makes an appropriate title for the passage?

(A)   New Health Research on Colon Cancer

(B)   Colon Cancer: A Major Killer in the U.S.

(C)   Regular Vigorous Exercise May Prevent Colon Cancer

(D)   Results of Research on Colon Cancer

(E)   A Prescription for Preventing Colon Cancer

48.   Based on the result of the research, can one make a generalization regarding colon cancer for men and women?

(A)   Yes   (D)   It depends

(B)   No   (E)   Not applicable

(C)   Maybe

49. What important message did you get from the passage?

   (A) Regular exercise is good for the health.

   (B) Only middle-aged men get colon cancer.

   (C) Women need not worry about colon cancer.

   (D) Regular exercise is needed only by older people.

   (E) Children are too young to exercise.

50. What is the major limitation of the study?

   (A) It did not explain "vigorous exercise."

   (B) It did not include children.

   (C) It did not include men below 30.

   (D) It did not include women of the same age group.

   (E) None of the above.

Section II: Mathematics

TIME: 70 Minutes
50 Questions

> **DIRECTIONS:** Each of the questions or incomplete statements below is followed by five suggested answers or completions. Select the one that is best in each case.

1. What is the least common denominator of $\frac{2}{15}, \frac{1}{21}$, and $\frac{4}{35}$?

    (A) 105

    (B) 35

    (C) 415

    (D) 735

    (E) 175

2. On July 19, a Friday, Dick received a letter to have a class reunion exactly four years from that day. On what day of the week is his reunion?

    (A) Monday

    (B) Tuesday

    (C) Wednesday

    (D) Thursday

    (E) Friday

3. John and Mary are working on a job together. If John does it alone, it will take him 7 days, while Mary can do it alone in 5 days. How long will it take them to do it together?

    (A) 12 days

    (B) 2 days

    (C) 2 and $\frac{11}{12}$ days

    (D) 3 and $\frac{1}{2}$ days

    (E) 6 days

4. How much water is needed to add to a half-pint of syrup with 60% sugar to obtain a drink with 5% sugar?

    (A) 3 pints

    (B) 2.5 pints

(C) 4 pints   (D) 5.5 pints

(E) 7 pints

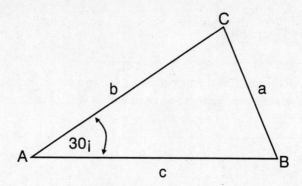

5. Which of the following is true about triangle ABC?

(A) Sides B and C are equal in measurement.

(B) Angle A is the smallest angle.

(C) Side A is not the longest side.

(D) Angle B or C must be a right angle.

(E) Side B must be greater than side A in measurement.

6. If the diameter of circle A is twice that of circle B, what is the ratio of the area of circle A to the area of circle B?

(A) 2 to 1   (D) π to 1

(B) 3 to 1   (E) 8 to 1

(C) 4 to 1

7. A solid cube has volume 8. What is the volume of the cube whose sides are twice that of this cube?

(A) 16   (D) 36

(B) 28   (E) 64

(C) 32

8. Jack flies from New York to Los Angeles. His plane leaves New York at 2:15 p.m. The flying time is 5 hours and 45 minutes. Since New York is three hours ahead of Los Angeles, what time does he arrive in Los Angeles?

(A) 11:00 p.m.   (B) 8:00 p.m.

(C)   7:45 p.m.   (D)   5:00 p.m.

(E)   4:45 p.m.

9.   Bob has 50 coins, all nickels and dimes, worth a total of $4.85. How many nickels does he possess?

(A)   30   (D)   37

(B)   15   (E)   3

(C)   7

10.   A steamboat goes 24 miles upstream and then returns to its original position. The round trip takes 6 hours. The water flows at three miles per hour. What is the speed of the boat in still water?

(A)   10 miles/hour   (D)   7 miles/hour

(B)   9 miles/hour   (E)   6 miles/hour

(C)   8 miles/hour

11.   If ten babies drink a total of ten gallons of milk in ten days, how many gallons of milk will 20 babies drink in 20 days?

(A)   20   (D)   35

(B)   25   (E)   40

(C)   30

12.   Jane has three kinds of coins, quarters, dimes, and nickels, totalling 24 in number and worth $3.00. How many coins of each kind does she have?

(A)   Jane has 12 nickels, 4 dimes, and 8 quarters.

(B)   Jane has 9 nickels, 8 dimes, and 7 quarters.

(C)   Jane has 6 nickels, 12 dimes, and 6 quarters.

(D)   Jane has 3 nickels, 16 dimes, and 5 quarters.

(E)   There is no unique answer; further information is needed.

13.   A parallelogram ABCD has all its sides measure 4, one of the diagonals AC also measures 4. What is its area?

(A)   Its area is 16.

(B)   Its area is 32.

(C)   Its area is $4\sqrt{3}$.

(D) Its area is $8\sqrt{3}$.

(E) Its area cannot be found; further information is needed.

14. Jack gave one-third of his money to his daughter and one-quarter of his money to his son. He then had $150,000 left. How much money did he have before he gave away some?

(A) $225,000

(B) $250,000

(C) $300,000

(D) $360,000

(E) $400,000

15. The fraction $\dfrac{1}{\left(\sqrt{3}-\sqrt{2}\right)}$ is equivalent to

(A) $\sqrt{3}+\sqrt{2}$.

(B) $\sqrt{3}-\sqrt{2}$.

(C) $\dfrac{1}{\left(\sqrt{3}+\sqrt{2}\right)}$.

(D) 1.

(E) None of the above.

16. If Don and Ron can paint a house in 5 days, and Ron can paint it alone in 7 days, how long will it take Don to paint it alone?

(A) 2 days

(B) 7 days

(C) 17.5 days

(D) 9.75 days

(E) 11.25 days

17. If the volume of a cube is 8, how long is its main diagonal (the line segment joining the two farthest corners)?

(A) $2\sqrt{2}$

(B) $3\sqrt{2}$

(C) $2\sqrt{3}$

(D) $3\sqrt{3}$

(E) The length of the main diagonal cannot be found for lack of information.

18. Norman lives 6 blocks north and 6 blocks east of Bob. The town is made up of all square blocks. How many ways can Bob walk to Norman's house walking only 12 blocks?

   (A)   2 ways   (D)   4096 ways

   (B)   924 ways   (E)   Infinitely many ways

   (C)   36 ways

19. If the area of a right isosceles triangle is 4, how long are its sides?

   (A) $2\sqrt{2}, 2\sqrt{2}, 4$ (B) $2, 2, 2\sqrt{2}$

   (C) $3, 3, 3\sqrt{2}$ (D) $3\sqrt{2}, 3\sqrt{2}, 6$

   (E)   The lengths of the triangle cannot be found for lack of information.

20. Donald gave Louie a number of marbles to share with Dewey and Huey. Making sure that he got his share, Louie took one-third of the marbles and hid them. Dewey, after hearing from Donald that he is entitled to one-third of the marbles as well, went and hid one-third of the remaining marbles. Not knowing what was going on, Daisy took two marbles from the pile. When Huey came, there were only 10 marbles left. How many marbles did Donald give to Louie in the beginning?

   (A)   18

   (B)   21

   (C)   24

   (D)   27

   (E)   That number cannot be found for lack of information.

21. A steamboat left Hong Kong on May 25, at 6 a.m., New York time. It sailed 400 hours and arrived in New York. When did it arrive?

   (A)   10 p.m., June 9   (D)   4 p.m., June 10

   (B)   10 p.m., June 10   (E)   4 p.m., June 11

   (C)   10 p.m., June 11

22. Joan is 8 years older than Georgette. Joan was twice as old as Georgette 8 years ago. How old are they now?

   (A)   Joan is 30 and Georgette is 22.

   (B)   Joan is 28 and Georgette is 20.

(C) Joan is 26 and Georgette is 18.

(D) Joan is 24 and Georgette is 16.

(E) Further information is needed to figure their ages.

23. A river flows at a speed of 5 miles per hour. A steamboat went upstream for 5 hours and stopped at a point 20 miles from where it started. What is the speed of the steamboat in still waters?

(A) 9 miles per hour

(B) 12 miles per hour

(C) 14 miles per hour

(D) 18 miles per hour

(E) The speed of the boat cannot be found for lack of information.

24. Sarah bought 10 pounds of apples and nuts. Apples are 89 cents a pound, and nuts are $1.29 a pound. She spent a total of $10.10. How many pounds of nuts did she buy?

(A) 1

(B) 2

(C) 3

(D) 4

(E) 5

25. Jim and Joe were running together. Jim's average speed was 400 meters per minute. Jim started running 4 minutes before Joe. Ten minutes after Joe started, he caught up with Jim. What was Joe's average speed?

(A) 440 meters per minute

(B) 450 meters per minute

(C) 480 meters per minute

(D) 500 meters per minute

(E) 560 meters per minute

26. If 96 chickens and rabbits are put together, they have a total of 312 legs. How many chickens are there?

(A) 36

(B) 60

(C) 72

(D) 24

(E) 42

27. Harold decided to cut down his sugar consumption in coffee, tea, and other drinks. He had been consuming 120 grams of sugar a day. He was determined

to cut down 2 grams per week until he no longer used sugar in his drinks. Starting from the first day that he began cutting down his sugar, how much sugar would he have consumed before he arrived at his goal?

(A) 92160 grams

(D) 8200 grams

(B) 10900 grams

(E) 24780 grams

(C) 72000 grams

28. John and Kevin have a total of $97. John has $9 more than Kevin. How much money does Kevin have?

(A) $40

(D) $46

(B) $42

(E) $48

(C) $44

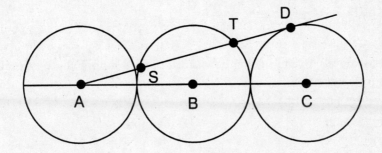

29. Three circles of equal radii with centers A, B, and C are lying on a straight line and tangent to each other as in the figure. A tangent line to circle C is drawn from A, meeting circle B at S and T, tangent to circle C at D. What is the ratio of the line segment ST to the radii?

(A) $\dfrac{\sqrt{3}}{2}$

(D) 1

(B) $\dfrac{3}{2}$

(E) $\sqrt{2}$

(C) $\sqrt{3}$

30. If a number times itself is added to five times itself, the result is 24. What could this number possibly be?

(A) 3 or 8

(B) −3 or 8

(C)   3 or –8   (D)   –3 or –8

(E)   –4 or 6

31.   Concerning the number π, which statement is the most accurate?

(A)   π = 3.14.   (D)   π cannot be calculated.

(B)   π = 3.1416.   (E)   π is an irrational number.

(C) $\pi = \dfrac{22}{7}$.

32.   What is the measurement of an angle of a regular pentagon?

(A)   72°   (D)   84°

(B)   108°   (E)   104°

(C)   100°

33.   A boat travels 15 mph going downstream and 8 mph going upstream. How fast is the waterflow?

(A) $\dfrac{7}{2}$ mph   (D)   4 mph

(B)   3 mph   (E) $\dfrac{5}{2}$ mph

(C) $\dfrac{9}{2}$ mph

34.   The longest side of a triangle measures 2 and the shortest side measures 1. What cannot be the measurement of the angle between them?

(A)   30°   (D)   20°

(B)   60°   (E)   90°

(C)   70°

35. Which of the following is closest to the graph of the equation $y = x^2$?

(A)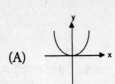

(D)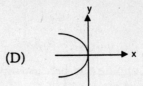

(B)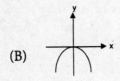

(E)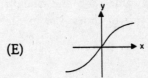

(C)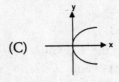

36. Roger took off at 8:00 a.m. driving 45 mph. Bill went after him two hours later and caught up with him at 4:00 p.m. How fast did Bill drive?

(A) 70 mph

(D) 55 mph

(B) 65 mph

(E) 50 mph

(C) 60 mph

37. The expression $\dfrac{x+1}{x-1} - \dfrac{x-1}{x+1}$ simplifies to

(A) -1.

(D) $\dfrac{4x}{x^2-1}$.

(B) 1.

(E) $\dfrac{x}{x^2-1}$.

(C) $\dfrac{2x}{x^2-1}$.

38. If an equilateral triangle has area $\sqrt{3}$, what are the lengths of its sides?

(A) 1

(B) $\dfrac{3}{2}$

(C) 2

(D) $\dfrac{5}{2}$

(E) 3

39. Jane went shopping. On her first trip, she bought six pairs of shoes, all at the same price, and three pairs of socks, also at the same price (shoes and socks are not necessarily of the same price), and she spent $96. On her second trip, she went to the same shop and bought four more pairs of the same socks and returned a pair of shoes; she spent $2. How much does a pair of her shoes cost?

(A) $10

(D) $16

(B) $12

(E) $18

(C) $14

40. Triangle ABC is inscribed in a circle with center O at the midpoint of the side BC. If angle B measures 47°, what is the measurement of angle C?

(A) 43°

(D) 37°

(B) 47°

(E) Insufficient information

(C) 53°

41. Dan flies north at a speed of 200 miles per hour, and Tom flies east at a speed of 150 miles per hour. Head wind and air resistance all having been taken into consideration, how far are they apart two hours later?

(A) 300 miles

(D) 450 miles

(B) 350 miles

(E) 500 miles

(C) 400 miles

42. The sum of the base and altitude of a triangle is 12 and the area is 16. What are the base and altitude of the triangle?

(A) 2 and 10

(D) 3 and 9

(B) 6

(E) 5 and 7

(C) 4 and 8

43. The repeating decimal 0.36363636...., when written as a fraction, is

(A) $\dfrac{9}{25}$.

(B) $\dfrac{4}{11}$.

(C) $\dfrac{63}{175}$.

(D) $\dfrac{8}{13}$.

(E)   Not expressible as a fraction.

44.   An isosceles triangle ABC is inscribed in a circle with center O in such a way that OBC forms an equilateral triangle. The measurement of angle B is

(A)   80°.

(D)   65°.

(B)   75°.

(E)   60°.

(C)   70°.

45.   If subtracting 13 from a number is the same as taking $\dfrac{3}{4}$ of the number, what is the number?

(A)   52

(D)   76

(B)   39

(E)   97

(C)   48

46.   Mr. Jones is nine times as old as his grandson. If they are 56 years apart, how old is his grandson?

(A)   9

(D)   6

(B)   8

(E)   5

(C)   7

47.   Bob is lending money at 6% simple interest. How much does he need to lend at the beginning of the year to yield $1,000 by the end of the year? (Figure to the nearest dollar.)

(A) $850

(D) $943

(B) $950

(E) $927

(C) $894

48.   The expression $x^n - y^n$

(A)   can be factored only when n is odd.

(B)   can never be factored.

(C)   can always be factored.

(D)   can be factored only when n is a power of 4.

(E)   can be factored only when n is twice an odd integer.

49.   If one root of the equation $ax^2 + bx + c = 0$ is 2, the other root must be

(A) $\dfrac{c}{2}$.

(D) $\dfrac{b}{2c}$.

(B) $\dfrac{c}{2a}$.

(E) $\dfrac{a}{2c}$.

(C) $\dfrac{c}{2b}$.

50.   If five gallons of 50% alcohol solution is mixed with three gallons of 20% alcohol solution, what is the resulting solution?

(A)   38.75%

(D)   42.25%

(B)   37.5%

(E)   32.25%

(C)   35%

Section III: Essay Writing

TIME: 60 Minutes
        2 Essays

DIRECTIONS: Carefully read the two writing topics below. Plan and write an essay on each, being sure to cover all aspects of each topic. Allow approximately 30 minutes per essay.

Topic 1

Ideologies, or ways of looking at things, range from very liberal to very conservative views of how lives should be lived and what is good and bad for society. A prevailing ideology in our culture holds that women's primary responsibilities are homemaking and child rearing; that men are primarily responsible for the financial support of the family; that women with children should ideally not work outside the home; and that a double standard in these social customs is acceptable.

You may not hold these views personally, but they have pervaded our culture for many years and have influenced everyone to some degree. What is your position on the issue of male and female roles in the home and society?

Topic 2

Sometimes you want something badly and then when you get it, it's not what you expected. Discuss such an event in your life, and analyze why it was disappointing.

CBEST TEST 3 – ANSWER KEY

Section I: Reading Comprehension

1.	(D)	14.	(B)	27.	(B)	40.	(C)
2.	(E)	15.	(E)	28.	(A)	41.	(B)
3.	(B)	16.	(C)	29.	(D)	42.	(D)
4.	(A)	17.	(B)	30.	(E)	43.	(B)
5.	(B)	18.	(A)	31.	(A)	44.	(E)
6.	(C)	19.	(B)	32.	(C)	45.	(C)
7.	(C)	20.	(A)	33.	(C)	46.	(A)
8.	(B)	21.	(E)	34.	(A)	47.	(C)
9.	(D)	22.	(C)	35.	(E)	48.	(E)
10.	(D)	23.	(B)	36.	(C)	49.	(A)
11.	(C)	24.	(E)	37.	(E)	50.	(D)
12.	(B)	25.	(E)	38.	(E)		
13.	(D)	26.	(D)	39.	(E)		

Section II: Mathematics

1.	(A)	14.	(D)	27.	(E)	40.	(A)
2.	(C)	15.	(A)	28.	(C)	41.	(E)
3.	(C)	16.	(C)	29.	(C)	42.	(C)
4.	(D)	17.	(C)	30.	(C)	43.	(B)
5.	(C)	18.	(B)	31.	(E)	44.	(B)
6.	(C)	19.	(A)	32.	(B)	45.	(A)
7.	(E)	20.	(D)	33.	(A)	46.	(C)
8.	(D)	21.	(B)	34.	(E)	47.	(D)
9.	(E)	22.	(D)	35.	(A)	48.	(C)
10.	(B)	23.	(A)	36.	(C)	49.	(B)
11.	(E)	24.	(C)	37.	(D)	50.	(A)
12.	(E)	25.	(E)	38.	(C)		
13.	(D)	26.	(A)	39.	(C)		

DETAILED EXPLANATIONS OF ANSWERS

Section I: Reading Comprehension

1. **(D)** The question asks for the best synthesis of the passage and (D) is the best and most complete answer. Choices (A), (B), (C), and (E) are not as complete. For example, (A) left out the duration of the conference, (B) left out the number of the nations represented at the summit, (C) left out both the duration of the conference and the number of the nations represented at the summit, and (E) left out the number of nations represented and support for Gorbachev's "new thinking."

2. **(E)** Of the choices provided, (E) gives the most logical and sound implication of the passage. (A) falls short of the capabilities of Gorbachev's leadership, in (B) the "new thinking" referred to already has the support of the seven leaders at the summit, (C) is a rather sweeping, unfair statement; and (D) left out support for economic and political reforms.

3. **(B)** The mention of banking and energy did not rule out technical assistance in other fields, hence, (B) is the correct answer. Answer (A) limited the assistance to only the fields of banking and energy, in (C) the statement is only partly true—the U.S. is not alone in providing support, in (D) the statement implies that there is no consensus among the seven nations, in (E) technical assistance can likewise come from other nations outside of the seven.

4. **(A)** The question asks for the main idea in the passage and (A) gives the best and complete main idea. Choices (B), (C), and (D) are generalizations derived from the passage and (E) while it is true and specific to the passage, is stated in the negative.

5. **(B)** (B) gives the most specific consequence for California. The other choices, while all plausible or possible answers, do not get to the "root" of the issue specific to California.

6. **(C)** Based on the passage read, the answer to this question is (C)—two things are mentioned that could affect California and these are federal funding and the number of congressional seats. While (A) and (B) are correct, they are incomplete. Choices (D) and (E) are consequential generalizations which are both correct but lack the preciseness of answer (C).

7. (C) The question asks for the "message" conveyed in the passage. Choice (C) is the correct answer, as it gives a warning. In choice (A), pesticides cannot necessarily be dangerous to all living things—some are good for the protection of plants, for example; in (B), water can be contaminated by something other than pesticides; the statement in choice (D) may be true, but it is certainly not the best answer.

8. (B) The train is definitely a cargo train, hence, (B) is the correct answer. In (A), if it were a passenger train, hundreds would have been killed; in (C) and (D), according to the clues, the answers here don't apply; and in (E) the answer used "special train" but could have appropriately used "cargo train" instead.

9. (D) The question here asks for the most "serious problem" that can come about; so, of all the choices, (D) provides the most serious problem resulting from the pesticide spill for Californians. Answers (A), (B), (C), and (E) are not life-threatening as is answer (D).

10. (D) The answer (D) is the most logical and straightforward answer. (D) prioritizes which action should be first taken, and is therefore the correct answer. While the choices in (A), (B), (C), and (E) are sound answers, they don't list the most urgent thing to do.

11. (C) The correct answer here is (C) because this choice synthesizes the key or main idea in the passage. The other choices, while partly true, don't give the main idea.

12. (B) Before World War II, which were the depression years, one can easily presume that people were more practical or money minded, hence, Labor Day as celebrated then could mean the loss of a day's pay for working people. Hence, (B) is the correct answer. While choices (A), (C), (D), and (E) are also possible answers they don't get to the "root" of the issue.

13. (D) Explicitly given in the passage is (D), the correct answer. Choices (A), (B), (C), and (E), while they may all be true and correct, are not what is precisely given in the passage.

14. (B) The question asks for implication. The most straightforward implication of the choices provided has got to be (B). Choice (A) is too general and is actually given in the passage. Choice (C) is an eventual consequence of the proposed program and the same can be said of (D) and (E).

15. (E) The gold content found in the volcanic ash from Mt. Pinatubo could easily stir or trigger a "gold rush." However, people are warned that the gold content found is not at a "commercial level." Hence, (E) is the correct answer. The other choices provided are all mere speculations.

16. **(C)**   Choice (C) is the most appropriate answer—it also synthesizes the content of the reading passage; hence, it is the correct answer. Choices (A) and (B) are both incorrect. Choices (D) and (E) are somewhat applicable as titles but do not really synthesize the main idea of the passage as choice (C).

17. **(B)**   If priorities will have to be established, to determine the most immediate research needed on the ash content from Mt. Pinatubo, choice (B) will have to be the most logical choice because there is already some data with which to work. Other research possibilities such as those in choice (A), (D), (C), and (E) will have to come later.

18. **(A)**   The best and correct answer here is (A)—it's the main idea of the passage. Choice (B) is incorrect. Choice (C) is partially correct—if it has to be specific, it should refer to the brake lights on the helmet. Choice (D) is incomplete as a key or main idea of the passage and the same could be said of choice (E).

19. **(B)**   It would follow that the rationale behind the new brake light requirement for cars in California is the same for all other vehicles on the road. Hence, choice (B) is the correct answer. The implication provided in (A) is not necessarily true; (C) is illogical; in (D) any car driven in California, wherever its been bought, cannot be exempted from the requirement; and in (E) Harris can go on inventing while remaining a farmer—he'll make more money doing both.

20. **(A)**   Choice (A) is the most logical and appropriate answer, hence, it is the correct answer. Choice (B) can be, but is not necessarily true; (C) is a logical possibility but will not drastically raise car prices beyond affordability; (D) may be true, but not as road hazards; and (E), the contrary may also be true.

21. **(E)**   All the choices in this question are possible answers, however, since the question asks for what lead poisoning, if not detected early "can lead to," it calls for the ultimate consequence. Hence, (E) is the correct answer inasmuch as the passage states "life-threatening disorders" as among the possible consequences.

22. **(C)**   The correct answer to this question is choice (C)—it gives the complete and precise category. Other choices are incomplete—(A) left out the age group and the medical eligibility; (B) is narrowed down and all inclusive of "children with learning disabilities," choices (D) and (E) are incorrect.

23. **(B)**   As indicated by figures in the passage, the correct answer is (B). Other choices (A), (C), (D), and (E) are obviously incorrect. This is an example of a question in which the incorrect choices are not possible answers. The correct answer is derived from the figures provided in the passage.

24. **(E)**   The implications provided in choices (A) through (E) are correct. However, each of the implications for (A) through (D) are narrowed down to only one specific

category of children—not any one is inclusive of all that need to be addressed. Hence, (E) is the best and appropriate answer because it addresses the thousands who will not be screened which include those in the answers to (A) through (D).

25. **(E)**   If schools exist to serve the best interest of students, then the correct answer for this question is (E). Choices (A) through (D) are also correct, however, the group that will be most affected by the financial crisis in California would have to be the "students." The fact remains that schools exist to serve the best interest of students.

26. **(D)**   A title is supposed to synthesize the main idea and (D) does. Choice (A) left out the main idea of a commemorative stamp; choice (B) is incorrect because it implies Columbus discovered the Americas; choice (C) is not the main idea of the passage; and choice (E), while it may be implied in the passage, does not synthesize its focus.

27. **(B)**   The underlying fact behind the passage is explicitly implied, therefore, (B) is the correct answer. Choice (A) while true, is a generalized implication, not addressing the specific issue; choice (C) is debatable and so is choice (D); choice (E) like (A) is also a generalized implication.

28. **(A)**   Of the choices given (A) is the most historically significant, and therefore, the correct answer. Choice (B) is significant but left out the fact that Columbus was not the first to arrive in the New World, the main point in the passage; choice (C) is a mere commemoration day; choice (D) remains a debatable assumption; and choice (E) is not specific enough as an historically significant fact.

29. **(D)**   Since zoology is the study of animals (D) is the correct and appropriate answer. The other choices which are other subject areas, as in (A), (B), (C), and (E) while they may be used by the classroom teacher, they are not quite the most appropriate subject areas.

30. **(E)**   A study of a 150 million-year-old fossil will require digging up into history, hence, (E) is the correct answer. Choice (A) could be used if there is a problem focus in the passage; choices (B), (C), and (D) are poor and incorrect choices—survey applies to a descriptive study, deductive is an approach that proceeds from a generalization or theory, and comparative requires two things to compare which is not addressed in the passage.

31. **(A)**   The answer in (A) clearly synthesizes the main idea in the passage, hence, it is the correct answer. Choice (B) is more of an implication, hence, the wrong answer; choice (C) is merely stating a fact which does not speak of the main idea; the same can be said of choice (D); and choice (E), while it may be true, is not really the passage's main idea.

32. **(C)** The most sound and significant implication of the passage is stated in (C), hence, this is the correct answer. Choices (A) and (B) are not sound, they reflect a rather immature reasoning; choice (D) merely states some degree of competitiveness which is not the issue focus; and (E) is a "so what" kind of statement and not a sound implication.

33. **(C)** The passage is really on global tourism providing comparisons and implying some inter-nation balance in tourism trade, hence, (C) is the appropriate and correct answer. Choices (A), (B), (D), and (E) are stated in general terms, missing out on the specific focus or topic of the passage, hence, not the logical and immediate topics to discuss.

34. **(A)** The most appropriate and complete title is expressed in (A), hence this is the correct answer. Choice (B) merely states a planned activity and does not address the main idea; choice (C) is incomplete—it does not specify basis for ranking; the same can be said for choices (D) and (E), likewise, incomplete titles.

35. **(E)** The best answer in considering "practical terms" will have to be (E) which is the correct answer. Choice (A) is an implication that does not apply to San Francisco; choice (C) is a possible consequence but an undesirable one; choice (D) is a true implication but the "practicality" is merely implied. (E) says this explicitly.

36. **(C)** The suggestion in (C) is the most sound and logical if equal opportunity for all students is to be our nation's priority, hence, this is the correct answer. Choice (A) is a mere statement of concern and does not provide a plan for action; choice (B) is illogical—you cannot cut down the number of minority students who are already in the system; choice (D) disregards other languages existing in the school system and in the community at large; and (E) is only secondary to the major issue.

37. **(E)** Since the passage points out the fact that there will soon be more minority students in the classroom, priority should be in providing the appropriate teacher preparation, hence, the correct answer is (E). Choice (A) is a need but secondary to those who are already in the system; choice (B) has always been an issue even before the rapid changes in the demographics; choice (C) is something that has triggered legislations since the 1950s—the natural composition of the classroom today is already desegregated. While the other choices are a need, the one that needs immediate action is (E).

38. **(E)** The answer to this question has to tie in with the foregoing answer, hence, the correct choice should be (E). Choices (A), (B), (C), and (D), while also problems arising from the changes in demographics, are secondary to (E).

39. **(E)** The most complete summary of the passage is stated in (E), hence, this is the correct answer. Choice (A) is not true, therefore, is incorrect; choice (B) is rather put in general terms—the U.S. pullout is not the only issue related to the Philippine economy. The interdependence of nations will remain no matter what, i.e., trade relations will

continue; choice (C) is incorrect. The U.S. military strategy will have to be relocated elsewhere in the Asia-Pacific region, the same can be said for choice (D)—the Philippines will not be completely on its own—it continues to maintain its trade relations with the U.S. and other trading partners.

40. (C) The passage is quite explicit in stating that the U.S. presence on the Philippines has been an impediment to the nation's capability in joining East Asia's "economic boom," hence, the the correct answer is (C); choices (A), (B), (D), and (E) are all possible consequences but are all quite debatable.

41. (B) Again, this question requires an answer that has to be consistent with the answers in the foregoing questions and, therefore, the answer has to be (B). The other choices—(A), (C), (D), and (E) are all possible and acceptable answers but do not directly relate to the key message in the passage.

42. (D) The answer in (D) states the most complete main idea in the passage, hence, it is the correct answer. Choice (A) addresses only one part of the correct answer; choices (A) and (C) are incorrect; and choice (E) is an incomplete answer.

43. (B) Of the choices provided,(B) provides the most complete answer—namely, the two things that the computer program does: predicts the aging process and predicts how an unborn child will look. The other choices, (A), (C), (D), and (E) while all true, are incomplete in providing the main capability of the new computer program developed in Japan.

44. (E) A logical answer to this question has got to be (E), the correct answer. With this new computer system it certainly will follow that Japan will do a more refined and sophisticated system next. Choices (A) and (B) are related—the answers are natural outgrowths of the competitive market among nations; and choices (C) and (D) have been an on-going trend anyway.

45. (C) In an emergency situation, the most sound and logical thing to do would have to be (C), the correct answer. Choice (A) is not the best thing to do in the situation; choice (B) is running a risk of consuming the fuel; same could be said of choice (D); and choice (E) is too risky, hence, incorrect.

46. (A) For air travelers who are aware of possible communications breakdown due to a power failure, choice (A) is the best and correct answer. Choice (B) could be true only to certain people; choice (C) is a good answer but does not relate to the specific incident; choice (D) is besides the point; and choice (E) is an incorrect generalization—delays are caused by other reasons besides a power failure.

47. (C) A title is supposed to synthesize the main idea of a passage. In this passage the best synthesis is (C), hence, the correct answer. Choices (A), (B), (D), and (E) are possible titles but are all incomplete as titles.

48. **(E)** The question is inappropriate to the passage—it addresses men and women. However, the research addressed in the passage was done on men only. Hence, the correct answer is (E); all the rest of the answers (A), (B), (C), and (D) are incorrect.

49. **(A)** The answer in (A) is sound and is the best and correct answer. Choice (B) is an incorrect answer; choice (C) is an incorrect implication; the same can be said of choices (D) and (E).

50. **(D)** The study covered only men, hence, a major limitation is the fact that it did not include women of the same age group. The correct answer, therefore, is (D); choice (A) may not be an essential in the study, hence, definitely not a major limitation; choice (B), while a limitation, cannot be considered "major." Besides, "children" could include babies through young adolescents—a rather wide age range; choice (C) is also a limitation, but it does not state the precise age range.

Section II: Mathematics

1. **(A)** The least common denominator of the fractions is the least common multiple of their denominators: 15, 21, and 35. Since 15 = 3 x 5, 21 = 3 x 7, and 35 = 5 x 7, we see that their least common multiple is 3 x 5 x 7 = 105.

2. **(C)** Since his reunion will be 365 x 4 +1 = 1461 days from a Friday, dividing 1461 by 7 yields a remainder of 5. Therefore, his reunion is 5 days from a Friday, which makes it on a Wednesday.

3. **(C)** In one day, John can do $\frac{1}{7}$ of the work, and Mary can do $\frac{1}{5}$; together, they can do $\frac{1}{5} + \frac{1}{7} = \frac{12}{35}$ of the job. To finish the whole job, it takes $\frac{35}{12} = 2$ and $\frac{11}{12}$ days.

4. **(D)** Since the sugar content is 60% of $\frac{1}{2}$ pint and will not be changed after the water is added, we obtain an equation by equating the sugar content before and after adding in x pints of water. The equation is then

$$\left(\frac{1}{2}\right) \bullet 60\% = \left(\frac{1}{2} + x\right) \bullet 5\% \text{ or}$$

$$30 = \frac{5}{2} + 5x$$
$$60 = 5 + 10x$$
$$55 = 10x$$
$$\text{and } 5.5 = x.$$

5. **(C)** Since the only information we have concerning the triangle is that angle A measures 30°, we know that in a triangle, the largest angle faces the longest side, the sum of the three angles of a triangle is 180°, and a 30° angle is not the largest angle. Therefore, A is not the longest side.

6. **(C)** The diameter of circle A is twice that of circle B, so if the radius of B is r, then the radius of A is $2r$. Since the area of a circle with radius r is πr^2 the area of B is πr^2, while the area of A is $\pi(2r)^2 = 4\pi r$.

7. **(E)** Since the cube has volume 8, its sides have length 2. The cube whose sides are twice that would be of length 4, so the volume of the other cube is 4 x 4 x 4 = 64.

8.   (D)   2:15 + 5:45 = 8:00 means he arrives in Los Angeles at 8 p.m. New York time. But New York is 3 hours ahead of Los Angeles, so the Los Angeles time of arrival is 5 p.m.

9.   (E)   We set up two equations. Let n be the number of nickels, and let d be the number of dimes. We have $n + d = 50$. Since each nickel is worth 5 cents and each dime is worth 10 cents, we have $5n + 10d = 485$. Multiplying the first equation by 10, we obtain $10n + 10d = 500$. Subtracting the second equation from it, we obtain $5n = 15$, or $n = 3$.

10.   (B)   Let s be the speed of the boat in still water. Then the speed of the boat upstream is $(s - 3)$ miles per hour, and the speed of the boat downstream is $(s + 3)$ miles per hour. Therefore, the time going upstream, $24/(s - 3)$ hours plus the time going downstream, $24/(s + 3)$ hours, equals 6 hours. Solving for s gives $s = 9$ miles/hour.

$$\frac{24}{s-3} + \frac{24}{s+3} = 6$$

$$\frac{(s+3)}{(s+3)(s-3)} + \frac{(s-3)}{(s-3)(s+3)} = \frac{6}{24} = \frac{1}{4}$$

$$\frac{2s}{(s+3)(s-3)} = \frac{1}{4} \qquad 8s = (s+3)(s-3) = s^2 - 9$$

$s^2 - 8s - 9 = 0$; $(s - 9)(s + 1) = 0$; $s = 9$ or -1, but we require $s > 0$. Thus $s = 9$ miles per hour.

11.   (E)   Since 10 babies drink 10 gallons of milk in 10 days, each baby drinks $\frac{1}{10}$ gallon of milk per day. Each baby drinks 2 gallons of milk in 20 days, so 20 babies will drink 2 x 20 = 40 gallons of milk in 20 days.

12.   (E)   Let x be the number of nickels, y be the number of dimes, and z be the number of quarters. We have two equations: $x + y + z = 24$ and $5x + 10y + 25z = 300$ and three unknowns. Therefore, no unique answer can be found without one more equation.

13.   (D)   Draw both diagonals to divide the parallelogram into four equal parts. Each part is a right triangle with hypotenuse measuring 4 and one side measuring 2. Therefore, the other side must measure $2\sqrt{3}$ by the Pythagorean Theorem. The area of this triangle is $\left(\frac{1}{2}\right) \cdot \left(2 \text{x} 2\sqrt{3}\right) = 2\sqrt{3}$, and the area of the parallelogram is four times that, which is $8\sqrt{3}$.

14. **(D)** Let the amount of money he had before be x. We have $x - \left(\dfrac{1}{3}\right)x - \left(\dfrac{1}{4}\right)x = 150,000.$ Or, $\left(\dfrac{5}{12}\right)x = 150,000.$ Therefore, $x = 360,000.$

15. **(A)** If we multiply both the numerator and denominator by the conjugate of the expression $\sqrt{3} - \sqrt{2}$, namely, $\sqrt{3} + \sqrt{2}$, the numerator becomes $\sqrt{3} + \sqrt{2}$, and the denominator becomes $3 - 2 = 1$.

16. **(C)** Since Don and Ron can paint the house in 7 days, they finish $\dfrac{1}{5}$ of the job in a day. Now Ron's contribution in a day is $\dfrac{1}{7}$ of the job, so $\left(\dfrac{1}{5}\right) - \left(\dfrac{1}{7}\right)$ is Don's contribution in a day, which amounts to $\left(\dfrac{2}{35}\right)$. Therefore, if Don is to do it alone, it will take him $\left(\dfrac{35}{2}\right) = 17.5$ days.

17. **(C)** Since the volume of the cube is 8, each side has a measure 2, and the main diagonal is found with the Pythagorean Formula.

18. **(B)** Each way for Bob to walk to Norman's consists of 6 blocks northward and 6 blocks eastward in different orders. The total number of ways of walking is then the same as the number of ways to choose 6 out of 12 things, and the number is 12 x 11 x 10 x 9 x 8 x 7 divided by 6 x 5 x 4 x 3 x 2, or 924.

19. **(A)** For a right isosceles triangle, the area is half of the product of the two equal sides. Therefore, each of the equal sides measure $\sqrt{8}$, or $2\sqrt{2}$, and the hypotenuse must be 4.

20. **(D)** Let the number of marbles in the beginning be x. We have $x - \left(\dfrac{1}{3}\right)x - \left(\dfrac{1}{3}\right)\left(\dfrac{2}{3}\right)x - 2 = 10.$ Solving the equation, $x = 27.$

21. **(B)** We divide 400 by 24 (number of hours in a day), we obtain a partial quotient of 16 and a remainder of 16. This means that it takes 16 days and 16 hours for the trip. With 31 days in May, the boat must arrive on June 10. And 16 hours from 6 a.m. is 10 p.m.

22. **(D)** If we let Joan's age be x, then Georgette's age is $(x - 8)$. Solving the equation $(x - 8) = 2[(x - 8) - 8] = 2x - 32$, we obtain $x = 24$.

23. **(A)** Since the boat took 5 hours to go 20 miles, its speed upstream was 4 miles per hour. But the water effect was 5 miles per hour. If that effect had been taken away, the boat would have been 5 miles faster; therefore, the boat in still waters goes 4 + 5 = 9 miles per hour.

24. **(C)** Suppose Sarah bought x pounds of apples and y pounds of nuts. We have the following equations to solve:

$$x + y = 10$$
$$89x + 129y = 1,010$$

Solving these equations give $x = 7$, $y = 3$.

25. **(E)** When Joe caught Jim, Jim had been running for $(10 + 4) = 14$ minutes, at the rate of 400 meters per minute. So the total distance covered was $(14 \times 400) = 5600$ meters. But Joe covered this distance in 10 minutes. Thus his average speed was

$$\frac{5600}{10} = 560 \text{ meters per minute.}$$

26. **(A)** Since a chicken has two legs and a rabbit has four legs, letting x be the number of chickens and y be the number of rabbits, we have the following equations to solve: $x + y = 96$; $2x + 4y = 312$.

27. **(E)** In the first week, he consumed 118 grams of sugar daily, in the second week, he consumed 116 grams of sugar daily, etc. We are then to add $118 + 116 + 114 + \dots + 2$ and since there are seven days in a week, the result must be multiplied by 7. Observing

that $118 + 116 + 114 + \dots + 2 = 2 \cdot (1 + 2 + 3 + \dots + 59) = 2 \cdot (1 + 59)\left(\dfrac{59}{2}\right) = 3540$.

And $3540 \cdot 7 = 24780$.

28. **(C)** Let x be the amount of money Kevin has, and let y be the amount of money John has. Then $y + x = 97$, and $y - x = 9$. Subtracting the two equations, we have $2x = 88$, or $x = 44$.

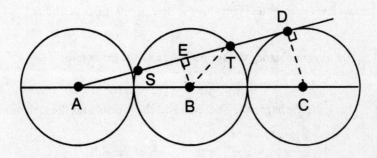

29. **(C)** If we draw a perpendicular line from B to the tangent line, say BE, then the

right-angled triangles ABE and ACD are similar, so BE equals half of CD, the radius. BET is also a right-angled triangle, and BT is a radius. Using the Pythagorean Theorem, ET measures $\dfrac{\sqrt{3}}{2}$ of the radius. Thus ST measures $\sqrt{3}$ of the radius.

30. **(C)**   Letting this number be x, we have $x^2 + 5x = 24$, or $x^2 + 5x - 24 = 0$, or $(x + 8)(x - 3) = 0$, so $x = 3$ or $x = -8$.

31. **(E)** π is an irrational number, while (A), (B), and (C) are all approximate rational values of π, and the statement (D) is vague.

32. **(B)**   We do not need to memorize any formula. If we inscribe the regular pentagon in a circle, the angle with the vertex at the center facing each side is $\dfrac{360°}{5} = 72°$, and each of the other angles of that triangle must be $\dfrac{(180° - 72°)}{2} = 54°$. Thus each of the angles is 108°.

33. **(A)**   Let x be the speed of the boat in still waters, and let y be the speed of the waterflow. Then $x + y = 15$ mph, and $x - y = 8$ mph, subtracting the equations, we get $2y = 7$, or $y = \dfrac{7}{2}$.

34. **(E)**   Since a 90° angle must be the largest in a triangle, it must face the longest side, and the angle between the longest side and the shortest side is not facing the longest side.

35. **(A)** $y = x^2$ has graph like (A). (B) is the graph of $y = -x^2$, (C) is the graph of $x = y^2$, (D) is the graph of $x = -y^2$, and (E) is not even the graph of a second degree equation.

36. **(C)**   Since Bill took 6 hours to catch up, and Roger has gone 90 miles, Bill was $\dfrac{90}{6} = 15$ miles closer each hour. Thus he was driving 60 miles per hour.

37. **(D)**   The common denominator is $x^2 - 1$, and the numerator is $(x + 1)^2 - (x - 1)^2 = 4x$.

38. **(C)**   Using the Pythagorean Theorem and the formula for the area of a triangle, $b = a$ and $h = \sqrt{a^2 - \left(\dfrac{1}{2}a\right)^2}$ where a is the length of the sides.

$$\frac{1}{2}bh = \text{area}$$

$$\frac{1}{2}a\sqrt{a^2 - \frac{1}{4}a^2} = \sqrt{3}$$

$$\frac{1}{2}a\sqrt{\frac{3}{4}a^2} = \sqrt{3}$$

$$\frac{1}{4}a^2\left(\frac{3}{4}a^2\right) = 3$$

$$a^4 = (3)\left(\frac{16}{3}\right)$$

$$a^2 = 2$$

39. **(C)** Let the price for a pair of shoes be x, and let the price for a pair of socks be y. Then, $6x + 3y = 96$, and $4y - x = 2$. Solving these equations, we have $x = 14$.

40. **(A)** Since BC is the diameter of the circle, angle A is a right angle. Therefore angle C is complementary to angle B, i.e., $90° - 47° = 43°$.

41. **(E)** Since they travel on the two sides of a right-angled triangle, Pythagorean Theorem yields $400^2 + 300^2 = 500^2$.

42. **(C)** Let b be the base and a be the altitude of the triangle. We have the equations: $a + b = 12$, and $\dfrac{ab}{2} = 16$. To solve these equations, substitute $b = 12 - a$ into the second equation, we have $a(12 - a) = 32$, or $12a - a^2 = 32$, or $a^2 - 12a + 32 = (a - 8)(a - 4) = 0$; thus $a = 4$ or 8, and $b = 8$ or 4 respectively.

43. **(B)** Since a two-digit repeating decimal is the two digits over 99, we have $\dfrac{36}{99} = \dfrac{4}{11}$.

44. **(B)** Since the angle BOC measures $60°$, angle BAC measures $30°$, angles B and C will be half of $\dfrac{(180° - 30°)}{2} = 75°$.

45. **(A)**   Since $x - 13 = \dfrac{3x}{4}$, or $4x - 52 = 3x$, we have $x = 52$.

46. **(C)**   Letting Mr. Jones' age be x, and his grandson's be y, we have $x = 9y$ and $x - y = 56$. Substitute the first into the second equation, $9y - y = 56$, $y = 7$.

47. **(D)**   His principle and interest need to be 1,000, which is 1.06 times his principle. Thus we divide 1,000 by 1.06 and it is close to 943.

48. **(C)**   In fact, $x^n - y^n = (x - y)(x^{n-1} + x^{n-2}y + x^{n-3}y^2 + \ldots + y^{n-1})$.

49. **(B)**   The original equation is equivalent to $x^2 + \dfrac{bx}{a} + \dfrac{c}{a} = 0$. The product of the two roots must equal $\dfrac{c}{a}$.

50. **(A)**   The alcohol content is $5 \times 0.5 + 3 \times 0.2 = 3.1$ gallons, and the total amount of solution is 8 gallons. $3.1 + 8 = .3875 = 38.75\%$.

Section III: Essay Writing

Topic 1 Sample Answer

Essay #1—Pass (Score = 4)

The ideology that "anatomy is destiny" is completely false. There are, however, explanations for the gap between boys and girls as they take their place in the world as masculine and feminine beings. Different sex role experiences and socializing forces may contribute to the differences in sex in ways far more powerful than the biological ones. The question recognizes ideologies as either liberal or conservative, but doesn't label any as discrimination. There is an unfortunate tradition of women's primary responsibilities as homemaking and child rearing, while men are responsible for the financial support of the family. That is discrimination against both men and women.

The question fails to acknowledge the social changes that have been occurring in contemporary history which have brought about equality and opportunity for women. The ideology of "happy family" is a fast fading one, for in a society of rising divorce rates, single parents, and latchkey kids, women are assuming the roles of sole parent, sole provider, and professional career persons. Beginning with the Voting Rights Act in the 1920s, women have become more independent and more outspoken. Masculine and feminine have become adjectives of the past; fashion has introduced blazers and slacks as the attractive female apparel, rather than the traditional skirts and blouses; the media is introducing a society of "Mr. Mom's," (motherly fathers) on shows such as "Silver Spoons," "Punky Brewster," and "My Two Dads." One final example that proves anatomy is not destiny is the sharp increase in woman professionals. More and more women are assuming managerial (rather than secretarial) positions.

Although I do not share the more traditional views about sex roles, I agree that they have pervaded our culture and influenced everyone to some extent. Thankfully, however, those views are quickly changing, and although women may always possess a certain "feminine" charm, hopefully they won't forever be labeled only mothers, wives, and homemakers, but have the ability and the right to be professional persons as well. And for the men who choose a homemaker's role, there won't be scorn but acceptance.

Scoring Explanation for Essay 1—Pass (Score = 4)

This essay demonstrates an understanding of the question that is quite sophisticated, arguing that sex roles, largely determined by society, are, in fact, a form of discrimination. The body of the essay goes on to demonstrate how both men and women have risen above the stereotypes tradition has dictated, and offers examples as diverse as manner of dress, television and changes in business management. All of this is done in a readable, reasonable fashion.

The writer's syntax is above average, demonstrating variety and complexity. Errors are few indeed, vocabulary used is broad and intelligent, and the voice of the writer is compelling.

Finally, both aspects of the question—sex roles in the home and society—are addressed. Thus, the essay is a clear pass.

Essay #2—Marginal Pass (Score = 3)

The society, in which we live, is filled with double standards, none so drastic or common as that between men and women. Throughout my growing up, I have witnessed these contradictions and I have come to find these standards to be unfair.

The programming that children receive, while growing up, is a major cause of established double standards. I have experienced times when my sister and I would be playing together and my father would scold one of us because either I shouldn't be playing with dolls, my sister shouldn't be playing with toy guns. I have also found that at a young age in school, society directs us into boy activities and girl activities. I remember that girls got in trouble for horsing around and boys would get in trouble for playing house. In school we learn that only daddies can be doctors, and that mommies must be nurses.

In high school years, this double standard first becomes challenged by the girls. As teenagers begin dating and going out with friends, I have noticed that guys have less restrictions and later curfews. However the most blatant and offensive double standard, to me, is that over sex. In plain terms, if a guy does it, he is a stud, but if a girl does it, she is a slut. I have observed this happen and have several times been guilty of this thinking myself. Besides the issue of sex, goals following high school also reveals this double standard. It is a common stereotype that guys should go to college or get a job, and that women should go out to raise a family. Despite the fact that increasing numbers of girls go to college and get a good job today, and that it's more common for a father to watch the kids, the double standard still exists.

In the workplace, there is a struggle by women and some men, to shatter the double standards and stereotypes. The typical image of a male boss with a female secretary is being toppled by the rising number of women executives and professionals. The question identifies the double standard of women raising families, and men working to support the family. This is beginning to be permanently altered with the huge efforts to fight that image seen in the business world and family situation every day.

Scoring Explanation for Essay #2—Marginal Pass

This essay largely draws on personal experience from childhood and school years to demonstrate that environmental conditioning in both home and school results in the double standard. While this is a more simplistic and expected treatment of the subject of sex roles, the writer is generally still clear. There are few errors, though the syntax and lexical choices are rather ordinary. The author does have a problem with comma use; the first sentence, for example, is over-punctuated.

There is enough information to illustrate the writer's position and to support his/her generalization of societal conditioning. This essay is a good example of an adequate essay that takes no risks and relies on the commonplace. Lastly, the essay lacks a real conclusion.

Essay #3—Marginal Fail (Score = 2)

Societies view points on the role of male and female are often caused by many standards and factors that are put on the male or the female upon birth.

At birth, the infant is placed in one of the categories, if it is a boy, or if it is a girl. Immediately after this is determined, the infant is wrapped in a blue blanket if it is a boy, and a pink blanket if it is a girl. Thus showing that one is taught at a very young age what he/she is *expected* to wear. Children learn early in the home what is right for them.

A point is that a women's primary responsibilities are homemaking and child rearing; that men are responsible for the financial support of the family; that women with children should ideally not work outside the home; and that a double standard in social customs is acceptable. I find that one generation ago this was true, but with todays generation I feel that this passage is not as accurate as it was one generation ago.

From my personal experiences I find the previous statement to be true. I was raised with my mother being a homemaker, my father being responsible for the financial support and there was definately a double standard present. These ideologies range from old customs and beliefs that women are inferior and they have their place in the home.

From my observations, however, I see that the women of today are more independant and defiant to the expectations that are sat upon them from birth. More women are proud to be women and there are not as many girls/women expressing dissatisfaction with the sex they are.

One issue in a family with one boy and one girl is the issue of the double standard. In most families I know, there is always a double standard present on certain issues. (i.e. going out, parties, curfues) The boy usually has more privileges than the girl and the girl is usually the one with the stricter rules. Even though women is trying to be more independent, old habit die hard and protection of their children, especially girls, is always on a parent mind.

The role of a male and a female in todays society is changing from their roles in the past. The female is becoming more independent and don't exactly live up to the expectations sat upon them.

Scoring Explanation for Essay #2—Marginal Fail

This essay draws on personal experience to demonstrate that male and female roles are the result of societal influences. The author has less control over organization than is desirable in a brief, analytic essay. The middle paragraphs show some repetition, and there is an absence of clear transitions between paragraphs. For example, the next-to-the-last paragraph raises the issue of the double standard imposed on teenagers, allowing boys more privileges and fewer restrictions. This paragraph more properly belongs earlier in the essay as support for the writer's claim that experiences in the home account for the double standard.

The author has inadequate control over punctuation and verb tense to a degree which is distracting for the audience: "The female is becoming more independent and don't exactly live up to the expectations sat upon them." Still, the writer does attempt to respond to the question, though the focus on sex roles in the home far outweighs the information offered about sex roles in society.

Essay #4—Fail (Score = 1)

The main point is that ideologies are more effective then the sex of an individual. For centuries traditions influence people more than the sex of a person does. People learn very young, what they think is right from wrong and what they think is sutable for the opposite sex.

Sex should not determine your futur. But everyone has the right to their own opinion. Everyone should always do what they think is best for them regardless of what society is used too. Ideologies of many people, especially young people will grow with open minds to what society should be like if everyone does what best for them and work to their full ability.

Customs and traditions are now changing because every individuals are doing whats best for them. Traditions such as women homemaking and men supporting the family has totally changed in some household. Now women are going out and bringing home the bread and men are at home taking care of the home. People are finally starting to realize that customs and traditions are just ideologies.

The new generation is growing up with different views because of what they see is going on our present society. The new generation sees that the idea that man and women can do just about the same. For example, women are now fighting in wars and trying to do just about everything a man could be.

In conclusion, Ideologies are more effective then a persons' sex.

Scoring Explanation for Essay #4—Fail

There is serious doubt that the writer has control of the language in this essay. The opening line, "The main point is that ideologies are more effective then the sex of an individual," is an unclear statement about the writer's thesis. It gradually becomes clearer that the writer believes that tradition determines sex roles, but the reader must work hard to arrive at that assumption.

There are many errors in diction and spelling, and several sentences are awkward and confusing, both syntactically and semantically. For example, in the next-to-the-last paragraph we read: "The new generation sees that the idea that man and women can do just about the same." The reader is left wondering if the author is discussing a matter of substance or degree.

The essay concludes with a no more lucid restatement of the thesis: "Ideologies are more effective then a persons' sex." There are errors of logic and language use that are impossible to ignore, contributing to the essay's essential failure.

Topic 2 Sample Answer

Essay #1—Pass (Score = 4)

Lee was the most attractive person that I had ever seen. He was tall and well-built, with dark brown hair and piercing hazel eyes. I had had my eye on him for a long, long time. In fact, everytime I went to the dance club, I went to see him. Although it seemed like it had taken forever, the momentous day finally arrived. Just when I least expected it, Lee came up from behind, tapped my shoulder, and asked me to dance. We swayed to the tune of "Take My Breath Away," exchanged telephone numbers, and then left for home. He called the following night at dinner time. Not only did Lee have a terrible sense of timing, but also a very boring personality. All he could talk about was his car. He was obviously not a conversationalist. Much to my disappointment, Lee and I had little in common and had trouble carrying on even a five-minute conversation. He was definitely not the guy that I had expected.

Many people claim that "sometimes when you want something badly and then when you get it, it's not what you expected." Obviously, in my situation, getting to know the "wondrous" Lee was definitely different than what I expected. He had represented a challenge for me and upon overcoming the challenge and actually talking with him, I found myself disappointed and regretful. Why did I feel this way after meeting this once-considered "dreamboat"? I can see two distinct reasons.

To begin with, Lee, after asking me to dance, no longer represented a challenge to me. The high-energy nights of watching and waiting and staring had come to an abrupt end. The was no longer an awe or a mystery to his character—he was a normal human being! The challenge was gone.

Another major reason for the disappointment was the fact that neither Lee, nor any other guy, could ever live up to the image that I had created in my mind of him. In my eyes, Lee could do no wrong. He had the looks of Mel Gibson, the personality of Chevy Chase, and the heart of Mother Theresa. After meeting him and realizing that he seriously lacked in all three areas, it is only obvious that I would be disappointed. True, Lee really did not have a chance, but I was still disappointed.

Disappointment is definitely a factor in wanting something badly and then finally getting it. Maybe because the challenge is gone, maybe because the expectations were too high or maybe because you really thought you would never get it to begin with—whatever the reason, more often than not, finally getting something that was previously desired can definitely be a letdown.

Scoring Explanation for Essay #1—Pass

This personal essay recounts, with much relevant detail, the anticipation of meeting a "dream date" and the subsequent disappointment the writer feels once she knows him better. The writer begins with a very descriptive anecdote of her first interaction with "Lee" and his failure to live up to her expectations. It is in the second paragraph that reference to the question (and the writer's thesis) first appears—an atypical and slightly more sophisticated approach than the usual order of the five-paragraph theme.

This essay is both well-written and interesting. The writer not only offers a well-developed narrative of her disappointment, but also analyzes her "letdown," speculating that she herself may have caused it by expecting too much. Finally, she uses this specific incident to speculate on the nature of the expectation/disappointment in general. Throughout, the writing is very competent, exhibiting sentence variety and a unique overall structure.

Essay #2—Marginal Pass (Score = 3)

If anyone where to ask me what my biggest dream in life was, I would have to say it was the hope for a perfect family. When I was young, I lived with only my mom because my father had left my mom, before I was born.

Together, mom and I, struggled to find enough money for food, and even a little peace of mind. I had always thought that the answer to our problems would be found in a complete family. By this I mean, I thought a family must consist of a father, mother, brother, and sister. I even included a family dog that would run in the yard that was enclosed by the white picket fence.

As a result of my mom having to work and worry so hard, we didn't have sufficient time to develop a good relationship. She was having a difficult providing for me, so I had to move in with another family. This family was friends of my mother, so I felt comfortable with them. I thought that this would be the perfect home. It included everything I had ever dreamed of. It had the mom, dad, siblings, and pets. I was sure that this family was perfect.

It was not soon before I realized how wrong I really was. This family had their share of problems to. For example, they found it hard to find adequate time together. They were always doing their own thing. I have to admit that initially I was shocked. However, I soon realized that there are many types of families and each of them has their own problems. The families protrayed on T.V. were not how family life really was. Of course it was sometimes difficult, buy I now know that what constituts a family is love. It is not always having enough time for eachother, or having a white-picket fence. It is not always being understood, or having all members present. It is about love. That love is demonstrated by the family trying to do the best they can.

Scoring Explanation for Essay #2—Marginal Pass

This essay, which focuses on the author's desire for a "perfect" family, is reasonably well-organized and usually competently written. There are only a few minor errors that offer the reader minimal distraction. But many of the sentences are simple and lack syntactic variety, contributing to an overall sense of only minimal success.

A key omission in this personal essay is sufficient exploration of the current family relationship the author finds deficient, as well as the ideal situation aspired to. The writer offers a limited description of the old situation he/she found lacking ("my mom [had] to work and worry so hard"), and an equally inadequate discussion of the disappointing new situation ("They were always doing their own thing."). Thus, the writer ignores opportunities to move from the general to the specific, to enliven the essay and to make it more convincing. Therefore, the essay passes, but only marginally.

Essay #3—Marginal Fail (Score = 2)

Growing up, I always wanted to be older. This had a lot to do with my older brothers and sisters. They never would let me play with them. I always looked forward to the following grade. It seemed like that being older had so much more freedom. And excitement.

That is why, after about the age of eight or nine, I couldn't wait til my sweet sixteenth birthday. I would have all the freedom I wanted. I never wanted something so much. I even wanted it more than my cabbage patch kid. When I was six.

I would go to extremes because I wanted my license. When I was fourteen I got caught one evening taking my brother's car for a little spin. Nothing major just a little ride to Carl's Jr. and back. Well the car got a flat on the way back and their was no way of avoiding the inevitable, but to call my parents. I wasn't intellectual enough to call triple A. I got an extreme punishment; that fit my crime perfect.

I was the oldest out of all my classmates because I was held back a year. So out of all my friends I was the luckiest because I would receive—my gold card to freedom—my driver's license.

I turned fifteen and you can bet that I was first in line to getting my permit that foggy cold morning at the DMV. After receiving this I was taxi service everywhere. I had to practice and practice because I wasn't going to fail my driver's test. Everytime I got behind the wheel, shivers tickled across my back. I was so excited be behind the wheel.

Finally, my sixteenth birthday rolled around. I took my drivers test—Passed with a 97. I already had a car waiting in the driveway when I came home. My little Jetta was crying out my name. The first month, I loved it. I could drive anywhere, anytime.

This got old real fast. I was soon driving friends home — home meaning an hour away. Picking up things for the family. I was basically, "slaves incorporated." The worse was having to drive to parties. I sat around watching everybody get drunk. It was not fun. Boy, was I wrong. Two years later, I still won't drive unless its' unavoidable. My friends know that. Now its' there turn to pay the piper.

Scoring Explanation for Essay #3—Marginal Fail

This essay is marked by a series of short, choppy sentences and several kinds of errors in grammar and syntax. There is also a rather confusing chronology that the writer uses as an organizational scheme. Much is made of the author's sixteenth birthday and the subsequent acquisition of a driver's license. But other ages (fourteen and fifteen) are described as "driving years" without needed clarification. The result is reader confusion and the necessity of several readings to achieve coherence. In short, the writer makes the reader work too hard. The essay might have been quite effective, since there are many interesting details.

The author concludes with the unexpected dismay he/she felt once his/her license was obtained. This section has potential, but is also underdeveloped and contains several errors. The final line ("Now its' there turn to pay the piper") is typical of the author's lack of control and reliance on inappropriate cliches.

Essay #4—Fail (Score = 1)

One time when I went to the store I had wanted to by a video cammra. So I went to the department where they were being sold and looked at the different types of cammra. I was surprised at the low prices they were asking. I picked out the one I wanted; and bought it.

When I got home I was messing around with the cammera to see what different type of things it could do. It had a zoom, it had a mic and had many other interesting function. When I was done playing around with it and finding out everything that it could do I went to the park with my little sister. She was only 3 years old I thought I could get some funny pictures. My older sister said that she wanted to go along also; just to watch. When we got to the park I had the cammera no more than 30 seconds and Kelly my older sister wanted to use my cammera. I let her but I said for only a couple. I went to get something to drink and when I came back I saw my cammera being passed around in a group of 15. I asked for it back but all I got was a black eye. Some guy didn't like the way I was trying to get my cammera. As it was being passed around some body dropped it. It broke into a thousand small pieces. I was very upset. I got to use my cammera for about 30 seconds; and I got a black eye.

As you could of told I was very dissappointed; with how much I got to use the cammera. One thing I did learn it if you ever buy a new "toy" than keep it to yourself; or let somebody you can trust.

Scoring Explanation for Essay #4—Fail

Lack of development and errors of many sorts (syntax, grammar, punctuation, and spelling) are, unfortunately, the most memorable features of this essay.

The writer begins with an overly simplistic and pedestrian accounting of the purchase of a "video cammra." The sentences are elementary and are surprisingly void of useful detail.

The longest, central paragraph in this too-brief personal essay is a narrative account of the "borrowing," misuse, and destruction of the camera. The reader feels little sympathy for the writer however, because very little effort has been made to make the camera a highly desired or valued object, and the story of its untimely end is lacking in relevant detail.

The author concludes with a typically awkward sentence: "As you could of told I was very dissappointed; with how much I got to use the cammera." The reader has little interest at this point, probably lacks understanding of the writer's disappointment, and is most certainly distracted by the writing errors. The essay fails on several levels.

CBEST

California Basic Educational Skills Test

ANSWER SHEETS

CBEST – TEST 1

Reading Comprehension

1. (A) (B) (C) (D) (E)
2. (A) (B) (C) (D) (E)
3. (A) (B) (C) (D) (E)
4. (A) (B) (C) (D) (E)
5. (A) (B) (C) (D) (E)
6. (A) (B) (C) (D) (E)
7. (A) (B) (C) (D) (E)
8. (A) (B) (C) (D) (E)
9. (A) (B) (C) (D) (E)
10. (A) (B) (C) (D) (E)
11. (A) (B) (C) (D) (E)
12. (A) (B) (C) (D) (E)
13. (A) (B) (C) (D) (E)
14. (A) (B) (C) (D) (E)
15. (A) (B) (C) (D) (E)
16. (A) (B) (C) (D) (E)
17. (A) (B) (C) (D) (E)
18. (A) (B) (C) (D) (E)
19. (A) (B) (C) (D) (E)
20. (A) (B) (C) (D) (E)
21. (A) (B) (C) (D) (E)
22. (A) (B) (C) (D) (E)
23. (A) (B) (C) (D) (E)
24. (A) (B) (C) (D) (E)
25. (A) (B) (C) (D) (E)
26. (A) (B) (C) (D) (E)
27. (A) (B) (C) (D) (E)
28. (A) (B) (C) (D) (E)
29. (A) (B) (C) (D) (E)
30. (A) (B) (C) (D) (E)
31. (A) (B) (C) (D) (E)
32. (A) (B) (C) (D) (E)
33. (A) (B) (C) (D) (E)
34. (A) (B) (C) (D) (E)
35. (A) (B) (C) (D) (E)
36. (A) (B) (C) (D) (E)
37. (A) (B) (C) (D) (E)
38. (A) (B) (C) (D) (E)
39. (A) (B) (C) (D) (E)
40. (A) (B) (C) (D) (E)
41. (A) (B) (C) (D) (E)
42. (A) (B) (C) (D) (E)
43. (A) (B) (C) (D) (E)
44. (A) (B) (C) (D) (E)
45. (A) (B) (C) (D) (E)
46. (A) (B) (C) (D) (E)
47. (A) (B) (C) (D) (E)
48. (A) (B) (C) (D) (E)
49. (A) (B) (C) (D) (E)
50. (A) (B) (C) (D) (E)

Mathematics

1. (A) (B) (C) (D) (E)
2. (A) (B) (C) (D) (E)
3. (A) (B) (C) (D) (E)
4. (A) (B) (C) (D) (E)
5. (A) (B) (C) (D) (E)
6. (A) (B) (C) (D) (E)
7. (A) (B) (C) (D) (E)
8. (A) (B) (C) (D) (E)
9. (A) (B) (C) (D) (E)
10. (A) (B) (C) (D) (E)
11. (A) (B) (C) (D) (E)
12. (A) (B) (C) (D) (E)
13. (A) (B) (C) (D) (E)
14. (A) (B) (C) (D) (E)
15. (A) (B) (C) (D) (E)
16. (A) (B) (C) (D) (E)
17. (A) (B) (C) (D) (E)
18. (A) (B) (C) (D) (E)
19. (A) (B) (C) (D) (E)
20. (A) (B) (C) (D) (E)
21. (A) (B) (C) (D) (E)
22. (A) (B) (C) (D) (E)
23. (A) (B) (C) (D) (E)
24. (A) (B) (C) (D) (E)
25. (A) (B) (C) (D) (E)
26. (A) (B) (C) (D) (E)
27. (A) (B) (C) (D) (E)
28. (A) (B) (C) (D) (E)
29. (A) (B) (C) (D) (E)
30. (A) (B) (C) (D) (E)
31. (A) (B) (C) (D) (E)
32. (A) (B) (C) (D) (E)
33. (A) (B) (C) (D) (E)
34. (A) (B) (C) (D) (E)
35. (A) (B) (C) (D) (E)
36. (A) (B) (C) (D) (E)
37. (A) (B) (C) (D) (E)
38. (A) (B) (C) (D) (E)
39. (A) (B) (C) (D) (E)
40. (A) (B) (C) (D) (E)
41. (A) (B) (C) (D) (E)
42. (A) (B) (C) (D) (E)
43. (A) (B) (C) (D) (E)
44. (A) (B) (C) (D) (E)
45. (A) (B) (C) (D) (E)
46. (A) (B) (C) (D) (E)
47. (A) (B) (C) (D) (E)
48. (A) (B) (C) (D) (E)
49. (A) (B) (C) (D) (E)
50. (A) (B) (C) (D) (E)

CBEST – TEST 1
Essay Writing Grid

CBEST – TEST 2

Reading Comprehension

1. Ⓐ Ⓑ Ⓒ Ⓓ Ⓔ
2. Ⓐ Ⓑ Ⓒ Ⓓ Ⓔ
3. Ⓐ Ⓑ Ⓒ Ⓓ Ⓔ
4. Ⓐ Ⓑ Ⓒ Ⓓ Ⓔ
5. Ⓐ Ⓑ Ⓒ Ⓓ Ⓔ
6. Ⓐ Ⓑ Ⓒ Ⓓ Ⓔ
7. Ⓐ Ⓑ Ⓒ Ⓓ Ⓔ
8. Ⓐ Ⓑ Ⓒ Ⓓ Ⓔ
9. Ⓐ Ⓑ Ⓒ Ⓓ Ⓔ
10. Ⓐ Ⓑ Ⓒ Ⓓ Ⓔ
11. Ⓐ Ⓑ Ⓒ Ⓓ Ⓔ
12. Ⓐ Ⓑ Ⓒ Ⓓ Ⓔ
13. Ⓐ Ⓑ Ⓒ Ⓓ Ⓔ
14. Ⓐ Ⓑ Ⓒ Ⓓ Ⓔ
15. Ⓐ Ⓑ Ⓒ Ⓓ Ⓔ
16. Ⓐ Ⓑ Ⓒ Ⓓ Ⓔ
17. Ⓐ Ⓑ Ⓒ Ⓓ Ⓔ
18. Ⓐ Ⓑ Ⓒ Ⓓ Ⓔ
19. Ⓐ Ⓑ Ⓒ Ⓓ Ⓔ
20. Ⓐ Ⓑ Ⓒ Ⓓ Ⓔ
21. Ⓐ Ⓑ Ⓒ Ⓓ Ⓔ
22. Ⓐ Ⓑ Ⓒ Ⓓ Ⓔ
23. Ⓐ Ⓑ Ⓒ Ⓓ Ⓔ
24. Ⓐ Ⓑ Ⓒ Ⓓ Ⓔ
25. Ⓐ Ⓑ Ⓒ Ⓓ Ⓔ
26. Ⓐ Ⓑ Ⓒ Ⓓ Ⓔ
27. Ⓐ Ⓑ Ⓒ Ⓓ Ⓔ
28. Ⓐ Ⓑ Ⓒ Ⓓ Ⓔ
29. Ⓐ Ⓑ Ⓒ Ⓓ Ⓔ
30. Ⓐ Ⓑ Ⓒ Ⓓ Ⓔ
31. Ⓐ Ⓑ Ⓒ Ⓓ Ⓔ
32. Ⓐ Ⓑ Ⓒ Ⓓ Ⓔ
33. Ⓐ Ⓑ Ⓒ Ⓓ Ⓔ
34. Ⓐ Ⓑ Ⓒ Ⓓ Ⓔ
35. Ⓐ Ⓑ Ⓒ Ⓓ Ⓔ
36. Ⓐ Ⓑ Ⓒ Ⓓ Ⓔ
37. Ⓐ Ⓑ Ⓒ Ⓓ Ⓔ
38. Ⓐ Ⓑ Ⓒ Ⓓ Ⓔ
39. Ⓐ Ⓑ Ⓒ Ⓓ Ⓔ
40. Ⓐ Ⓑ Ⓒ Ⓓ Ⓔ
41. Ⓐ Ⓑ Ⓒ Ⓓ Ⓔ
42. Ⓐ Ⓑ Ⓒ Ⓓ Ⓔ
43. Ⓐ Ⓑ Ⓒ Ⓓ Ⓔ
44. Ⓐ Ⓑ Ⓒ Ⓓ Ⓔ
45. Ⓐ Ⓑ Ⓒ Ⓓ Ⓔ
46. Ⓐ Ⓑ Ⓒ Ⓓ Ⓔ
47. Ⓐ Ⓑ Ⓒ Ⓓ Ⓔ
48. Ⓐ Ⓑ Ⓒ Ⓓ Ⓔ
49. Ⓐ Ⓑ Ⓒ Ⓓ Ⓔ
50. Ⓐ Ⓑ Ⓒ Ⓓ Ⓔ

Mathematics

1. Ⓐ Ⓑ Ⓒ Ⓓ Ⓔ
2. Ⓐ Ⓑ Ⓒ Ⓓ Ⓔ
3. Ⓐ Ⓑ Ⓒ Ⓓ Ⓔ
4. Ⓐ Ⓑ Ⓒ Ⓓ Ⓔ
5. Ⓐ Ⓑ Ⓒ Ⓓ Ⓔ
6. Ⓐ Ⓑ Ⓒ Ⓓ Ⓔ
7. Ⓐ Ⓑ Ⓒ Ⓓ Ⓔ
8. Ⓐ Ⓑ Ⓒ Ⓓ Ⓔ
9. Ⓐ Ⓑ Ⓒ Ⓓ Ⓔ
10. Ⓐ Ⓑ Ⓒ Ⓓ Ⓔ
11. Ⓐ Ⓑ Ⓒ Ⓓ Ⓔ
12. Ⓐ Ⓑ Ⓒ Ⓓ Ⓔ
13. Ⓐ Ⓑ Ⓒ Ⓓ Ⓔ
14. Ⓐ Ⓑ Ⓒ Ⓓ Ⓔ
15. Ⓐ Ⓑ Ⓒ Ⓓ Ⓔ
16. Ⓐ Ⓑ Ⓒ Ⓓ Ⓔ
17. Ⓐ Ⓑ Ⓒ Ⓓ Ⓔ
18. Ⓐ Ⓑ Ⓒ Ⓓ Ⓔ
19. Ⓐ Ⓑ Ⓒ Ⓓ Ⓔ
20. Ⓐ Ⓑ Ⓒ Ⓓ Ⓔ
21. Ⓐ Ⓑ Ⓒ Ⓓ Ⓔ
22. Ⓐ Ⓑ Ⓒ Ⓓ Ⓔ
23. Ⓐ Ⓑ Ⓒ Ⓓ Ⓔ
24. Ⓐ Ⓑ Ⓒ Ⓓ Ⓔ
25. Ⓐ Ⓑ Ⓒ Ⓓ Ⓔ
26. Ⓐ Ⓑ Ⓒ Ⓓ Ⓔ
27. Ⓐ Ⓑ Ⓒ Ⓓ Ⓔ
28. Ⓐ Ⓑ Ⓒ Ⓓ Ⓔ
29. Ⓐ Ⓑ Ⓒ Ⓓ Ⓔ
30. Ⓐ Ⓑ Ⓒ Ⓓ Ⓔ
31. Ⓐ Ⓑ Ⓒ Ⓓ Ⓔ
32. Ⓐ Ⓑ Ⓒ Ⓓ Ⓔ
33. Ⓐ Ⓑ Ⓒ Ⓓ Ⓔ
34. Ⓐ Ⓑ Ⓒ Ⓓ Ⓔ
35. Ⓐ Ⓑ Ⓒ Ⓓ Ⓔ
36. Ⓐ Ⓑ Ⓒ Ⓓ Ⓔ
37. Ⓐ Ⓑ Ⓒ Ⓓ Ⓔ
38. Ⓐ Ⓑ Ⓒ Ⓓ Ⓔ
39. Ⓐ Ⓑ Ⓒ Ⓓ Ⓔ
40. Ⓐ Ⓑ Ⓒ Ⓓ Ⓔ
41. Ⓐ Ⓑ Ⓒ Ⓓ Ⓔ
42. Ⓐ Ⓑ Ⓒ Ⓓ Ⓔ
43. Ⓐ Ⓑ Ⓒ Ⓓ Ⓔ
44. Ⓐ Ⓑ Ⓒ Ⓓ Ⓔ
45. Ⓐ Ⓑ Ⓒ Ⓓ Ⓔ
46. Ⓐ Ⓑ Ⓒ Ⓓ Ⓔ
47. Ⓐ Ⓑ Ⓒ Ⓓ Ⓔ
48. Ⓐ Ⓑ Ⓒ Ⓓ Ⓔ
49. Ⓐ Ⓑ Ⓒ Ⓓ Ⓔ
50. Ⓐ Ⓑ Ⓒ Ⓓ Ⓔ

CBEST – TEST 2
Essay Writing Grid

CBEST – TEST 3

Reading Comprehension

1. Ⓐ Ⓑ Ⓒ Ⓓ Ⓔ
2. Ⓐ Ⓑ Ⓒ Ⓓ Ⓔ
3. Ⓐ Ⓑ Ⓒ Ⓓ Ⓔ
4. Ⓐ Ⓑ Ⓒ Ⓓ Ⓔ
5. Ⓐ Ⓑ Ⓒ Ⓓ Ⓔ
6. Ⓐ Ⓑ Ⓒ Ⓓ Ⓔ
7. Ⓐ Ⓑ Ⓒ Ⓓ Ⓔ
8. Ⓐ Ⓑ Ⓒ Ⓓ Ⓔ
9. Ⓐ Ⓑ Ⓒ Ⓓ Ⓔ
10. Ⓐ Ⓑ Ⓒ Ⓓ Ⓔ
11. Ⓐ Ⓑ Ⓒ Ⓓ Ⓔ
12. Ⓐ Ⓑ Ⓒ Ⓓ Ⓔ
13. Ⓐ Ⓑ Ⓒ Ⓓ Ⓔ
14. Ⓐ Ⓑ Ⓒ Ⓓ Ⓔ
15. Ⓐ Ⓑ Ⓒ Ⓓ Ⓔ
16. Ⓐ Ⓑ Ⓒ Ⓓ Ⓔ
17. Ⓐ Ⓑ Ⓒ Ⓓ Ⓔ
18. Ⓐ Ⓑ Ⓒ Ⓓ Ⓔ
19. Ⓐ Ⓑ Ⓒ Ⓓ Ⓔ
20. Ⓐ Ⓑ Ⓒ Ⓓ Ⓔ
21. Ⓐ Ⓑ Ⓒ Ⓓ Ⓔ
22. Ⓐ Ⓑ Ⓒ Ⓓ Ⓔ
23. Ⓐ Ⓑ Ⓒ Ⓓ Ⓔ
24. Ⓐ Ⓑ Ⓒ Ⓓ Ⓔ
25. Ⓐ Ⓑ Ⓒ Ⓓ Ⓔ
26. Ⓐ Ⓑ Ⓒ Ⓓ Ⓔ
27. Ⓐ Ⓑ Ⓒ Ⓓ Ⓔ
28. Ⓐ Ⓑ Ⓒ Ⓓ Ⓔ
29. Ⓐ Ⓑ Ⓒ Ⓓ Ⓔ
30. Ⓐ Ⓑ Ⓒ Ⓓ Ⓔ
31. Ⓐ Ⓑ Ⓒ Ⓓ Ⓔ
32. Ⓐ Ⓑ Ⓒ Ⓓ Ⓔ
33. Ⓐ Ⓑ Ⓒ Ⓓ Ⓔ
34. Ⓐ Ⓑ Ⓒ Ⓓ Ⓔ
35. Ⓐ Ⓑ Ⓒ Ⓓ Ⓔ
36. Ⓐ Ⓑ Ⓒ Ⓓ Ⓔ
37. Ⓐ Ⓑ Ⓒ Ⓓ Ⓔ
38. Ⓐ Ⓑ Ⓒ Ⓓ Ⓔ
39. Ⓐ Ⓑ Ⓒ Ⓓ Ⓔ
40. Ⓐ Ⓑ Ⓒ Ⓓ Ⓔ
41. Ⓐ Ⓑ Ⓒ Ⓓ Ⓔ
42. Ⓐ Ⓑ Ⓒ Ⓓ Ⓔ
43. Ⓐ Ⓑ Ⓒ Ⓓ Ⓔ
44. Ⓐ Ⓑ Ⓒ Ⓓ Ⓔ
45. Ⓐ Ⓑ Ⓒ Ⓓ Ⓔ
46. Ⓐ Ⓑ Ⓒ Ⓓ Ⓔ
47. Ⓐ Ⓑ Ⓒ Ⓓ Ⓔ
48. Ⓐ Ⓑ Ⓒ Ⓓ Ⓔ
49. Ⓐ Ⓑ Ⓒ Ⓓ Ⓔ
50. Ⓐ Ⓑ Ⓒ Ⓓ Ⓔ

Mathematics

1. Ⓐ Ⓑ Ⓒ Ⓓ Ⓔ
2. Ⓐ Ⓑ Ⓒ Ⓓ Ⓔ
3. Ⓐ Ⓑ Ⓒ Ⓓ Ⓔ
4. Ⓐ Ⓑ Ⓒ Ⓓ Ⓔ
5. Ⓐ Ⓑ Ⓒ Ⓓ Ⓔ
6. Ⓐ Ⓑ Ⓒ Ⓓ Ⓔ
7. Ⓐ Ⓑ Ⓒ Ⓓ Ⓔ
8. Ⓐ Ⓑ Ⓒ Ⓓ Ⓔ
9. Ⓐ Ⓑ Ⓒ Ⓓ Ⓔ
10. Ⓐ Ⓑ Ⓒ Ⓓ Ⓔ
11. Ⓐ Ⓑ Ⓒ Ⓓ Ⓔ
12. Ⓐ Ⓑ Ⓒ Ⓓ Ⓔ
13. Ⓐ Ⓑ Ⓒ Ⓓ Ⓔ
14. Ⓐ Ⓑ Ⓒ Ⓓ Ⓔ
15. Ⓐ Ⓑ Ⓒ Ⓓ Ⓔ
16. Ⓐ Ⓑ Ⓒ Ⓓ Ⓔ
17. Ⓐ Ⓑ Ⓒ Ⓓ Ⓔ
18. Ⓐ Ⓑ Ⓒ Ⓓ Ⓔ
19. Ⓐ Ⓑ Ⓒ Ⓓ Ⓔ
20. Ⓐ Ⓑ Ⓒ Ⓓ Ⓔ
21. Ⓐ Ⓑ Ⓒ Ⓓ Ⓔ
22. Ⓐ Ⓑ Ⓒ Ⓓ Ⓔ
23. Ⓐ Ⓑ Ⓒ Ⓓ Ⓔ
24. Ⓐ Ⓑ Ⓒ Ⓓ Ⓔ
25. Ⓐ Ⓑ Ⓒ Ⓓ Ⓔ
26. Ⓐ Ⓑ Ⓒ Ⓓ Ⓔ
27. Ⓐ Ⓑ Ⓒ Ⓓ Ⓔ
28. Ⓐ Ⓑ Ⓒ Ⓓ Ⓔ
29. Ⓐ Ⓑ Ⓒ Ⓓ Ⓔ
30. Ⓐ Ⓑ Ⓒ Ⓓ Ⓔ
31. Ⓐ Ⓑ Ⓒ Ⓓ Ⓔ
32. Ⓐ Ⓑ Ⓒ Ⓓ Ⓔ
33. Ⓐ Ⓑ Ⓒ Ⓓ Ⓔ
34. Ⓐ Ⓑ Ⓒ Ⓓ Ⓔ
35. Ⓐ Ⓑ Ⓒ Ⓓ Ⓔ
36. Ⓐ Ⓑ Ⓒ Ⓓ Ⓔ
37. Ⓐ Ⓑ Ⓒ Ⓓ Ⓔ
38. Ⓐ Ⓑ Ⓒ Ⓓ Ⓔ
39. Ⓐ Ⓑ Ⓒ Ⓓ Ⓔ
40. Ⓐ Ⓑ Ⓒ Ⓓ Ⓔ
41. Ⓐ Ⓑ Ⓒ Ⓓ Ⓔ
42. Ⓐ Ⓑ Ⓒ Ⓓ Ⓔ
43. Ⓐ Ⓑ Ⓒ Ⓓ Ⓔ
44. Ⓐ Ⓑ Ⓒ Ⓓ Ⓔ
45. Ⓐ Ⓑ Ⓒ Ⓓ Ⓔ
46. Ⓐ Ⓑ Ⓒ Ⓓ Ⓔ
47. Ⓐ Ⓑ Ⓒ Ⓓ Ⓔ
48. Ⓐ Ⓑ Ⓒ Ⓓ Ⓔ
49. Ⓐ Ⓑ Ⓒ Ⓓ Ⓔ
50. Ⓐ Ⓑ Ⓒ Ⓓ Ⓔ

CBEST – TEST 3
Essay Writing Grid

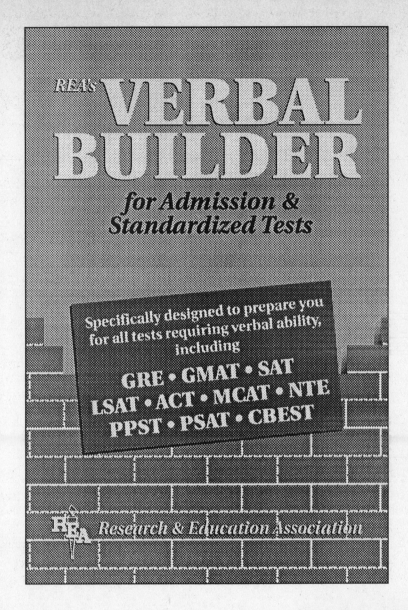